Not Quite Hope
and Other Political Emotions
in the Gilded Age

OXFORD STUDIES IN AMERICAN LITERARY HISTORY

Gordon Hutner, Series Editor

Not Quite Hope
and Other Political Emotions
in the Gilded Age

Nathan Wolff

OXFORD
UNIVERSITY PRESS

OXFORD

UNIVERSITY PRESS

Great Clarendon Street, Oxford, OX2 6DP,
United Kingdom

Oxford University Press is a department of the University of Oxford.
It furthers the University's objective of excellence in research, scholarship,
and education by publishing worldwide. Oxford is a registered trade mark of
Oxford University Press in the UK and in certain other countries

Published in the United States of America by Oxford University Press
198 Madison Avenue, New York, NY 10016, United States of America

British Library Cataloguing in Publication Data
Data available

Library of Congress Control Number: 2018949488

ISBN 978-0-19-883169-3

Printed and bound by
CPI Group (UK) Ltd, Croydon, CR0 4YY

Links to third party websites are provided by Oxford in good faith and
for information only. Oxford disclaims any responsibility for the materials
contained in any third party website referenced in this work.

{ ACKNOWLEDGMENTS }

After the sometimes anxious and exhausting process of writing a book about messy, complicated emotions, it's a joy to now focus on giving thanks—a simpler, if no less intense feeling.

First off, I am pleased to acknowledge Lauren Berlant, Bill Brown, and Kenneth Warren for their supervision of the dissertation that became this book. I hope they will see how much it remains indebted to their guidance while also appreciating how it has evolved. An extra thank you to Lauren for ongoing feedback, advice, and inspiration.

A number of friends and colleagues generously read portions of the text over the years, served as respondents to my work in public forums, or convened panels that provided the occasion to sharpen key ideas. Those include Jason Berger, Russ Castronovo, Peter Coviello, Theo Davis, Elizabeth Freeman, Heather Keenleyside, Maurice Lee, and Hilary Strang. Thanks, especially, to Joshua Kotin who read multiple chapters over multiple years and provided much-needed camaraderie and grounding during the final stretch of work on this book.

When I was an undergraduate, Joseph Litvak provided one of my earliest models for academic life; his intellect, decency, and sense of humor continue to set the gold standard. I am honored to be his colleague and am grateful for his support. Sincere thanks, as well, to the rest of the faculty and staff in the Department of English at Tufts, some of whom deserve special mention as welcoming hosts, lunch companions, pedagogical examples, collaborators, and interlocutors, in particular: Liz Ammons, Linda Bamber, Ricky Crano, Lee Edelman, Sonia Hofkosh, Jess Keiser, Lisa Lowe, John Lurz, Modhumita Roy, Natalie Shapero, Christina Sharpe, and Ichiro Takayoshi. I am also grateful for the committed students at Tufts, especially the members of my "Political Emotion" and "O, Democracy" graduate seminars, whose challenging questions and observations made this a better book.

An early version of material that now makes up portions of Chapters 1 and 5 first appeared in *ELH*, Volume 81, Issue 1, Spring, 2013, pages 173–97. Copyright © 2013 The Johns Hopkins University Press. An earlier version of Chapter 3 first appeared in *J19: The Journal of Nineteenth-Century Americanists*, Volume 2, Number 2, Fall 2014, pages 225–52. Copyright © 2014 C19: The Society of Nineteenth-Century Americanists. I thank the editors of these journals for their votes of confidence in my work and their permission to reprint.

Many thanks to Gordon Hutner for his faith in this project and for extending the privilege of joining the Oxford Studies in American Literary History series. Thank you, too, to the anonymous reviewers who provided generous feedback and encouragement, to Jacqueline Norton and Aimee Wright at Oxford University Press for seeing the book through production, to Christine Ranft for copy-editing, and to Derek Gottlieb for preparing the index.

Although their only interest in this book was that it made me a reliable couch companion, it makes me happy to acknowledge two beloved pets. Sprout was a strange and devoted friend. I miss him very much. Clementine makes me laugh, livens up office hours, and paws my keyboard when I've spent too long inside.

Finally, thank you to my family. To my parents, Fred and Kathy; siblings, Jake and Genevieve; sister-in-law, Lesley; and parents-in-law, Leon and La Juana: Your confidence in me across this long haul meant and means a lot. And to Jennifer Wehunt: Your love and support deserves more acknowledgement than I have room to express. Breaks have been too few and far between, but I have cherished every adventure—whether hikes and paddles or fried clams and beers. What's more, your careful attention to each chapter in this book, multiple times over, sharpened the prose, elevated the ideas, and made me feel that finishing was possible. I dedicate this book to you with gratitude and love.

{ CONTENTS }

{ LIST OF FIGURES }

Agitation

{ Introduction }

Bureaucratic Vistas

*Democratic institutions awaken and flatter the passion for equality without
ever being able to satisfy it entirely.... [T]he people become heated in the search
for this good, all the more precious as it is near enough to be known, far enough
not to be tasted. The chance of succeeding stirs them, the uncertainty of success
irritates them; they are agitated, they are wearied, they are embittered.*

—ALEXIS DE TOCQUEVILLE

Politics is What Hurts

In 1881 the neurologist George Beard offered a clinician's take on the adverse effects
of political participation, closely echoing Alexis de Tocqueville's 1835 assessment,
in the epigraph above, of American democracy's affective toll.[1] According to Beard,
"politics and religion appeal mostly to the emotional nature of men ... and in consequence, the whole land is at times agitated by both these influences, to a degree
which ... is most exciting to the nervous temperament."[2] Unlike Tocqueville, Beard
does not observe this distress as linked to a "passion for equality"—a painful-but-
praiseworthy democratic feeling. Instead, Beard sees nervous agitation as the annoy-
ing side effect of a much more grievous communal ailment: a fundamentally irrational political process. Similarly, in her 1881 novel of postbellum life in Washington,
DC, *Through One Administration,* the writer Frances Hodgson Burnett has her protagonist offer a catalog of devastations that results from spending even one season
in the capital's atmosphere of political power-brokering and social intrigue: "She
had seen so many weary faces, so many eager ones, so many stamped with care and
disappointment.... [S]he had read of ambitions frustrated and hopes denied, and
once or twice had seen with a pang that somewhere a heart had been broken."[3]
When measuring the sentiments that animate and sustain the nation's leaders or
when gauging citizens' collective mood, one might hope to find patriotic pride,
democratic fellow feeling, even idealistic enthusiasm. According to the Gilded Age
observers above, however, political participation only frustrates, disappoints, agi-
tates, and depletes.[4]

The late-nineteenth-century lament that democracy is wearying, upsetting, or
disheartening surely isn't novel to twenty-first-century readers, many of whom

inevitably grapple with their own bouts of political depression. Despite this striking resonance between Gilded Age and present-day discourses on the phenomenology of politics, I will argue that at least three major blind spots in American literary criticism have obscured our view of postbellum literature's investigation into the intersection of emotion and democracy. These involve: first, an overly narrow vocabulary for conveying the full range of "political emotions" (and some confusion about what this term could mean); second, a persistent suspicion of conservatism lurking in any specifically *institutional* politics (given an aesthetic and political preference for radical breaks from convention or forms); and, finally, a literary-historical discomfort with the generic irregularities (in works fusing romance, sentimentality, and realism) and ideological eccentricity (a surprising mix of populist critique, republican nostalgia, and bureaucratic pragmatism) peculiar to the transitional postwar moment.[5] These three cases of nearsightedness are deeply intertwined, as the literature's uniquely negative tone and its discomfiting focus on institutional politics unite texts that otherwise defy easy generic taxonomies.

Hoping to correct this oversight, this book aims to develop a conceptual framework for analyzing the affective-political work of the occasionally well known but consistently understudied Gilded Age political novel. "The Gilded Age"—roughly the period from the election of President Ulysses S. Grant in 1869 through the end of that century—is ripe for such an analysis, given that it is defined both by a phenomenon, political corruption, and a set of feelings about it. Mark Summers has argued persuasively that rapid government expansion after the Civil War did indeed produce prime conditions for political venality, but bribery, vote buying, lobbying, and profiteering were not new. Indeed, the increased intensity of the public's focus on corruption was in many ways more consequential than the misdeeds themselves.[6] Reformers zeroed in on the failings of politicians and the political process while also worrying about the widespread disgust with politics and its potential impact on civic participation. Along with other popular nicknames, such as "The Era of Good Stealings" and "The Great Barbecue," "The Gilded Age" denotes a period of rampant greed and appetitive excess while also capturing the cynicism, bitterness, and exhaustion that attended the period's major scandals.

The remainder of this Introduction will sketch, and the chapters will flesh out, my understanding of literature's role in defining and exploring the emotional contours of this fraught moment. My overarching claim is that Gilded Age political satires, "Washington novels," and reform-minded historical romances reveal the opposition of cool reason vs. warm enthusiasm to underdescribe the emotional life of postbellum US democracy. These novels dramatize and perform myriad affective strategies for modulating distance from and proximity to politics, a realm of social life that did and does provoke feelings of exhilaration and exhaustion, optimism and pessimism, passionate attachment and disgusted withdrawal. In making this claim, *Not Quite Hope* seeks to move beyond the threadbare opposition of emotional versus rational politics, a binary that continues to shape present-day diagnoses of our pathological public sphere. I further argue for a shift in scale from those dramatic, positive, and object-oriented emotions we might associate with the goals of reform literature (i.e., to incite strong emotions for or against a cause, or to cultivate empathy for a person or group) to a more diffuse, often negative, set of feelings that structure citizens' relation to the political as such. But before delving further into this thesis, I offer a pair of questions that put into relief the Gilded Age novel's unique affinity to an earlier canon of political fiction, which serves as both a model and a foil.

Which Feelings are Democratic? What Does Democracy Feel Like?

For the last thirty years or so, the field of nineteenth-century American literary studies has pursued several variations on the first question. Does Harriet Beecher Stowe's famous call for her readers to "feel right" about slavery mobilize a denigrated "feminine" emotionalism for radical democratic ends, or does it privatize a properly political problem?[7] Does Walt Whitman's vision of "adhesive love" offer an intimate counterpoint to the failures of official politics, or does it reproduce the sleight of hand by which the white male body claims exclusive right as the (paradoxically specific) embodiment of abstract, democratic citizenship?[8] In other words, sympathy and adhesiveness may describe an affective tool for political work, but is this work "democratic"? Studies that take up these and related questions about sentiment, sympathy, compassion, and intimacy have clustered around binding and cathartic feelings (largely focused on "positive" emotions, but also including grief, anger, and mourning), the power and pitfalls of which lie in the ethical relationships they foster or erode between people, especially across racial, gender, and economic boundaries.[9] Work in this vein has made emotion and affect fundamental components of how we understand literature's cultural impact. But it has also tended to subsume the topic of "political emotion" under the heading of "sympathy" or sentimentality, when "political emotion" writ large seems the more properly capacious category.[10]

This book thus proposes that we shift the discursive terrain by posing a related question: "What does democracy feel like?" Initially, this question might seem to invite only subjective accounts of political life. The Pew Research Center, for example, often plots the citizenry's mood along a political-affective spectrum characterized by the key benchmarks of "Content," "Angry," and "Frustrated," with the majority of respondents reliably choosing from among the two flavors of irritation.[11] On the other hand, the question, "Which feelings are democratic?" points to a particular strain of nineteenth-century literary criticism in which sentimentality, once denigrated as feminine and commercial, came to be seen as a complex set of aesthetic and affective strategies for shaping readers' democratic sensibilities. Yet the gap between these two sets of affects—negative, unsociable, and exhausting on the one hand; positive, binding, even therapeutic on the other—also presents potential problems for nineteenth-century American literary history and criticism. First, how did we decide that the emotions we associate with formal politics are, oxymoronically, not democratic? Second, when we explore affect in literature, what do we leave out if we see "political emotion" as roughly synonymous with "sympathy"?

Taken at face value, the first of these two questions is relatively easy to answer, although tracing its repercussions will be a major project of this book. The avoidance of negative emotions, or those seen as not properly democratic, has everything to do with the more fundamental irony that, for much of US history, politics itself has been seen as antidemocratic (and antipathetic). That is, if the nation was founded on a principle of popular sovereignty understood as the amalgamated opinion of free and equal individuals, then any form or institution for representing that popular will is potentially artificial, distasteful, and, to some degree, illegitimate.[12] We view this denigration of the political in at least three major strains of nineteenth-century literature and thought: in transcendentalism, where expressions of individual conscience (uncontaminated by formal participation in parties, elections, or reform movements) are praised as the pinnacle of intellectual courage and creativity; second, in the sentimental novel, where the failure of official politics to remedy the question of slavery demands a shift in moral authority to women, the domestic sphere, sentiment, and, just as importantly, to an affective public that will coalesce through reading the same literature, a form of commodity consumption; and finally in the romance, where the construction of an airy space of imagination and creativity requires distance from official politics. This last dynamic figures most memorably in Hawthorne's *The Scarlet Letter* (1850), with its author's prefatory "decapitation" and ejection from the custom house; but also in *Moby-Dick's* (1851) mariners, renegades, and castaways, whose short-lived homosocial utopia thrives in its distance from shore; and in Whitman's ideal democracy to come, explored throughout *Leaves of Grass* (1855) and its many iterations, which could begin to take poetic form only after his departure from the attorney general's office.[13]

This strain of antebellum literature is rightly prized for its call to challenge the inequities fossilized in political institutions. And critics have built on this canon's anti-institutional critique to stress that democracy and citizenship must be seen as encompassing a range of activity beyond the ballot box, as well as to underscore literature's role in exploring conceptions of morality or ethics that put into relief the injustices inherent to existing political structures. But the wholesale embrace of an anti-institutional politics has had some distorting effects on our literary historiography. In his essay "Revolutions in the Meaning and Study of Politics," Eric Slauter notes that "everywhere, it seems, studies of institutional and electoral politics are back in style, necessarily transformed by those revolutions in social and cultural analysis that were designed to shift attention away from politics."[14] And yet a sharp divide between early and postbellum American studies shapes this renewed interest in politics: "Early Americanists concentrate on the culture of politics, whereas later Americanists concentrate on the politics of culture."[15] Reviewing the tables of contents of two relevant anthologies, Slauter notes, "one might surmise that

American literature before 1865 was a political literature; and that after 1865, it was not."[16] To be sure, this pattern of scholarly output reveals real archival differences. Early American literature courses and anthologies routinely include texts that bear a close relation to political and social institutions: sermons, speeches, pamphlets, overtly political poetry, and polemical essays. "Literature" in this context is understood to encompass the whole of the early republic's print public sphere and as much of its oral culture as we can reliably access. By midcentury, a variety of literary and cultural movements had begun to emphasize the contributions of a distinctly literary mode of writing, and later criticism on this period naturally attends to this body of work's claims to aesthetic specificity and autonomy.

Yet this predominant storyline renders invisible a body of postbellum nineteenth-century literature that continued to imagine itself as intimately tied, for better or worse, to formal politics. Readers after the Civil War not only had a wide range of political literature from which to choose; they felt inundated by it. In August of 1883, a reader of the journal *The Literary World* shared his estimation of Madeleine Dahlgren's recent novel, *A Washington Winter*: "Oh dear, another Washington novel, and of the same type!"[17] This letter is dated only three years after the publication of Henry Adams's *Democracy* (1880), which the aggrieved reader goes on to charge with intensifying the worst features of a genre inaugurated by Mark Twain and Charles Dudley Warner's *The Gilded Age* (1873) and currently saturating the market with scandalous novels of life in the capital. For this frustrated reader, the Washington novel was to be dismissed on patriotic grounds due to the "essential falsity" of its negative view of democracy and the dangers of such cynicism. Henry James, in a review of William DeForest's 1875 novel, *Honest John Vane*, similarly worried that DeForest put the reader in a grotesque intimacy with democracy's underbelly. "[DeForest] has wished to overwhelm the reader with the evil odor of lobbyism. But the reader, duly overwhelmed...may be excused for wondering whether, if this were a logical symbol of American civilization, it would not be well to let that phenomenon be submerged in the tide of corruption."[18]

If Gilded Age literature joins its antebellum antecedents in denouncing the corruption of politics, its extended treatments of the sites, sights, and smells of official democracy clearly express an ambivalent investment in and attraction to political institutions. Authors working in the mode of the Washington novel adapted the comedy of manners, the *roman-à-clef*, and strains of regionalism and muckraking realism to explore the capital city's social spaces as a complex metonym for the workings of the federal government.[19] Simultaneously drawing on and denouncing the taste for political gossip, in particular, these novels suggest the public's affective relation to the democratic process was marked by attraction and repulsion, a conflicted fascination with what Frances Hodgson Burnett called the "romance" of scandal, "the magnitude of it...the social position of the principle schemers, all [of which] endeared it to the public heart."[20] The human heart—that seat of moral sentiments—figures here as the source of prurient curiosity.

The political literature of the 1870s and 1880s, then, inherits a profound distrust of democratic institutions from an earlier literary canon. Now, however, anxiety becomes the driving force for a nervous attachment to politics, not simply a renunciation of it. Underlying works such as *Honest John Vane* and *Through One Administration* is the question of how, precisely, these books' authors were to articulate a critique *without* abandoning the project of democracy all together.[21] A similar dynamic can be seen in other genres of Gilded Age political literature. Mark Twain and Charles Dudley Warner's *The Gilded Age: A Tale of Today* (1873), the anchor of my first chapter, is part Washington novel and part political satire, even as its subtitle announces the text as a historical novel of the unfolding present. For all of its many modes, it is, fundamentally, a critique of corrupt political and legal institutions, even as its most famous characters (namely, Laura Hawkins and "Colonel" Beriah Sellers) loom so large because they dramatize the *allure* of the capital as a field for idealistic, egalitarian visions—and an arena for brutal ambition and self-interested scheming. Likewise, Helen Hunt Jackson's *Ramona* (1884), which I examine in Chapter 3, is a historical romance modeled on antebellum sentimental literature; it often strives to bypass a corrupt political system by appealing directly to readers' feelings. But Jackson developed other affective strategies beyond "sympathy," reflecting an engagement with journalism, political pamphleteering, and the norms governing official correspondence to fight for a more just federal Indian policy. In other words, she explored diverse modes of political writing and activism within and to the side of formal politics, even as her experience with the Department of the Interior provided ample evidence that government bureaucracy was unlikely to be anything but a tool for nepotism, greed, and routinized violence.

One could view these examples of the Gilded Age novel as reviving an earlier approach to political literature that, Nancy Glazener has argued, was mostly subsumed by emerging eighteenth- and early nineteenth-century norms regarding literary autonomy. For Glazener, the career of the writer Charles Brockden Brown offers an especially illustrative case. His "conspiracy-filled novels of the [17]'90s...played out forms of fear, paranoia, and aggression" with explicitly "political dimensions."[22] But, Glazener argues, American authors increasingly deployed claims of autonomy as a defense against censorship, a promise of aesthetic distance that "would insulate readers from any very strong or direct promptings to action."[23] Brown's later works respond to this valorization of apolitical writing by "promote[ing] prudence and conventional ideas of personal responsibility."[24]

Glazener offers a crucial frame for understanding the fate of political literature in the early republic, but I would propose a slight revision of Brown's place in order to clarify his relevance to the Gilded Age novel. It is worth noting, for example, the necessarily abstract contention that Brown's earlier novels "played out" paranoia and fear. Critics have struggled to abstract a program of action from Brown's political writing, in part because he dramatizes the anxious undercurrents of American democracy from all angles. In *Wieland* (1798), readers are put on guard against religious enthusiasm, but also against Enlightenment hubris. In *Edgar Huntly* (1799), indigenous people are rendered as a threat, but so too are the descendants of Europeans who surpass the Indians in "savagery." Brown delicately balances an overt interest in political themes (often resonant with the Jacobin writings of his intellectual mentor, William Godwin) with a degree of autonomy vis-à-vis parties and platforms. His novels are deeply interested in the affective atmosphere of his political moment, but not exactly in the mode of "promptings" to action.

This is to say that Brown's fiction is broadly anxious in a way that, as I will show, the literature of the Gilded Age is, as well. The later literature's delicate balance of universal aspirations and specific reform impulses was facilitated by developments in the political press. The Gilded Age saw the emergence of independent newspapers alongside the continued power of party organs. Less partisan organizations were instrumental in reinforcing the picture of postbellum America as uniquely corrupt, since they staked their value on investigative reports into congressional misdeeds— reports that no partisan editor would bankroll.[25] In this context, literature could appear both autonomous *and* political as long as it wasn't overtly partisan. At its worst, this literature thereby adopts a nonpartisan posture that levels meaningful distinctions between parties and contributes to the notion that "all" politics is corrupt. On the other hand, the Gilded Age novel could further distinguish itself from both the partisan and independent press by exploring the crises of democratic faith provoked by journalistic coverage of political malfeasance.

With these contours of the Gilded Age and its literature in view, we can now return to the question of democracy and affect unresolved at the beginning of this section: What do we miss—historically, conceptually, and aesthetically—if we equate "political emotion" with "sympathy"? Literature making a direct appeal to readers' sentiments foregrounds the cultivation of empathy as an important political strategy, circumventing rigid institutions in favor of malleable cultural sensibilities. At the same time, however, political feelings of frustration, apathy, or cynicism can only be seen as the expected, even deserved, fallout from any debilitating attachment to degraded institutions or forms. My outline of the antebellum period's anti-institutional imaginary, and the anxious postbellum political literature that followed in its wake, already hints at how these negative emotions have an interest and a power of their own. After all, for many of the authors I study, it was the *absence* of any intense political feelings that was most disturbing and most threatening to the vision of a more just political system. Take, for example, the much-publicized Crédit Mobilier bribery scandal of 1872, which seemed to offer crystal-clear evidence of the deleterious effects of corporate finance on the political process but resulted merely in voter apathy—at least according to nearly every major political novel of the period.[26] Narratives of political cynicism, exhaustion, agitation, and depression might provoke a disaffected readership to recoil from fallen democracy. But some of this literature also pushes back against the lack of interest and attenuated attention diagnosed by "apathy." Tracking this tension, "political emotion" in the context of this book refers not only to those grander emotions targeted by classical rhetoric (anger, compassion, etc.) that spur actions and forge alliances, but also to the almost-always-negative feelings associated with everyday political activity, attentiveness, or involvement.

I thus position the works studied in this book—by Twain and Jackson, along with Walt Whitman, Harriet Beecher Stowe, Henry Adams, W.E.B. Du Bois, and Ignatius Donnelly, among others—as part of a nineteenth-century story about literature, politics, and emotion that includes, but does not end with, sentiment and sympathy. Indeed, as I will show, Stowe's *Uncle Tom's Cabin* was an implicit and explicit model for these authors—the exemplar of literature's capacity to yoke individual feeling to public concerns.[27] Yet Stowe's novel was also an object of suspicion. I hope to show that many of the political novels of this period must be understood as both "countersentimental," or critical of the insufficiencies of an intimate public structured by putatively universal feelings, and deeply affective.[28] These novels suggest, in one form or another, that emotion cannot be expunged from political life and that political emotions require representational forms for delineating their puzzling capacity to alternate between energizing new social imaginaries and fueling a retreat from politics.

A political public sphere that both attracts and repels, and a cast of characters starring seductive lobbyists, corrupt senators, heartless bureaucrats, and an apathetic electorate: These are the core ingredients of Gilded Age political literature. They are also early indicators of persistent similarities with our current political moment. Many recent commentators have declared ours to be a "second Gilded Age," noting the déjà vu character of our political and social ills: "Crony capitalism, inequality, extravagance, social Darwinian self-justification, blame-the-victim callousness, free-market hypocrisy: Thus it was, thus it is again!"[29] I borrow from contemporary political criticism and theory to see what those areas of study reveal of the first Gilded Age, even as I intend these historical novels to put pressure on what we think we know about our own political moment. This dialogue works both ways: Our contemporary experiences of twenty-first-century democracy may allow us to see the literature of the Gilded Age in a new light. While the anxiety-producing energies of American society at the end of the nineteenth century are largely familiar to historians (detailed, for example, in Beard's 1881 volume, *American Nervousness*, from which I quote in the first section above, and in critic and historian Tom Lutz's 1991 volume of the same name), this nationwide case of the nerves largely has been attributed to a single source: the intensity of the American moneymaking impulse.[30] Yet twenty-first-century readers—perpetually rediscovering the shocking intensity of partisan disagreement, the unseemly appetites of the politically ambitious, and the surprising emotional toll of the election season—are well poised to question if economic activity was truly the only source of this national anxiety. While the link between industrial capitalism and nineteenth-century neurasthenia is revealing and persuasive, I argue that critics and historians have paid insufficient attention to how the ambitions, passions, and rampant energies of nineteenth-century *political* life inspired its own dictionary of nervous disorders—and, as I will show, its own literature.[31] Washington after the Civil War was notorious for lacking any business other than politics. Some for-profit industry, however manic, could have provided a welcome reprieve from what Washingtonians of the day saw, but many critics have since overlooked, as a monomaniacal fixation on the institutional workings of democracy.[32]

My project, thus, has a direct connection to the current moment's second Gilded Age of widening inequality and crony capitalism, as well as its persistent anxieties about the intensity of political disagreement. The literature I study here details the everyday negotiations with political emotion that define times of ongoing crisis, when a cluster of wearying, anxious emotional states comes to seem like both a grave threat to citizens' agency and the primary way people feel political.[33] At the heart of *Not Quite Hope* is the claim that, even as these works articulate an often-cynical view of American democracy that threatened to provoke an anxious retreat from politics, they also sought to cultivate an affective attachment to the institutions they criticized. This pattern of recoil and return, which continues to define our ambivalent relationship to the political process, is what I call an aversive attachment to institutional democracy.[34]

You Know, *Politics* Politics

This, then, is a book about literature, emotion, and politics. The Gilded Age political novel builds on and responds to anti-institutional strains in antebellum literature; it explores an important cluster of ambivalent and negative emotions; and it cultivates a melancholy yet critical posture toward corrupt democracy. The word "emotion" surely requires fuller attention and explanation, and in the next section I clarify how I situate this book within the expanding "affective turn" in the humanities. Yet one further note remains to be said about the seemingly more straightforward term, "politics." As I have described this project over the years, I have often invoked the awkward iteration "*politics* politics" to emphasize its concern with institutional politics and to distance it from an understanding of all literature as political in the wider discursive context of power relations—a field that bumps up against and indirectly impacts the "political" in its narrower meanings. This is also to say that I examine authors' engagement with the state, not just the nation.[35] Most of the works considered here take on an especially complicated relationship to formal politics, thanks to their having been written by authors who had political careers. I have already suggested that this approach offers a crucial corrective to a literary historiography that shifts from the culture of politics to the politics of culture, resisting the impulse of the romance, the sentimental novel, and transcendentalism to seek real art and real politics far from degraded institutions.[36]

But it may be letting literary criticism off the hook to suggest that the field's turn away from politics is simply an effect of too thoroughly internalizing the lessons of our antebellum literary archives. In a polemical essay addressing this question, Sean McCann and Michael Szalay offer a critique of *why* critical accounts of American literature through the present day consistently eschew formal politics. They lambast what they call the academic left's "magical" thinking: a fantasy that literature, theory, and academic critique are at their most powerful when they strongly express a fundamental irrationality or unspeakability, seeing intuition and imagination as crucial, radical counterparts to the constraints of bureaucratic rationality. McCann and Szalay contend that such a notion is little more than a self-serving conception of political agency prized by an intellectual class that wields little political or economic power and thus has embraced theorists, Foucault chief among them, who lend credibility to a conception of culture as a higher order of politics, over and against formal institutions.[37]

In McCann and Szalay's account, to refocus on institutional democracy is to get real about politics and to wean oneself from the left's mystified fantasies of cultural radicalism.[38] From this perspective, the Gilded Age political novel's institutional obsessions might look like an important resource. Their account meets some trouble, however, in the authors I study here—nearly all of whom turned to literature to remedy the disappointments of direct political participation, reinforcing the idea that culture offers a better kind of politics. Henry Adams, frustrated over the failures of his many campaigns for reform, determined that "literature offers higher prizes than politics," and—in his retrospectively inaccurate account, anyway—abandoned politics in favor of writing histories and novels.[39] Twain remained steadily involved in political life, from delivering speeches for President Hayes to famously publishing Grant's biography, all the while upholding the oft-repeated truism that he "detested" the subject of politics.[40] Caught in the mire of party politics, Ignatius Donnelly yearned to escape to the realm of literature symbolized most powerfully for him, as for W.E.B. Du Bois, by Shakespeare. Finally, Helen Hunt Jackson, serving as an unpaid agent of the Indian Agency, famously tried writing nonfiction, and then a romance, to offset her failure to enact change in her official bureaucratic capacity.

The temptation to celebrate these novels' turn "back" toward institutional politics is further complicated by the perspective of recent political theory, which suggests that to focus on formal politics is a sure way to guarantee one is not thinking about "politics" at all. Indeed, "institutional politics" appears closer to what Jacques Rancière has recently designated as the *opposite* of a properly aesthetic politics. "[P]olitics is generally seen as the set of procedures whereby the aggregation and consent of collectivities is achieved, the organization of powers, the distribution of places and roles, and the systems for legitimizing this distribution."[41] In his account, this so-called politics is more like bureaucratic administration, and so he "propose[s] to give this system of distribution and legitimization another name. I propose to call it the police."[42]

Rancière thus critiques a conception of the public sphere as an administrative mechanism for producing consent, consensus, and minimizing disagreement. For Rancière, the desire for conflict-free consensus is antidemocratic and incompatible with the genuinely political act of reconfiguring the political-aesthetic field, such that those who are excluded from its workings—those who "have no part"—appear as political actors. Such an aesthetic redistribution is a necessarily antagonistic act, an act of disagreement, leading Rancière to propose we "reserve the term politics for an extremely determined activity antagonistic to policing: whatever breaks with the tangible configuration whereby parties and parts or lack of them are defined by a presupposition that, by definition, has no place in that configuration—that of the part of those who have no part."[43] If "consensus," in its etymological meaning, refers to a shared feeling or a sense in common, then to engage in the work of democratic politics necessarily is to have a commitment to dissensus, to interrupting the state of anesthetic repose in which current configurations of power appear stable and self-evident.[44]

How, then, do we proceed, given that the Gilded Age's overtly political literature could be seen as an important occasion to refocus on "real," institutional politics— *politics* politics—or, from another perspective, could dramatize the very turn away from politics that McCann and Szalay lament? Is it possible to heed a warning about the too-easy celebration of cultural politics while simultaneously attending to Rancière's caution that what passes for politics in formal settings may be its opposite: an administrative mechanism for minimizing the very antagonism and disagreement that define true democracy? Throughout, I argue that Gilded Age literature may be most valuable in disordering our critical desire to consistently map real versus magical politics, or politics versus the police, according to how a text highlights its proximity to or distance from institutions.

One step toward resisting such reductive schematizations is to develop a more flexible definition of institutions as such. As Lisi Schoenbach notes:

> It is difficult enough merely to define "institutions": the term combines conceptual complexity with seemingly limitless linguistic flexibility. Here is a word whose verb form, "institutionalize," evokes punishment, repression, and coercion, while its nominal form is equally likely to describe a beloved hamburger joint, a prison, a mental hospital, or a widely accepted social convention.[45]

Schoenbach thus "define[s] institutions broadly as structures that govern and codify collective behavior."[46] Note, however, that even this clear, if expansive, definition is an odd fit for one of her examples: a beloved burger joint. Does that kind of institution "govern and codify"? Such difficulties may motivate Lauren Berlant's much broader account, defining an institution as "a thing with resources to which we return to anchor our world as we move through it."[47] For Berlant, an institution is anything that persists with sufficient stability to seem like the same thing across time, thereby grounding some aspect of social life. To say a restaurant or a bar "governs" behavior may imply too intentional an implantation of norms, but it is easy to see how such a "joint" might suture various aspects of a community's idea of itself and the behaviors that stem from it.

While risking imprecision, this expanded sense of institutions prepares us to take seriously Fredric Jameson's use of the word in thinking about literary form: "Genres are essentially contracts between a writer and his readers; or rather ... they are literary institutions, which like the other institutions of social life are based on tacit agreements or contracts."[48] The unstated "contract" is simply an expectation that the genre will have recognizable features and seem, in some recognizable way, like other books that are similarly categorized. For Jameson, this recognizability derives from the relation among texts. He argues we should not think in terms of a "traditional logic in which a given item is ranged in the class appropriate to it" but rather of a "generic system ... [as] a constellation of ideal relationships" in relation to the "work itself ... [as] a concrete verbal composition. We must then understand the former as constituting something like an environment for the latter."[49] If we return to institutions because they offer resources for organizing social life, and if they are defined relationally, then late-nineteenth-century reform literature can be seen to take its shape from a complex web of both literary and nonliterary institutions. Marriage, the sentimental novel, and the US Congress are all examples of "institutions" that constitute the greater relational environment of the Gilded Age political novel, from which the genre gains an institutional stability of its own.

Formal politics and literary form thus meet in the Gilded Age novel. But as much as this literature differs from earlier democratic fictions by its relation with, rather than its rejection of, official politics, this "relation" is deeply ambivalent. The political romances encountered here often set out to structure their current-affairs analyses along legible partisan lines, fantasizing ontological solutions of merit or virtue, and bureaucratic solutions of order and stability, to "solve" the contingency at the heart of democratic politics. Thus, when at their most institutional, they can appear at their most anti- or post-political, in Rancière's sense.[50] At other moments, it is these texts' disgusted recoil from the grubby work of politics that is most likely to fuel post-political fantasies of transcending or escaping the realm of democratic disagreement. Ambivalence is rarely seen as an aesthetic or political virtue, but, as I explain, this literature's tonal qualities of pessimism, cynicism, and disgust stem from the novelists' fraught efforts to narrate the competing allures of post-political administration and democratic dissensus. In narrating the full spectrum of emotions experienced by those who plunge into politics, or even those affected by its margins, this literature illuminates the "plurality of antago-nisms and points of rupture" that Rancière considers "political" in its proper meaning. Much as I hope to challenge the reason/emotion binary by exploring a more complex continuum of affective relations that includes (rather than defined in opposition to) cool detachment, so too the Gilded Age novel refuses to be either for or against formal politics.[51] This literature drifts uncomfortably close to the police-like mechanisms of institutional politics, but in so doing it reveals surprising scenes of negotiation, bargaining, risk-taking, and world-making that persist within and alongside the political public sphere.[52]

The Turn to Affect

I have sketched how Gilded Age Washington novels, satires, and reform romances require thinking about the role of emotion in politics. Rather than focusing only on those positive emotions that forge imagined communities, I have proposed that we attend more closely to the negativity and ambivalence these novels link to too-close-for-comfort contact with existing political institutions. Of course, even as nineteenth-century American literary history retains a strong focus on sympathy as the most important moral sentiment, there has been a wider range of studies outside this context, exploring in great detail the complex range of bodily intensities that theorists have placed under the headings of emotion and affect.

This "affective turn" is vast and diverse; any account of its philosophical lineage and later disciplinary inflections will be necessarily incomplete. Studies of affect generally are seen as building on a theoretical tradition that began with thinkers such as Baruch Spinoza and, later, William James and Henri Bergson—a tradition then revitalized by Gilles Deleuze.[53] This work attends to the body, its receptivity, and its capacity to affect and be affected by a world of people and things with which one is engaged in constant sensorial transactions. The stakes of this focus on the body's affects can be framed in different ways, but for nearly all of these philosophers and their followers, the corporeal rubric poses a challenge to Cartesian conceptions of the self, to Enlightenment valorizations of abstract reason, to liberalism's celebration of individual autonomy and self-containment, and to misogynist and racist denigrations of embodiment.[54] While affect's intensities are almost always linked to thinking and judgment, these theories usually emphasize components of bodily experience that are pre-, sub-, or quasi- cognitive, bearing both directly and obliquely on agency and action without equating to a fully rational thought or decision. In their most utopian register, such affects help describe the possibilities of a body politic that is fundamentally intersubjective and social.[55] Yet a language of affect also draws attention to the ways in which politicians, the media, and others manipulate the body's feeling faculties.[56]

Even the most basic shared assumptions about affect pose challenges for placing this "turn" in the context of other critical genealogies. "Affect" might be seen as a departure from Marxism (because a language of the body and its feelings privatizes properly political problems) or its supplement (because, in Raymond Williams's hands, "structures of feeling" provide a way to analyze emerging structural and historical transformations in the arrangement of society under capitalism).[57] Affect may seem to pose an alternative to psychoanalysis (because it shifts focus from a "subject" of language or discourse to an embodied intersubjectivity), or it may look like a complement to it (because affect extends a theory of libidinal drives and attachments to account for aspects of social life beyond the individual's familial, psychosexual dramas). Many influential works within queer theory and critical race studies, for example, have drawn on a powerful mix of Marxism, psychoanalysis, and affect theory to highlight feelings of melancholia, depression, and shame as indexes of structural inequalities and institutional violence. These pressures register affectively on marginalized bodies, producing forms of othered subjectivity.[58]

Needless to say, this book cannot sustain an engagement with all of these strands while also undertaking a detailed literary history of the Gilded Age political novel. Yet it is equally true that these ongoing critical conversations have fundamentally shaped this project. It is worthwhile, then, to highlight those facets of the affective turn with which I attend most directly, and to explain those aspects of its terminology and methodology from which I do and do not draw. Most obviously, I am interested in work that emphasizes an interest in *social* affect but de-emphasizes the taxonomic intricacies of the affect/emotion debate by speaking in terms of "political emotion." This body of work pays "close attention to the microdynamics of the everyday and the ordinary," seeking to attend to the "richness of emotional experience," including being "honest about moments of boredom or exhaustion or depression but also alert to what makes us feel energized or hopeful."[59] One central claim of *Not Quite Hope* is that a concern with everyday political emotion was very much present in the period after the Civil War, although I specify the crucial distinction that this concern frequently found articulation in a largely phobic rhetoric. I share with Sianne Ngai an interest in feelings beyond the canonical emotions (sympathy, fear, anger), although these "ugly feelings" (being underwhelmed, overwhelmed, cynical, tired, agitated, and embittered) emerge as uncomfortable states in late-nineteenth-century novels that, in their polemical focus and reformist zeal, seem reluctant to recognize improvisation or uncertainty.[60]

As my citation of critics employing discourses of affect, emotion, feelings, and sentiments indicates, I do not insist on a strict distinction between "affect" (understood generally as impersonal bodily intensities not fully captured by an emotional lexicon) and what Fredric Jameson calls simply "named emotions" (feelings, however intense, with a relatively clear subject and object, and a relatively stable linguistic referent within a historical period and cultural location).[61] In part, this is because speaking of both affect and emotion puts the critical energy of the affective turn in dialogue with nineteenth-century American studies' longstanding interest in sympathy, sentiment, and feeling.

For example, thinking in terms of affect and emotion together offers an occasion to revisit some of literary criticism's own suspicions about the political effects of affects in nineteenth-century America. Christopher Castiglia has argued that a range of antebellum authors and political theorists described the self-management of one's emotional inner life as a kind of civic responsibility, thereby displacing properly political modes of public agency. He calls this "reformist interiority, one that brought about the loss of social participation in public life while giving citizens the impression that they had lost nothing at all."[62] What's more, this unruly inner life then was used to justify greater institutional control: "If the people of the United States cannot be trusted to regulate their relation to sexual, much less social, reproduction, institutions…without the complication of wills or desire, happily fulfill that function."[63] Castiglia's account helps us see how, even as Gilded Age political novels decry the excessive emotionality of politics, they offer an important alternative to the antebellum conception of emotion and feeling as private affairs. For better or worse, in these novels affect is always and explicitly a feature of *public* life, one that saturates institutions no less than it does individuals. Put another way, these texts see feeling as not only an "interior state." Anticipating the social component of emotional life underscored by recent theories of "affect," the novels studied here anxiously depict DC politics as a contagious atmosphere that enshrouds feeling, permeable subjects.

I also hesitate to draw a strict affect/emotion distinction in these novels because they repeatedly reveal a great deal of affective noise and counterintuitive connotations—even within seemingly stable feelings. In Twain's novels, for example, "hope" attains a debilitating, crazy-making intensity, while for Adams, "pessimism" and "disgust" color an intense attachment to the *promise* of political life.[64] Unlike some of the founding works of affect theory—critiqued so powerfully but, I submit, imprecisely, by Ruth Leys—I am not invested in identifying the indeterminacy of affect as an "autonomous" space of pure potentiality.[65] In most cases, I use "affect" to emphasize the corporeal experience of emotion and its unstable relationship to language, noting again that this project's novels rarely see instability as a virtue. A profound postbellum craving for bureaucratic order and unity means many political novels of the period make overt gestures toward a public sphere cleansed of partisan passions, old grudges, and destabilizing enthusiasms.[66] At the same time, the period's genre experiments stand as an archive of the forms of political ambivalence through which American authors negotiated a hesitant commitment to the project of democracy.

The final strain of this broader "affective turn" with which I contend is the body of work that thinks about the affective tone of critical reading itself, a self-reflexive focus on our own critical dispositions. Queer theorists, for example, have long critiqued naïve postures of optimism and happiness as hegemonic, embracing the critical power of negativity and, in a related but distinct bibliography, the social creativity mediated by shame, melancholy, and even depression. An apparent contradiction reveals itself: I've suggested that nineteenth-century literary studies focus too exclusively on the power and pitfalls of positive feeling, yet the more common complaint within one strand of affectively attuned queer theory is that critics have focused *only* on negative affect.[67] But this tension reinforces my claim that negative affect has come to look like either the necessary cost or the just punishment of any engagement with real and existing political institutions. While imaginative literature can explore ideal realms of feeling and community, affect theory as a strain of contemporary cultural studies focuses on the bad feelings of present politics. In advocating a renewed focus on the anxious affects of nineteenth-century political literature, my appeal might be seen as the mirror image of calls by queer theorists for counterhegemonic critique that makes room for more hopeful critical postures.[68]

This debate perhaps is most interesting as part of a wider cycle of concerns over our critical temperaments. Too much critical negativity sparks calls for a renewed optimism conducive to political action. This in turn re-energizes commitments to forms of negativity that appear less seduced by the normativity masquerading as "hope" or happiness. Versions of this back-and-forth play out in very different contexts. Wendy Brown famously critiqued leftist theory as too "melancholic," debilitated by a nostalgic attachment to class-based politics.[69] More recently, however, Amanda Anderson has attempted to *redeem* liberalism (sometimes associated with a naïve faith in individual autonomy and social progress) by emphasizing its melancholic "bleakness" and unexpected affinities with the Frankfurt school's critical pessimism.[70] Eve Sedgwick made an oft-cited call for reading practices of repair, hope, and attachment as alternatives to the suspicion and bitterness of ideology critique.[71] Yet some of Sedgwick's later readers have worried that this seemingly optimistic call for repair is itself too depressed.[72] Rita Felski and Bruno Latour have diagnosed ideology critique as exhausted, or "out of steam."[73] But forms of "surface reading," a kind of modest attentiveness sometimes advanced as an alternative to critique, have left some pining for the force, the political engagement, and even the suspicion of critique, which may have some steam left after all.[74]

Such a quick overview doesn't do the nuances of these arguments justice, yet a bird's-eye view of the conversation's circularity should push us to question the value of pessimism and optimism as ready terms of approbation or condemnation. All of these modes of reading and interpretation are united in an effort to stay invested in political projects (critiquing capitalism, patriarchy, heteronormativity, etc.) while also refusing debilitating attachments to bad objects (hegemonic cultural narratives, overused critical methodologies, shopworn vocabularies). If we see "optimism" less as a hopeful feeling and more as a persistent structure of attachment, nearly all of these efforts to challenge our critical temperaments desire an "optimism" that is also smart and critical.[75] Likewise, if "pessimism" is seen less as a depressive affect and more as a detachment that makes space for reflection and critique, nearly all of these critics seek forms of skepticism and distrust that stop short of apathetic collapse. I don't mean to say the literature I study here solves this impasse; nor do I advance a new candidate for what comes after critique. But the fact that the ambivalent disposition of Gilded Age political literature so directly mirrors our own critical gridlock makes it impossible to apply any of these competing modes of "reading" in a doctrinaire fashion. Literature of this period gains much of its force from a deep suspicion of emotion's role in democratic politics. The novels themselves are engaged in something like ideology critique.

Yet these texts also fight to maintain an emotional attachment to the very institutions they criticize, an attachment articulated in a paradoxically negative idiom. Whether one calls this a reparative reading of critique-y texts or a reaffirmation of critique in the face of the texts' own cruel optimism, these novels' apprehensive efforts to sustain a desire for the political is alternately threatened and energized by excesses of both optimism and cynicism.[76] My title (taken from a line in Helen Hunt Jackson's *Ramona* discussed in my third chapter) should thus be understood as emblematic of the Gilded Age political novel's affective negotiations. Menaced on one side by apathetic pessimism, and on the other by naïve or even crazy optimism, they arrive at a productively unsettled state: "something, not quite hope."

Fits of Reason

Before providing an overview of the structure of this book (and by way of an intro-duction to the same), one last word remains wanting about a final term that haunts this study of literature and emotion: namely, "reason." Anyone familiar with post-bellum literature might wonder what all this talk of affect and feeling has to do with a canon that often seems explicitly rationalistic. After the Civil War, a variety of reform communities expressed a sober desire to fix what ailed democracy, often positioning this overt rationalism against earlier strands of "sentimental" reform. The growth of the federal government in the postbellum years seemed to call for a measure of patriotic idealism, but, more importantly, for some effective and scien-tific solutions. As one author and critic put it in 1870: "The questions of slavery and the war were perfectly simple. The people comprehended them. In contrast, the questions which are now pressing upon us are technical, and call for the exercise of statesmanship . . . the people do not understand the subjects."[77] As the notion of moral philanthropy became increasingly relegated to churches and private organi-zations, technical statesmanship soon required its own institutional organization and found its home in an expanding government bureaucracy: "Problems that had formerly been considered largely private and best solved by moral suasion now became candidates for government solutions."[78]

As the government grew more hands-on in managing social ills, private citizens seeking reform found themselves making direct appeals to the ever-expanding federal bureaucracy: "Spokesmen for the poor and the sick, for the abolition of capital punishment, for civil rights for Negroes, for justice for American Indians, for women's suffrage, and for fair treatment of laborers converged on Washington to plead their cases before the new agencies, committees, and departments."[79] This proliferation of federal agencies and subagencies made the government, in its institutional and bureaucratic functions, a more immediate presence in citizens' lives than it had been at any point before the war. While such "technical" governance might have been a welcome reprieve after the intense sectional passions of the war, many observers also sensed an antidemocratic aspect to the new, obscure topics of debate. The editors of *The New York Sun*, for example, worried that "tariff treatises are for the college room, not for the open field of a great popular controversy."[80] Likewise, a historian analyzing the trend noted "pure deliberative rhetoric educated the voters on policy but it alienated them from politics."[81] Even more worrisome, the new bureaucratic rationality not only threatened to replace inspiration with paperwork; it revealed the enormous potential for abuse in party-patronage practices, a form of corruption that treated the thousands of low-level political appointments as bargaining chips and viewed the budgets of small committees tasked with development projects as cash dispensaries.

What, in this context, would count as expert solutions to the rampant corruption that had already come to characterize the age? And how could literature, which had demonstrated its power to dramatize the putatively simple subjects of slavery and war, now engage with this new science of politics? The dearth of concrete answers may explain why one specific, if seemingly yawn-inducing, proposal had such a surprisingly strong imaginative pull on many of the authors in this book: civil service reform.[82] From the first discussion on the 1869 Jenckes Bill to the passage of the Pendleton reform act in 1883, many reform-minded citizens, mostly eastern Republicans and "mugwumps," called for the institution of competitive exams that would determine government appointments.[83] In actuality, such exams applied only to clerkships and other low-level roles, but the notion of an enforced merit-based system was frequently extended in the popular imagination to cover cabinet positions and even congressional and presidential elections. This rationalizing solution, however, threatened to mechanize a process in which sectional and party loyalties, as well as moral judgments of character, intuition, and other less quantifiable and testable virtues, were not always unwelcome. As one opponent of reform insisted, such a quantification of government appointments reduced the masses to "mere machines."[84]

This sketch of the period's burgeoning bureaucratic imaginary thus partly answers the question that began this section: why focus on emotion in a period obsessed with reason? In the context of the civil service debate, as well as in nineteenth-century efforts to regulate the criminal justice system, the currency system, and the administration of Indian affairs and western territories, intense emotion was often designated a contaminant, although it could also be seen as an antidote to the dehumanizing, reifying process of bureaucratic rationalization.[85] But this answer still doesn't capture the deep imbrication of reason and emotion with which this book is concerned. As I have shown, recent studies of emotion and affect draw attention to the capacity for feelings to be contagious and extravagant, to exceed the boundaries of the individual, to surpass proper measure, and to unsettle our notion of a stable subject.[86] I will argue, however, that a primary lesson of the ostensibly rational but generically playful, ambivalent, conflicted, insightful, and phobic novels to be examined in the coming chapters is that the desire for cool, rational politics generates an intensity of its own. As Susan Wells notes, "practices of rationality can take the relations of desire as their subject or employ those relations as one of their motives; desire can be articulated in the discourses of rational practices."[87] Discourses of overt, even ostentatious, rationality might themselves be a medium for the cultivation of intense attachments, the expression of utopian desires, or attempts to manage the aftereffects of traumatic anguish.

Such a complex mix of reason and emotion structures all of the texts herein. I introduce each chapter in this book with a heading—madness, disgust, depression, suspicion, cynicism, and exhaustion—that might be seen as the primary text's or texts' dominant affective "tone," even as the instability and contagiousness native to affect ensures that these feelings bleed across chapters.[88] An abiding bitterness, apathy, and disappointment, as well as surprising moments of exuberance, arousal, and optimism, pervade the works studied here. At the same time, most of the authors I consider sought a zone outside the realm of political conflict and uncertainty: a fantasmatic space, often in the legal system or even the political bureaucracy, where complex political and ethical problems could be adjudicated by the light of reason.

In my first chapter, "Crazy Love: Emotional Insanity in the Gilded Age," I argue that a desire to expunge the law and politics of their passionate intensity led Mark Twain and Harriet Beecher Stowe, each in his or her own way, to employ an overly capacious discourse of "emotional insanity" in analyzing the failings of the Gilded Age public sphere. Examining Stowe's *My Wife and I* (1871) and Twain's *The Gilded Age* (1873), I show how both authors respond to the perceived threat of the free love movement as an assault on private property and individual responsibility, with Twain calling for a renewed commitment to the norms governing legal reason, while Stowe advocates an ascetic vigilance to restrain unruly passions. Stowe's and Twain's antipassional diagnoses overlook the nuances of various forms of public, political enthusiasm, choosing instead to standardize and taxonomize the entire spectrum, from vigilante mobs to political demonstrations, as—in the language of nineteenth-century medical jurisprudence—"emotional insanity." And yet, in their struggles to conceptualize love as a political emotion, the authors are surprisingly productive. Twain can see love only as a threat to the law. Stowe sees love as a power that reinforces institutions but wants to yoke it to "traditional" marriage alone. Together, Twain and Stowe dramatize the difficulty but also the necessity of theorizing desire and love as simultaneously institutional adhesives and solvents—a way out of the false choice between lifeless institutions and a pure, unmediated multitude.

The need to insulate legal and political rationality from disruptive emotions permeates the literature of this book. Ultimately, however, these novels are far more successful at offering unwitting demonstrations of the untenability of such a rigid territorialization, demonstrated perhaps most powerfully by the novelists' frequent recourse to a visceral sense of right as the proper measure of justice or injustice. This is just one way sentimentalism and realism, romance and rationality, coincide in these works.[89] And so in my second chapter, "Desire, Disgust,

Democracy: or, Aversive Attachments," on Henry Adams's *Democracy: An American Novel* (1880), I explore how Adams's commitment to civil service reform expresses a utopian wish that competency exams could sanitize the political process of the antidemocratic exclusivity of intimate attachments. Evoking an affective atmosphere of disgust, Adams cultivates in his reader a shared repulsion for the excessive political appetites that strike him as abandoning the disinterested reason his presidential progenitors embodied. By the novel's close, "disgust" looks like the only affective posture that refuses to passively accept democracy's failings, offering an idiom for expressing, not squelching, a desire for the political. In making this claim, I challenge political philosophers, such as Martha Nussbaum, who repudiate disgust out of hand, and I revisit a related strain of literary criticism, focused on Walt Whitman, that celebrates without reservation the suppression of disgust as a necessarily democratic act.

In my third chapter, "Strange Apathy: Sentiment and Sovereignty in *Ramona*," the rational-emotional intensity initially takes shape in Helen Hunt Jackson's avowedly calm-headed effort to distinguish between good and bad, high and low, measured and mawkish styles of sentimentality. Even so, Jackson's *Ramona* (1884) ultimately registers the ways such taxonomies played into the hands of the Department of the Interior's biopolitical mandate to stay "cool" and reasonable about native suffering. Critics usually think of Jackson as undertaking a project modeled on *Uncle Tom's Cabin*, in that sympathy for her American Indian protagonists promises to bring them into the fold of personhood and citizenship. I contend that the novel's most searching affective strategies are, in fact, counter-sentimental, insofar as designating Indians as persons was fully in keeping with "assimilation era" efforts to individuate the Indian and dissolve native tribes. In my account, Jackson's novel can be seen as an affective fleshing out of the theorist Giorgio Agamben's later notion of "bare life": the biological remainder of fractured political lives. *Ramona* lingers with animal-like desperation and depression to register the loss of tribal forms of political life and to disturb bureaucratic visions of efficiently managed populations and incrementally improved feelings.

If realism is understood (problematically) as "as an antidote to sentimental representation" then each of these novels looks broadly "realist."[90] Yet I also draw attention to a cynical intensity and eccentricity of aesthetic style in the novels themselves—a zeal that seems at odds with the rationalist pretension of the reform programs the books directly or indirectly endorsed.[91] For example, my fourth chapter, "On the Hatred of Hypocrites: Donnelly, Du Bois, Race, and Representation," first turns to *Doctor Huguet* (1891), by Ignatius Donnelly, a best-selling novelist and leading founder of the American People's Party. This novel depicts a white, southern reformer who suppresses his feelings of solidarity with African Americans in order to gain elected office. In an act of divine retribution, Huguet is turned black for betraying his principles, providing Donnelly's readers with a troubling, if eccentric, allegory about the importance of the populist project of building a cross-racial alliance.

Like many populists, Donnelly dreamed that economic interest might offer a route to overcome sectional passions and racial prejudice, and to displace the dominance of the Republican Party. His wariness of political struggles, passions, and frustrations, however, threatens to fuel a full-on retreat from the political process. Drawing on a range of theorists who have grappled with the unusually intense hatred and suspicion provoked by the figure of the hypocrite, I seek ways to re-evaluate the cluster of negative affects that seem to always follow in the archetype's wake. Accordingly, I turn to W.E.B. Du Bois, focusing especially on *Black Reconstruction*'s (1935) account of the fleeting promise of an alliance between black and white laborers, which was derailed by Andrew Johnson's hypocritical policies. Du Bois joins Donnelly in a deep suspicion and condemnation of white hypocrisy, but he also reimagines hypocrisy as less of an individual moral failing and more the result of a political system that is itself disjointed. This chapter ends with an examination of what I call "structural hypocrisy," and Du Bois's counterintuitive proposition that an idiosyncratic form of pity may be the only way to defuse a debilitating hatred of political hypocrites.

Given that all of these texts exhibit some pessimism about democracy's future, they collectively contribute to what observers of the period had begun to call the "new cynicism."[92] Indeed, "cynical" may be the most common affective adjective leveled at the literature and culture of the Gilded Age. My final chapter, "Cynical Reason in the Cranky Age," examines the question of cynicism head on, returning briefly to Twain's *The Gilded Age* in order to measure the shift in the author's thinking on political emotion and madness by the writing of his later novel *The American Claimant* (1892). After the assassination of President Garfield by Charles Guiteau in 1881, many commentators looked back to Twain's first novel for his satiric take on the insanity defense. Yet when Twain returns to a character from *The Gilded Age,* the eccentric Colonel Sellers, in *The American Claimant*, he unexpectedly affirms a species of the lunacy he had earlier rejected. In my first chapter, I focus on Twain's heavy-handed embrace of legal reason and his sweeping denigration of all political emotion as madness. In my last chapter, I argue that the historical aftermath of Twain's novel made him newly aware of the insane violence of cynical reason itself.

Specifically, I claim that Twain helps us understand how cynicism is paradoxically defined by the intensity of its own affective involvement in politics (expressed aversively as a smart form of bitterness, pessimism, and exasperation, etc.) and a deep suspicion of others' positive affects as signs of unthinking credulity. By turning to *The American Claimant* and building on theoretical accounts, such as Peter Sloterdijk's *Critique of Cynical Reason* (1983), I show how this discomfort with political emotion yields the snake-eating-its-tail aspect of cynical critique, wherein a revelation of elite corruption on behalf of the people circles back to denigrate the people themselves, and how a fearful rejection of enthusiasm as a sign of suspended agency ends up substituting ardor with apathy—the cynic's own disease of will.

The main argument of this book thus begins and ends with Twain, the author whose work not only gave the period its singular epithet but also provided us with some of the most vivid evocations of politics' affective "atmospheres." In a final coda, I expand on this atmospheric metaphor by turning to time. The title of *Through One Administration* (1881), Frances Hodgson Burnett's Washington novel, invokes a unit of official time that also bookends her novel's love plots. Like Whitman's neologism "presidentiad," Burnett's "administration" privileges the rhythms of electoral politics while also imagining that such timeframes could organize alternative forms of intimacy. I show how the novel's temporal dynamic offers a crucial supplement to the "atmospheric" model developed thus far. Gilded Age fiction often promises to bring readers "behind the scenes" in Washington; these works rely on elite (or crafty) protagonists who secure our access to the parlors, lobbies, and private chambers where realpolitik takes place. Burnett's vision of a reading public moving alongside but not fully in step with administrative time, I argue, offers a rubric for describing how the mere fact of paying attention to the political process—even one with few opportunities for direct citizen access or agency—nonetheless ropes a wider public into the affective rhythms of the political.

This account puts pressure on recent queer theories of temporality, which often valorize asynchronous sociality as necessarily radical (an account that echoes the antebellum romance's distaste for institutions). If critics have often supposed the literary imagination to require distance from official politics, *Not Quite Hope* attends to the ways in which political creativity can survive, at least occasionally, in proximity to formal institutions and party politics. Dirty campaigning, brazen corruption, and partisan acrimony deaden our political sensorium. And yet, in such a fraught libidinal economy, a complex range of emotions—including, or even especially, negative and imprecise political affects—offers one idiom for expressing a fragile yearning for politics.

Madness

Crazy Love

EMOTIONAL INSANITY IN THE GILDED AGE

In one of the nested subplots in Mark Twain and Charles Dudley Warner's co-authored novel, *The Gilded Age: A Tale of Today* (1873), Ruth Bolton, an aspiring doctor, explains to her Quaker mother why she will consider marriage only after she has secured her own income: "Mother, I think I wouldn't say 'always' to any one until I have a profession and am as independent as he is. Then my love would be a free act, and not in any way a necessity."[1] Warner claimed responsibility for this chapter, and his contributions tend to steer Twain's raucous political satire toward more cautious moral pronouncements.[2] So it's no surprise Ruth's mother quickly offers a conventional corrective to Ruth's ambitions: "Margaret Bolton smiled at this new-fangled philosophy. 'Thee will find that love, Ruth, is a thing thee won't reason about, when it comes, nor make any bargains about'" (G, 185). For Ruth's mother, love's suspension of logic offers a clear rebuke to what Harriet Beecher Stowe called—in her novel *My Wife and I* (1871)—"very alarmingly rational women-reformers" who hoped their reasoned ideas about female dress, careers, and sexual freedom could alter women's putatively natural role as mothers and homemakers.[3] In Warner's account, love pays little heed to reformers' rational theories.

Yet this message sits uncomfortably in *The Gilded Age,* a novel that not only is deeply anxious about the total suspension of rational faculties recently categorized by medical experts as "emotional insanity" but insistently traces vexing connections between love and madness.[4] A few chapters before Laura Hawkins, the novel's possibly crazy protagonist, attempts to murder her married paramour, she offers a disturbing echo of Mrs. Bolton's homely advice: "She wanted love, this woman. Was not her love for [him] deeper than any other woman's could be?... Did he not belong to her by virtue of her overmastering passion? His wife—she was not his wife, except by the law" (G, 277).

In Gilded Age debates over the definition of marriage, "love" is a complex concept. For both traditionalists and radicals alike, love names a relation of intimacy in which enthusiasm, irrationality, unexpectedness, and self-disruption are taken to be signs of legitimacy. Yet the meaning of love's antinomian power varies widely. For Stowe, as for Warner, love's madness could be a conservative force, reminding radical women of gender's hard facts. But Stowe was also committed to expanding women's political and economic freedom by upending the idea that women must marry, or that economic considerations were in and of themselves grounds to wed. In this light, love's craziness was critical to expanding opportunities for women's agency: Sane love might be a bill of sale in affective disguise; it might be something men had reasoned over or made bargains about.[5] But the pact that moderate reformers, like Stowe, made with love relied on insanity knowing its place, keeping love's states of thrilling vulnerability contained within the parameters of monogamous heterosexual domesticity.

For the period's more radical feminists, designated "free lovers" by their contemporaries, this was a bargain worth breaking.[6] For them, that same irrationality instilled sexuality with a force that might open up new political horizons once love was released from the gilded cage of compulsory domesticity. Meanwhile, an observer like Twain—anxiously chronicling the influence of money on politics and the law, and skeptically eyeing the links between emotion and insanity drawn by mercenary medical "experts"—saw love's madness in a different light. In a ripped-from-the-headlines series of high-profile lovers' spats turned violent, the so-called "insanity dodge" threatened to provide a court-sanctioned alibi for wealthy criminals and jealous cuckolds alike. The real lunacy, in Twain's eyes, was the madness of the masses that seemed ready, even eager, to acquit elite defendants who claimed to be in love's thrall.

Tracking these complex relays between love and madness and between passion, politics, and the law, this chapter examines Stowe's *My Wife and I; Or, Harry Henderson's History* and Twain and Warner's *The Gilded Age: A Tale of Today* as cognate efforts to explore the madness of love but also to insulate politics from its lunacy. In the Introduction to this book, I claimed that studying political emotion in the Gilded Age requires attending to a variety of "ugly," in-between affects we might miss if we focused only on sociable feelings (sympathy and compassion) or on any of the more canonical emotions (anger, happiness, grief) that generally are directed toward a stable object. Why, then, should I begin with "love," perhaps the conventional emotion par excellence, and one that immediately—in a nineteenth-century American literary context, anyway—calls to mind Walt Whitman's celebration of amative and adhesive attachment as the libidinal glue binding the nation together?[7] As the scenes sketched above suggest, one answer is that love's adhesive qualities do not fully account for its status as a political emotion. The cluster of intensities my title shorthands as "crazy love" remind us that love binds people to some institutional forms (marriage, family) even as it threatens others (the law). Love assembles and it shatters; it grounds you and it drives you mad.

This tension haunts a long history of efforts to harness "love" for politics.[8] Theorists often locate love's utopian force in its anti-institutional power, as it drives subjects into relations and scenes that upset the restrictions of existing legal, ethical, and political norms. Michael Hardt and Antonio Negri, for example, posit that love is political because it is about "producing a new social world." Love "is an ontological event in that it marks a rupture with what exists and the creation of the new."[9] To produce a world, however, love must do more than rupture—a point with which Alain Badiou grapples in his *In Praise of Love*. He exalts love as "a cosmopolitan, subversive, sexual energy," which "transgresses frontiers and social status at a time normally devoted to the Army, the Nation and the State."[10] Later, however, Badiou distinguishes his approach from, for example, a "surrealism [that] exalts 'l'amour fou' as the power of an event that is beyond any law" but has "little interest in that which endured."[11] The key question for Badiou becomes how love can produce social forms that *persist*. Lauren Berlant keeps this multivalent relation to disruption and stability in view by attending to love's genres. She considers love as a rare vernacular idiom for articulating a desire to be undone and transformed. In this way, love might model a potentially political desire to risk destabilization in hope of a better life.[12] But "the love plot" more often stirs self-defeating desires to be in closer alignment with romantic conventions, guarding against various forms of social precarity.[13]

This is a condensed overview of one strain of love theory. But it helps us begin to track how the Gilded Age political novel's love plots are also—always—stories about political emotion writ large. In particular, as I will show, the emerging prominence in the 1870s of the notorious "free lover" Victoria Woodhull (a profound influence on Stowe's sister, Isabella Hooker, who was a neighbor to Stowe, Twain, and Warner) brought to the fore love's fraught relationship with institutions. Free love threatened to dissolve the marriage form while also raising questions about love's role in shaping group behavior. Public kissing and hugging were given a new political force by Woodhull and other radical feminists as signs of a specifically political enthusiasm, potentially able to generate lasting democratic institutions. In those same signs, the movement's detractors saw a worrying, crazy-making mode of mass agitation.

The novel *The Gilded Age* has been celebrated for its "critical realism," but I will show how the authors' avowed rationalism committed them to denounce affective counterpublics as a species of insanity, to the detriment of the novel's wider political critique. *The Gilded Age* is an ambitious assault on political corruption and crony capitalism, but it lapses with alarming regularity into a critique of the emotionality of the masses, with particular vitriol reserved for women in public. By contrast, Stowe's fiction, focusing on love in the home, looks less obviously political. But I will demonstrate how her advocacy for marriages founded on cautious "enthusiasm" reveals that if the institution of marriage was widely understood to require both unreason and stability, this insight failed to carry over into her (and Twain's) thinking about the role of affect in political institutions. In the latter arena, these authors theorize emotions only as madness: a disruptive threat to deliberative rationality.

Twain and Warner's extravagant realism is well suited for debunking the emotional and appetitive excesses of democracy, but it is less adept at delineating feelings that sustain people's relation to political life. Stowe's guarded sentimentality knows a lot about love as an institutional affect, but it disavows what it knows about the laws love will break. Taken together, Twain and Stowe dramatize the difficulty, but also the necessity, of theorizing desire and love simultaneously as institutional solvents and adhesives. In the late-nineteenth century's atmosphere of corrosive partisan acrimony and speculative fervor, it was tempting to point to intense emotion as the gravest threat to democracy. But, then as now, this diagnosis ignores how often we ask the madness of love to dissolve bad social forms, only to call on sane love to forge new ones.[14] I ultimately argue that Twain and Stowe reveal a pervasive Gilded Age fantasy of a more perfect democracy (a vision that could just as easily apply to romantic love or to twenty-first-century politics, for that matter), where reason and emotion achieve perfect balance: neither too hot nor too cold, destabilizing but secure in its institutions, passionate but conventional, unruly and idiosyncratic but expertly managed.

Insanity: The New Crime

In the coming section, I will trace the complex routes by which insanity law became Twain's privileged realm for thinking about Gilded Age democracy, and I will ultimately argue that this idiosyncratic crossover from law to politics has troubling consequences for the force and focus of his critique. First, however, it is worth reviewing how surprisingly capacious Gilded Age legal and medical discourses were toward mental illness, even before falling into Twain's hands. Indeed, the topic of the insanity defense quickly became a touchstone for a range of concerns about widespread corruption, a flashpoint for reigniting age-old debates about gender roles, and a catch-all vocabulary for conceptualizing the limits of "responsibility" in a social world threatened both by attenuated corporate liability and citizens' overmastering emotions.[15]

In 1838 Dr. Isaac Ray, an ambitious autodidact from Maine, offered one of the earliest accounts of insanity as a systematic medical and legal problem in *A Treatise on the Medical Jurisprudence of Insanity*. Ray sought to provide more rational, humane standards for judging insanity in legal cases.[16] But much to his frustration, the year in which he published his second edition saw the trial, in England, of Daniel McNaughton, an event that set an international precedent in direct contradiction to Ray's recommendations.[17] This "McNaughton Test," as it came to be known, dictated that: "To establish a defence on the grounds of insanity, it must clearly be proved that, at the time of committing the act, the party accused ... did not know that he was doing what was wrong."[18] Ray countered that an awareness of wrong could be compatible with insanity, and in 1869 he issued a challenge to the McNaughton Test with the help of a long-time admirer of his work, Associate Justice Charles Doe of the Supreme Court of New Hampshire.[19] Doe presided over the case of Josiah Pike, a confessed ax murderer, and based his instructions to the jury on Ray's theories: "[T]he verdict should be 'not guilty by reason of insanity' if the killing was the offspring or product of mental disease in the defendant."[20] Doe thereby upheld Ray's argument that it was not the law's place to define the medical condition of mental illness as confusion over right and wrong, but only to affirm that a person could not be held criminally responsible for an act committed as the result of insanity.

While Ray and Doe's "New Hampshire Rule" was widely commended by medical and legal experts for discarding the false positivism of the "right/wrong test," their challenge to the McNaughton ruling introduced a crisis of authority in the courtroom that highlighted other major shortcomings of America's legal system. The prominent attorney Francis Wharton, for example, questioned the capacity of a lay jury to judge complex medical questions but also lamented the importance placed on the testimony of experts who could not agree on the nature of insanity.[21] Most importantly, the absence of firm legal or scientific guidelines for identifying mental illness opened the door to a variety of corrupting influences that could shape a trial's outcome. Especially in New York, where the power of the Tammany political machine extended into the courts, a verdict of guilty or not guilty was often thought to have less to do with the facts of the case than with the defendant's political connections.

Twain was at the forefront of the attack on new legislation such as the "New Hampshire Rule" and its attendant problems. In his earliest story on insanity, 1870's "The New Crime," which followed soon after *State v. Pike,* Twain expresses initial concern over "how many really crazy people are hanged" because they lack the financial and social resources to mount an insanity defense.[22] Yet he is far more incensed by "how many [people] that never were crazy a moment in their lives are acquitted of crime in the plea of insanity" (C, 354). For example, there was "the Baldwin case, in Ohio, twenty-two years ago" (C, 350), in which a wealthy young man accused of murder finagled an acquittal on the grounds of insanity. The defendant went on to kill several more times, and Twain, feigning concern over Baldwin's expenses, bitterly reports that "[I]t required all his political and family influence to get him clear in one of the cases, and cost him not less than ten thousand dollars to get clear in the other" (C, 351). For Twain, as for other American and British commentators, the insanity defense morphed from a subtle medical and legal discourse on the limits of criminal responsibility to a much wider reflection on the inroads of inequality into law and politics: "If a person of high standing squanders his fortune in dissipation and closes his career with strychnine or a bullet, 'Temporary Aberration' is what was the trouble with *him*" (C, 353).[23]

By 1873, insanity and political corruption were deeply inscribed in Twain's imagination as the go-to shorthand for the failures of American civilization. Remarking wryly on the forms of enlightenment America could share with her imperial conquests, Twain sarcastically encouraged the annexation of the Sandwich Islands by remarking that the United States could enrich the islanders with "leather-headed juries, the insanity law, and the Tweed ring."[24] At the time of this remark, Twain was writing his contributions to *The Gilded Age*, the plot of which is saturated with imbricated discourses on corruption and madness, dramatized most strikingly in the novel's concluding scenes of "temporary insanity."

The novel begins by recounting impoverished farmer Silas Hawkins's fantasies of the wealth to be gained from the sale of his family's Tennessee property. Silas dies before these dreams come to fruition, and his family disperses, with each child setting off to seek his or her own fortune. The plot primarily follows his adopted daughter, Laura, accepted into the family in the aftermath of a steamboat explosion, as she travels to Washington, DC, with her brother, Washington. In the capital, Laura hopes to use her significant beauty and charm as a lobbyist, and convince the government to purchase the family's land. Meanwhile, the chapters authored by Warner relate the exploits of two young friends seeking their fortunes out West. The first youth, Harry Brierly, is seduced by the fever of speculation and easy money. The second, Philip Sterling, is more or less consistent in his desire to learn the trade of engineering and to mine coal and mineral deposits: hard work backed by hard science, and the signs of a steady character that ultimately per-suade Ruth Bolton to marry him. The stories are united by "Colonel" Beriah Sellers, a lovable but compulsively speculative businessman and inventor who is Silas Hawkins's oldest friend. Sellers goes into business with Sterling and Brierly, and he mentors Laura in the art of politics. The plots' tracks further converge in Washington, DC, where nearly all of the characters' fortunes rise or fall with the fate of the Knobs University Bill and Colonel Sellers's Colombus River Navigation Fund, two corrupt schemes intended to persuade the government to purchase or improve land of questionable value. Thanks to Laura's successful lobbying, the bills seem to be on the point of passing until damaging gossip arises surrounding her resumed relations with Colonel Selby, a man who had previously tricked her into a sham marriage before abandoning her. Laura initially forgives Selby but soon learns he has discarded her yet again and left the capital with his wife. Distraught over this second desertion, Laura boards a train to New York, finds Selby in a hotel lobby, and shoots him dead. The subsequent farcical trial predictably centers on a crucial question: Can Laura plead insanity?[25]

Despite Twain's frequent protests against the insanity defense, the novel initially seems to endorse Laura's plea of innocence. She is introduced, after all, as a victim of others' insanity: The steamboat explosion in which she was orphaned was the result of a contest between two passenger vessels attempting to outpace each other on the Mississippi; the captains are implicitly relieved of culpability because they were caught up in the throes of competition—a momentary insanity.[26] Further, the novel hints repeatedly that the father Laura lost in the blast may well have been insane, supplying the strongest evidence in favor of her insanity for the likes of Isaac Ray and his contemporaries: hereditary madness.[27]

Most importantly, however, by framing Laura's act of violence in the context of her mistreatment at the hands of her seducer, Twain and Warner offered a new twist on a question central to the mid-nineteenth-century women's movement, about women's violent retribution for sexual assault and seduction. For example, the subject of one of the most well-known entries from Lydia Child's column "Letter from New York," the 1844 trial of Amelia Norman for the attempted murder of her seducer, crystallized for Child the law's institutionalized gender inequality.[28] A woman tricked or coerced into a sexual relationship was rendered socially dead, while her attacker would face few legal or social consequences. Yet when Norman violently avenged herself on the man who seduced her, the legal system's machinery sprang to life, holding her to strict account. Andrea Hibbard and John Parry have argued that popular novels, such as *The Coquette* and *Charlotte Temple*, supplied the sentimental moral framework that allowed for Norman's ultimate acquittal.[29] Child made this enabling logic explicit when she opined that widespread popular sympathy for Norman forecast the eventual "triumph of moral sentiments over legal technicalities."[30]

As though to appeal to Child and her readers, the narrator of *The Gilded Age* initially reports that Laura is, like Amelia Norman, acquitted of all charges. But it soon becomes clear that Twain and Warner echo the sentimental plot and its elevation of feeling over law only to underscore how vehemently they reject it. After the jury pronounces the verdict of not guilty, Twain disparages the decision as the result of "some occult mental process." He then exults in describing Laura's fate, which is revealed to be far less hopeful than her legal success seemed to promise. The narrator explains that, having freed Laura by virtue of insanity, the judge "in accordance with the directions of the law in such cases…and in obedience to the dictates of a wise humanity…commit[s] Laura Hawkins to the care of the Superintendent of the State Hospital for Insane Criminals" (G, 410). Laura, who "had expected to walk forth in freedom in a few moments," is instead whisked off to the train station and then to the "small, bare room that was to be her home." Faced with the reality of her situation, her apparently feigned madness threatens to become all too real: "She wondered if she *were* not mad; she felt that she soon should be among these loathsome creatures" (G, 411).

But then the story takes another strange turn, marking with a simple em-dash a disorienting narrative reversal in which the preceding paragraphs, and their commitment to rational justice, are suddenly undone:

> —We beg the reader's pardon. This is not history, which has just been written. It is really what would have occurred if this were a novel. If this were a work of fiction, we should not dare to dispose of Laura otherwise….The novelist who would turn loose upon society an insane murderess could not escape condemnation….But this is history and not fiction….What actually occurred when the tumult in the court room had subsided the sagacious reader will now learn. Laura left the court room…amid the congratulations of those assembled, and was cheered as she entered a carriage, and drove away….Were not these following cheers the expression of popular approval and affection? Was she not the heroine of the hour? (G, 411–12)

Twain and Warner were part of the elite Nook Farm literary salon that, in a series of lectures and discussions, had worked out a bifurcated critique of the failings of the modern novel.[31] In their account, "sentimental" literature was to blame for a dangerously idealistic and tepid picture of romantic life. This was objectionable in its own right, but also because it left young readers ripe for seduction by the literary market's other threat: "sensational" fantasies of immense wealth and immoral affairs. To claim to have written a "history" and not a novel is thus not to denounce literariness or fictionality as such, but rather to announce a commitment to a form of realism that opposes two paired styles of literary excess. Well before the widespread popularity of naturalism and muckraking exposés, Twain and Warner suggest that a text's response to the insanity defense is a key litmus test for its author's capacity to offer sharp, critical realism over moralistic, gullible sentimentalism, and tawdry sensationalism.

The narrative thus exacts its own fictional, extrajudicial justice, as if to make up for the emotional failings of the jury and of popular literature: After her acquittal, Laura takes to the lecture circuit to capitalize on her popularity but dies almost immediately of nervous strain after her premiere performance is disrupted by a boisterous and insulting mob. In a letter he wrote after composing the scene in which Laura dies, Twain reports with glee, "I have killed my heroine dead as a mackerel yesterday," exulting in imagined forms of punishment for a character he initially depicted as a victim.[32] In Twain's earlier writing on the insanity defense, he positions "emotional insanity" as neither emotional nor insane. It is a calculated ruse to exploit a legal loophole. *The Gilded Age* makes a risky gambit by feigning a belief in the capacity of past emotional traumas to suspend responsibility, only to then double down on a rationalist rejection of Laura's insanity plea. In effect, it seems, the text stages the temptations of sympathy only to sternly refuse the enticement. It's as though the authors supply so many plausible sources for Laura's madness precisely in order to stress that none of those possible explanations matter: The public must not become contaminated by emotional insanity, whatever its origin.

I will have more to say about the consequences of this tactic in the coming section, where I argue that a rationalist denunciation of popular emotion has odd effects for a novel that, elsewhere, tries to speak on behalf of the democratic masses. But for now we can note how a realist and sentimental hermeneutic converge in the novel, creating a palimpsest of two very different ways of conceptualizing love as a political emotion. While Child celebrated "the sympathies of all who approached" Norman as being "excited in her favor," Twain and Warner scoff at emotional "expression[s] of popular approval," which they see as revealing a public complicit in the erosion of rational, legal norms and political equality. In the sentimental view, literature offers a medium to affirm deeply felt norms of fairness and justice that transcend formal law. In Twain and Warner's realist view, literature must take over the institutional commitment to reason that has been forfeited by a legal system corrupted by feeling. With the "congratulations of those assembled," Laura is showered with "cheers" and "affection," and gets off scot-free—or would have done so, if not for Twain and Warner's narrative retribution. In a major shift that the text nearly obscures, we move from a dynamic in which the madness of love must be protected by law and democracy to an approach in which law and democracy must be protected from crazy love.

The Free Love Incubus

Twain and Warner muddy their critique by combining two distinct strains of writing about the insanity defense. One, exemplified by Twain's earliest works, denounced the naked inequality enabled by the jury system and the misplaced sympathies of the crowd. The other, exemplified by Child's defense of Amelia Norman, celebrated the capacity for sympathy to transcend the limitations of written law. But transposing the skepticism of the former approach into a plot that more closely parallels the latter underscores the surprising ways the target of Twain's critique shifted from corruption and inequality to mass emotion and female publicity.[33] This shift is enabled by the instability of "insanity" discourse itself, but it is also politically motivated. While Laura Hawkins's "insanity" is shown to have hereditary and post-traumatic roots, the novel ultimately suggests the most immediate cause of her murderous insanity is, in fact, her flirtation with "free love" doctrines. Even when faced with the knowledge of Selby's previous marriage, Laura reveals her "free love" creed by maintaining, "God would not have permitted her to love George Selby as she did, and him to love her back, if it was right for society to raise up a barrier between them" (*G*, 277). Love, for Laura, is something that transcends the legal, conventional definition of marriage and by extension authorizes her "insane" breach of the law.[34]

The novel reveals that she came to these "theories of the tyranny of marriage" by hearing women "besieging congress…utter[ing] sentiments that fully justified the course she was marking out for herself" (*G*, 277). Louis Budd suggests that readers of these lines "at the time…would think first of Victoria Woodhull, then of Elizabeth Cady Stanton, Susan B. Anthony, and Lucy Stone" (*G*, 473). Recovering the history of radical women's rights advocate Victoria Woodhull adds nuance to our understanding of Laura, Twain and Warner's unusual heroine, and reveals the power and flexibility of the insanity discourse as it was marshaled against the scandal of affective publics in late-nineteenth-century America. Emotional insanity is the discursive pivot that allows *The Gilded Age* to shift almost imperceptibly from a concern with elite men to fallen women, from cunning and selfish rationality to love in the streets, from a critique of political institutions on behalf of the lives they fail to protect, to a critique of forms of group affection and intimacy on behalf of the institutions those feelings are said to threaten.

In *The Gilded Age*, Laura's personal charm is so powerful, she is described as being on the brink of becoming the "queen of America…applauded, and honored, and petted by the whole nation" (*G*, 326). Crowned one of the "Queens of Finance" by the press, the real-life Victoria Woodhull might similarly have seemed on track to become a kind of American royalty.[35] Woodhull first grabbed national attention in 1870, when she reportedly earned Commodore Cornelius Vanderbilt $1.3 million, thanks to financial advice based on a visionary prophecy, establishing Woodhull and her cross-dressing sister, "Tennie C.," as New York's "Bewitching Brokers" (*O*, 189, 192). At the height of her political respectability, Woodhull was invited by Benjamin Butler to address Congress on women's rights issues; her 1871 speech entitled *The Victoria Woodhull Memorial* dazzled audiences and received the enthusiastic praise of Susan B. Anthony and Elizabeth Cady Stanton (O, 253). By May of 1872, however, Woodhull's name had become more widely known but also more divisive. A public that had tolerated the eccentricity of her political activity came to perceive her radical social philosophy and personal power as more threatening than charming. Rumors circulated in which Woodhull figured as a seductive lobbyist. Perhaps even more scandalously, her political activity became increasingly ambitious and overt with the founding of the People's Party (later the Equal Rights Party) and her nomination as its candidate for president in 1872 (O, 320). As details of her unconventional personal life, including her own open marriage, became public, Woodhull was increasingly vocal in her critique of gender inequality and marriage, and more openly avowed a doctrine of "free love," arguing that traditional marriage equated to state-sponsored ownership of women and that marriage for money was merely legalized prostitution. With this radical-ization, the women's rights movement that had welcomed her celebrity and money splintered (O, 32). Thomas Nast vilified Woodhull as a devil tempting women to "be saved by Free Love" (O, 329), and Susan B. Anthony's *Woman's Journal* responded to the negative attention by urging the National Woman Suffrage Association to expel Woodhull, the " 'Free Love' incubus" (O, 328).

Woodhull's influence on *The Gilded Age* helps account for Laura's strange status in that novel as both wronged woman (and possibly insane murderess) and influ-ential political provocateur. Although Woodhull provided much inspiration, Laura's other immediate model was the real-life Laura Fair of San Francisco, an accused murderer whose 1871 acquittal was initially met with popular fanfare. But opinion soon shifted, as Fair attempted to profit from her beauty and fame on the lecture circuit.[36] Early legal cases trying wronged women thus already contained seeds of a fear that was intensified by Woodhull's arrival on the public stage. Charismatic, lawless women could use their sexual attractiveness to pivot from legal notoriety to political power.

Figures like Woodhull and Fair embodied ambiguous, overlapping forms of power: financial, sexual, political, and charismatic. For Twain and Warner and other elites casting a wary glance at corruption, an almost mystical concept of "political influence" grouped these and other seemingly disparate forms of immoral inducement into a false unity:[37]

> [O]ne of the first and most startling things you find out [upon arrival] is, that every individual you encounter in the City of Washington almost...from the highest bureau chief, clear down to the maid who scrubs Department halls, the night watchmen of the public buildings and the darkey boy who purifies the Department spittoons—represents Political Influence.   (G, 174)

The insidious means by which insiders gain access to the spoils of political power precipitates an upheaval of gender and class norms; the presumably white male "you" who arrives in the nation's capital is confronted by an inverted political hierarchy in which "maids" and "darkies" occupy a privileged position inside the halls of power, while the naïve newcomer is denied entrance to these hidden sites of authority. Forged and wielded in backrooms and lobbies, "political influence" is immune to individual talent or capacity, as well as to the formal rights putatively granted to the citizen: "Mere merit, fitness and capability, are useless baggage to you without 'influence'" (*G*, 174).

Beginning with a spectacle of race and class inversion, Twain and Warner sharpen the focus of their critique of "influence" on gender, finding the most emblematic figure of the new, informal, occult power networks is that of the unique late-nineteenth-century invention, the "female lobbyist":[38]

> I was only thinking, as to this appropriation, now, what such a woman could do in Washington.... Common thing, I assure you in Washington; the wives of senators, representatives, cabinet officers, all sorts of wives, and some who are not wives, use their influence. You want an appointment? Do you go to Senator X? Not much. You get on the right side of his wife. Is it an appropriation? You'd go straight to the Committee, or to the Interior office, I suppose? You'd learn better than that. It takes a woman to get any thing through the Land Office.   (*G*, 139)

The fictional Laura Hawkins, heir to the real-life Laura Fair's beauty and Victoria Woodhull's eloquence and political savvy, is uniquely suited to wield such female influence by virtue of her "fascination." It's rumored she could "fascinate an appropriation right through the Senate" (*G*, 139). Etymologically related to enchantment by witchcraft, "to fascinate" is more generally "to enslave (the faculties), the judgment" of a person.[39] Again, a key shift has taken place almost without remark. Twain and Warner often seem committed to stern-minded judgment as the solution to the era's corruption. But by positing an affective solution to a political crisis they lose the capacity to distinguish between "influence" as a problem unique to a system of crony capitalism and "influence" as any suasion that bypasses judgment in its address to the feeling body.[40]

All This Ridiculous Idea About Loving: Stowe Vs. Woodhull

Twain and Warner were not alone in their nervousness over Woodhull's quasi-demonic sexuality. Much as those authors hoped a better sort of novel might remedy the immorality and over-emotionality stoked by popular fiction, Harriet Beecher Stowe penned a tale of love and marriage intended to draw subtle but clear distinctions between those reforms she endorsed and those which threatened to erode the sanctity of the domestic sphere.[41] It's worth considering Stowe's fictional response to Woodhull in detail, both for how it reinforces the connection between love, sexuality, and madness in Twain's oeuvre and Gilded Age mass culture more broadly, and for how her strategy of containment puts into relief key differences in Twain's understanding of political emotion, and vice versa.

Stowe's *My Wife and I: Or, Harry Henderson's History*, first published serially in *The Christian Union* from 1870 to 1871 and then as a novel the latter year, recounts the romantic history of its titular protagonist from his earliest childhood romance through his adult marriage to Eva Van Arsdel, the daughter of a wealthy but soon-to-be impoverished New York importer. *My Wife and I*'s plot is willfully dull, with Stowe positioning the novel's lack of thrills as a rebuke to "the sensational novel, the blood and murder and adultery story, of which modern literature is full" (*M*, 94). What dramatic tension there is derives from the myriad false conceptions of marriage that threaten to confuse the lovers and those around them. Chief among Stowe's targets are the mercenary notion that a wealthy husband is always the best catch and the insistence that any marriage is better than spinsterhood. Thanks to a sound foundation of true love based on personal attraction and mutual respect, and the promise of future comfort secured by Eva's domestic frugality and Harry's burgeoning career as an author, the novel's conclusion depicts a couple well situated to flourish in matrimony despite their reduced circumstances. Stowe's novel is thus engaged in a project of fine-tuning: It aims to make a strong claim for a woman's right to a career and financial independence (worked out in a parallel plot about Harry's cousin, Caroline), to choose a lover based on personal attraction and sympathy of intellect, and to opt to remain single should no suitable mate present himself. Stowe also makes an explicit assault on the more extreme veins of reform advocacy by having her "progressive" hero and heroine encounter the sex radicalism embodied by Woodhull and her followers.[42] As the novel's preface states, "[it is] the author's purpose to show the embarrassment of the young champion of progressive principles, in meeting the excesses of modern reformers" (*M*, iv).

To differentiate her novel's own principles from others' immoderation, Stowe introduces the character of Audacia Dangyereyes, whose broadly satiric name indicates how out of place she is in the genre of anti-sensational moral fiction. To readers of the era, it was so clear Audacia was meant to parody Woodhull that, when Stowe published the story in novel form, she appended a prefatory disclaimer denying the portrait was of any one person. Before getting to the novel's attack on Woodhull's "free love" advocacy as a mode of political insanity, however, it's important to understand the case Stowe makes *for* love as a species of necessary madness.

In *My Wife and I*, many of Eva's friends and relatives urge her to accept the hand of Wat Sydney, "a rich man [who] owns all sorts of things" (*M*, 164) and who would secure Eva a comfortable home, a place in society, and would save her family from financial ruin. Eva's Aunt Maria is the alliance's leading champion and the most outspoken foe of the importance placed by "modern reformers" on personal attraction and love:

> "It's all this ridiculous idea about loving. Why, girls can love anybody they'd a mind to, and if I had a daughter she should." "Oh! I don't know, Maria," said Mrs. Van Arsdel. "I think it is a pretty serious thing to force a daughter's affections." "Fiddlestick upon affections, Nelly, don't you begin to talk. It makes me perfectly sick to hear the twaddle about it." (*M*, 363)

Eva, keenly aware of her aunt's wish and the positive effect such a marriage would have on her family's prospects, deeply regrets her inability to love Sydney: "Oh, dear, if I only could get up some enthusiasm for him! He likes me, but he don't like the things that I like, and it is terribly slow work entertaining him" (*M*, 172).

Luckily for her, Eva has other advisers who confirm her intuitive sense that a love without intense feeling is no love at all. If Aunt Maria's advice rests on sneering at the "twaddle" of love and affections, the case *for* love hinges insistently on the concept of "enthusiasm." As her "dear friend and teacher" Mrs. Courtney writes:

> You say you can get up no enthusiasm for this man....It is out of just such [passionless] marriages...that come all these troubles that are bringing holy marriage into disrepute in our times. A woman marries...a man whom she consciously does not love, hoping that she shall love him....[T]hen by accident or chance she is thrown into the society of the very one whom she could have loved with enthusiasm....The modern school of novels are full of these wretched stories, and people now are clamoring for free divorce, to get out of marriages that they never ought to have fallen into....A woman who has what you call an enthusiasm for a man, can do much with him. She can bear with his faults; she can inspire and lead him; she can raise him in the scale of being. But without this enthusiasm, this real love, she can do nothing of the kind; it is a thing that cannot be dissembled, or affected. (*M*, 174)

For Twain, "modern novels" offer either idealistic, sentimental platitudes or immoral, sensational excess. In both cases, the solution is clear-headed critical realism. Stowe, however, focuses on overheated sensational romances, but her solution is more, not less, emotion. In Stowe's vision, "enthusiasm" is risky but crucial because it overcomes two forms of instrumental rationality: the aforementioned "alarmingly rational" reformers who think they can mold human nature to conform to their theories of equality, and the naked greed of those would place a dollar value on a sacred and ineffable component of human desire. Despite its intensity, "enthusiasm" properly understood *reinforces* the institution of marriage, as Stowe takes a not-so-subtle swipe at "free love"—implicitly a doctrine of unbridled enthusiasm—by acknowledging it only as "free divorce."

Stowe's protagonist and Eva's eventual husband, Harry, likewise undergoes an education in love's necessary irrationality. For Harry, who has taken to writing what we might call "think pieces" on modern love, language itself provides a clue to love's true power. Musing on "the philosophical justice of popular phrases," he explains:

> The ordinary cant phraseology of life generally represents a homely truth because it has grown upon reality like a lichen upon a rock. "Falling in love" is a phrase of this kind; it represents just that phenomenon which is all the time happening...in most unforeseen times and seasons, and often when the subject least intends it, and even intends something quite the contrary. The popular phrase "falling in love" denotes something that comes unexpectedly....[O]ne falls in love as one falls down stairs in a dark entry.... (*M*, 216)

Harry thinks of himself as "a thorough-paced philosopher," with "all his passions and affections under most perfect control" (*M*, 216). But like Ruth's mother in the vignette of *The Gilded Age* discussed in the opening paragraphs of this chapter, Stowe questions Harry's new-fangled philosophy and overly confident fantasies of self-mastery. One falls in love; one does not argue himself into it. In Harry's case, he must learn that, much as one should not marry *for* money, the presence of money is not therefore an *obstacle* to love. Similar to Hawthorne's reformer Holgrave in *The House of the Seven Gables*, Harry finds himself drawn by love's irresistible enthusiasm toward unexpectedly conventional forms of marriage and domesticity.

As Jon Mee has shown, "enthusiasm" had a complex history through the eighteenth and nineteenth centuries, when it named not only the transcendent delights of poetry and a curative alternative to the soullessness of the market, but also the sensual excesses of erotic and religious ecstasy and the unthinking violence of the mob. In Mee's account, literary romanticism sought ways to chasten or regulate enthusiasm, claiming the power of its unreason while differentiating itself from the madness of the crowd.[43] Similarly, love as a species of unreason makes precise, definitional demands on Stowe's romantic theory of love. First, although she gives a condescending wink to Harry's fantasies of rational self-possession, Stowe is deeply invested in the idea that only strong-minded men and women can handle the responsibility of love's overmastering passions. Take Mr. Bolton, Harry's friend and colleague at the newspaper, and a recovering alcoholic who commits himself to a life of bachelorhood because he worries the "temporary insanity" of his addiction could return at any time. Bolton lives in perpetual fear that his rational self-possession could be upended by even the tiniest drop of alcohol: "[T]he idea at last flashed upon me that I had indeed become the victim of a sort of periodical insanity in which the power of the will was overwhelmed by a wild unreasoning impulse" (*M*, 314). He holds fast to his radical self-denial of companionship even after the true love of his youth, Harry's cousin, suddenly arrives in New York: "The danger is one I cannot comprehend and provide for. It is like that of sudden insanity'" (*M*, 418).

Stowe does hold out hope for Bolton's eventual marriage, if predicated on strict conditions: "I, the sane and sound, I hope to provide for the insane and unsound intervals of my life. And my theory is, briefly, a total and eternal relinquishment of the poisonous influence, so that nature may have power to organize new and healthy brain-matter, and to remove that which is diseased" (*M*, 316). In other words, Bolton may eventually wed if he can literally rebuild his brain, reclaiming his sanity so as to have the strength to bear love's madness, and to respect and care for the woman whose mad love for him would place her in a state of intimate dependence. Revealingly, this language of well-composed brain matter closely parallels Stowe's account of why the women's movement should aim for gradual reform rather than sudden enfranchisement. As Eva's sister muses, "I am, on the whole, very well pleased that there is no immediate prospect of the suffrage being granted to women until a generation with superior education and better balanced minds... shall have grown up among us" (*M*, 261). Like the romantic poet's deft regulation of "enthusiasm," balanced minds set the necessary limit on love's lunacy.[44]

Stowe's imprecise materialization of rational self-governance as reconstructed brain matter might be seen as a particularly idiosyncratic and anxious version of what Chris Castiglia has described as the early-nineteenth century's reconceptualization of citizenship as an interior process: "Citizens were encouraged to understand the incessant labor of vigilant self-scrutiny and self-management as effective democratic action."[45] Castiglia tracks antebellum literature's imagination of deep interiority as compensation for lost democratic sociality, and no substitute was richer than romantic love: "Love as a broad social affect—the tie that binds one family to others or, more important, one member of a society to others—is thus sacrificed in favor of the romantic couple."[46] Stowe, however, departs from Castiglia's paradigm by seeking to maintain "enthusiasm" as a public feeling—one that, properly embraced, would directly challenge gender norms and alleviate women's suffering. *My Wife and I*, much like her earlier *Uncle Tom's Cabin*, strives to depict a domestic sphere that is secure yet permeable, a safe foyer to the wider world of political action. For Stowe, establishing relays between the psychological interior, the domestic interior, and formal politics is necessary but is only tenable if there are precise parameters for delineating legitimate and illegitimate forms of political emotion.

Indeed, Stowe's project of setting boundaries on love's enthusiasm is urgent because the greatest danger to her theory of love is so closely related to the "enthusiasm" she champions. At first, Henry is charmed and invigorated by the circle of reformers he meets through Eva's sister, Ida, who frequents meetings run by a Mrs. Cerulean: "I must confess that I found my evening at Mrs. Cerulean's salon a very agreeable one; the conversation of thoroughly emancipated people has a sparkling variety to it.... Everybody was full of enthusiasm, and in the very best of spirits" (*M*, 238). Soon thereafter, however, Henry meets Stowe's Woodhull stand-in, Audacia, who barges into his office, brags of her smoking habit, makes barely disguised sexual advances, and pressures Harry into subscribing to her magazine, a fictionalized version of the *Woodhull and Claflin's Weekly*.[47] Harry reports, "I had heard before of Miss Audacia Dangyereyes, as a somewhat noted character in New York circles, but did not expect to be brought so unceremoniously, and without the least preparation of mind, into such very intimate relations with her" (*M*, 241).

This new "intimacy" so repulses Harry and unsettles his unprepared mind that he begins to question his own convictions regarding the "woman question." Once again, Stowe is teasing out distinctions between seemingly like concepts, and Harry's friends reassure him that a movement is not to be judged by its eccentric outliers:

> You're not the first reformer that has had to cry out, "Deliver me from my friends."...[D]on't be ashamed of having spoken the truth, because crazy people and fools caricature it.... It is true that [women] ought, everywhere, to have equal privileges with men; and because some crack-brained women draw false inferences from this, it is none the less true. (*M*, 245)

The lively "enthusiasm" Harry first detected in the salon is shown to be a species of crack-brained craziness, an insane flood of reform energy.[48] His suspicion of Audacia's lunacy is confirmed when he reads the content of her journal, "an exposition of all the wildest principles of modern French communism...consist[ing] of attacks...against Christianity, marriage, the family state, and all human laws and standing order, whatsoever" (M, 257). True love always and necessarily suspends the lover's self-possession, but Audacia's "free love" unleashes a kind of enthusiasm in public that dissolves all institutions. Stowe's conception of *true* love's enthusiasm, on the other hand, captures this energy and links it insistently with existing social forms. While Justine Murison has delineated Stowe's earlier "longing for enthusiasm" as a disruptive political force in the context of abolitionism—and John Mac Kilgore tracks a longer history of enthusiasm's links to a "fervor for 'fanatical' democracy"—the threat of Woodhull's public passions provoked a nervous retrenchment.[49]

Mixed-Up-Ativeness

One of the most surprising features of *My Wife and I* is thus Stowe's highly nuanced efforts to theorize crazy love as essential to non-coercive domestic intimacy while also guarding against forms of emotional insanity that might undermine other institutions: Christianity, the state, the law. While it is tempting to denounce Stowe for pulling back from a radical embrace of women's rights, it's worth emphasizing that her lukewarm support of "enthusiasm" reveals a more refined understanding of the vicissitudes of affect than the aggressive rationalism on display in Twain's rejection of public emotion. That said, it is crucial to see how Stowe's obsession with the scandal of Woodhull's free love movement strains the author's project of containment. This emerges most clearly when, eager to challenge women's status as property, Stowe ends up devoting so much energy to affirming the importance of property as such.

Soon after Audacia's first encounter with Harry, Stowe parodies the Woodhull-surrogate's utopian vision as a free-for-all of boundary dissolving attachments:

> [S]he says, everything ought to be love, everywhere, above and below, under and over, up and down, top and side and bottom, ought to be love, LOVE. And then when there's general all-overness and all-throughness, and an entire mixed-up-ativeness, then the infinite will come down into the finite, and the finite will overflow into the infinite, and, in short, Miss Dacia's cock's feathers will sail right straight up into heaven.   (M, 267)

Far from a kind of Whitmanian "adhesiveness" that would produce a secular heaven on earth, "mixed-up-ativeness" for Stowe represents a terrifying threat to fundamental notions of privacy and private property. All private possession is eradicated in Audacia's "French" vision of communal living and promiscuous erotic attachments:

> The great mischief at present, she informs me, lies in possessive pronouns, which they intend to abolish. There isn't to be any *my* or *thy*. Everybody is to have everything just the minute they happen to want it....Marriage is an old effete institution, a relic of barbarous ages. There is to be no *my* of husband and wife, and no *my* of children....Love, she informed me, in those delightful days is to be free as air; everybody to do exactly as they've a mind to; a privilege...that she took now as her right. (*M*, 436)

Against this vision of oppressive freedom, Stowe clarifies that *her* conception of marriage is, to the contrary, devoted specifically to ownership: "There are certain characteristic words which the human heart loves to conjure with, and one of the strongest among them is the phrase, 'Our house'" (*M*, 448). The crucial word here is of course the plural possessive pronoun: "It is not my house, nor your house, nor their house, but Our House. It is the inseparable we who own it, and it is the we and the our that go a long way towards impregnating it with the charm that makes it the symbol of things most blessed and eternal" (ibid.).

If the phrase "my wife" seems to convey a kind of ownership incompatible with the novel's case for a "femininity in itself" or a right to remain single, Stowe waves away the dilemma by again insisting on a higher form of sentimental possession that is immune to abuse.[50] Calming Eva's qualms over the marriage vow's injunction to "obey" her husband, Harry assures her that "where...husbands and wives are intelligent companions and equals, the direction does no harm because it confers a prerogative that no cultivated man would think of asserting" (*M*, 412). Likewise, "our house" presupposes a utopia of conflict-free possession, a form of perfect joint ownership authorized by an instinct innate to the human heart. The novel's seemingly lifeless title, *My Wife and I*, all subjective pronoun and no verb, is thus, in Stowe's eyes, a forceful rejection of free love's challenge to matrimonial property.

Strangely enough, the novel troubles its own vision of possession-without-aggression when it dramatizes Eva's homemaking frugality, referring to the flotsam and jetsam of ruin:

> In fact, her excursions into the great sea of New York and the spoils she brought thence to enrich our bower reminded me of the process by which Robinson Crusoe furnished his island home by repeated visits to the old ship which was going to wreck on the shore. From the wreck of other homes came floating to ours household belongings, which we landed reverently and baptized into the fellowship of our own. (*M*, 457)

In subsequent decades, the *Oxford English Dictionary* traces "home-wrecking" as floating between connotations of financial ruin (a "home-wrecking" loan officer) and the work of any seductive adulterer ("in his business of home wrecking he seems to rejoice"), eventually coalescing in the twentieth-century figure of the "home-wrecker": "A person who ruins a family, home, or relationship; spec. a person who is blamed for the break-up of a marriage."[51] Stowe's evoking the "wreck of other homes" hints ominously at these untold sorrows, even in the midst of her celebration of Eva's nesting. Lori Merish has argued that Stowe's domestic and abolitionist writing expresses a theory of "sentimental materialism" in which "bringing things home...is an act of love, an act invested with emotional and moral urgency."[52] Yet if one might hope that a woman, a child, or a slave damaged by instrumental possession might have some physical and psychic wounds mended by a new domestic context, *My Wife and I* pushes that theory to its breaking point. It is as though Stowe wants readers to imagine not only that Harry and Eva are able to craft a home out of urban detritus but that the off-stage traumas of these items' previous owners are likewise healed by Eva's acts of sentimental reappropriation.[53]

Despite Stowe's stylistic commitment to restraint, *My Wife and I* ends up articulating a conservatively utopian—or outrageously moderate—vision of social life. First, she advocates an ascetic self-discipline and a committed gradualism that could produce something like a new kind of man and woman. This superior species can be saved *by* enthusiasm from the hyper-rationality of the reformer and the market but also saved *from* enthusiasm's "temporary insanity" by well-prepared minds and the underlying continuity of marriage and domesticity as social forms.[54] Second, she imagines modes of obedience that never authorize tyranny and forms of possession that never dispossess. While "free love" is cast as a crazy desire for the utter dissolution of all distinctions, for Stowe, the presence of *true* love serves as the guarantor of both sane self-possession and domestic property. "Love," with just a dash of crazy, becomes the most institutional of emotions, as it bears the extraordinary burden of healing or disavowing the violence that inheres in existing gender relations, the exclusions of the official political sphere, and market competition. But if enthusiasm can fracture the women's movement as easily as it can sustain the matrimonial bond, and if love can wreck a home as easily as it can create one, then Stowe's novel also hints at a persistent anxiety whether intense affect is, at heart, an institutional solvent. In this, she offers an inverted mirror image of *The Gilded Age*, which focuses on love's threat to the law but returns again and again to scenes in which love sustains potentially political relations.

Political Kissing

Despite her hints at the violence implicit in men's ownership of women, Stowe ultimately doubles down on the sanctity of ownership. I argue she was driven to these extremes by her urgency to make a case for true love over the craziness of free love, and to capture and tame simmering forms of public enthusiasm. For Twain, however, "enthusiasm" was already a defining feature of the Gilded Age public sphere, in which his ever-growing catalog of brands of insanity—elite privilege, speculative excess, female influence, mass sentimentality—expanded to indict "the people" as a whole. Like Stowe, Twain zeroes in on Woodhull as the primary icon of delusional forms of mass political action. Unlike Stowe, he expresses little confidence that rational individuals can temper their own enthusiasm. Notwithstanding their differences in approach, however, both authors' hostility toward and fascination with free love reached fever pitch around Woodhull's famed involvement in one of the greatest scandals of the nineteenth century: the accusation and trial of Henry Ward Beecher for adultery, an event that would test both authors' strategies of containment.

Even those who have heard of the scandal surrounding Henry Ward Beecher's affair may forget Woodhull's involvement and how the scandal was tied up with fantasies and anxieties about free love. Woodhull's exposé "The Beecher–Tilton Scandal Case" was published on November 2, 1872, in her own journal, *Woodhull & Claflin's Weekly* (*O*, 337). In a turn of logic too subtle for the population at large, Woodhull revealed the details of Beecher's affair not as a moral condemnation but as a reproach to unnatural restrictions on "amative impulses," asserting that the "marriage institution" had become "in a general sense injurious instead of benefi-cial to the community" (*O*, 338). For Woodhull, Beecher was *right* to seek love where he could find it and only wrong in disavowing this free love creed. Woodhull's steadiest supporter in her crusade was Beecher's own sister and Twain's neighbor, Isabella Hooker (*My Wife and I*'s "Stella Cerulean"), who had long worshiped Woodhull. Hooker, too, called upon her brother not to confess a sin but merely to articulate the theory that motivated his behavior: "My own conviction is that the one radical mistake you have made is in supposing that you are so far ahead of your time" (*O*, 356). Beecher, however, was clear: "I have no philosophy to unfold and no new theory of society" (ibid.). Beecher and Hooker's family, especially their sister Harriet Beecher Stowe, worked quickly to disparage Woodhull and to minimize her hold on Hooker. Stowe warned Hooker that rumor of Woodhull's lobbying activities included behavior bordering on prostitution and continued to attack Woodhull vociferously in print, building the case against Woodhull she had begun in *My Wife and I* (*O*, 255).

For Hooker, however, Woodhull's rise to political prominence promised to usher in a new era of passionate politics and affective attachments, making possible new forms of political and social life. Using the pseudonym "Broadway," Hooker wrote enthusiastically about one of Woodhull's political rallies in *Woodhull & Claflin's Weekly*:

> Mrs. Woodhull, the nominee for the Presidency, passed into an ante-room, where her friends crowded to congratulate her. She was in ecstasy...The ladies kissed her and embraced her, kissed each other and kissed her again. I never before saw so much kissing and hugging in public, nor, for that matter, in private either. Men were not afraid to pass hands round women who were not their wives, and women indulged in political osculation till they were tired.   (*O*, 321)

Susan B. Anthony was horrified and promptly wrote Elizabeth Cady Stanton: "What a ridiculous letter that is that Mrs. Hooker has published. It is too bad this kissing and hugging and putting away old men and getting new ones to hug and kiss emblazoned in print…[I]t's simply sickening—what can be Mrs. Hooker's object?" (*O*, 321). Hooker seemed nearly insane to mainstream feminists, and the kissing (or "osculation") she celebrates represented, to Anthony, the kind of reckless passion that threatened to dissolve a feminist claim to political participation based on reason. Hooker displays a rigorous naïvety throughout the scandal; she seems to have little sense that the scene she describes could be received as licentious abandon rather than as evidence of righteous political enthusiasm. It was precisely the former view that led Twain to forbid his wife from seeing Hooker and that caused him to (prematurely) celebrate Hooker's reported retreat from politics: "Well, anyway, I am glad she is out of 'public life,' & I have no doubt that all of her best friends are, also."[55]

Emotional insanity is implicit in these public vignettes of affective attachment. Earlier I claimed that Twain's critique of the insanity defense was partially motivated by a suspicion of mass affect more broadly. The Woodhull–Beecher affair clarifies that Twain's mapping of the insanity of the murderer onto the insanity of the crowd gives form to anxieties about modes of social organization arranged by passionate attachment instead of by traditional, legal categories of marriage. These discursive connections would soon be more explicit, as the scandal of "insanity" was repeatedly employed to police political intimacy.[56] Most notably, in order to contain Hooker's disturbing calls for her brother to tell the truth about his motivations, the Beecher family had Dr. Harold Butler declare Hooker's attraction to Woodhull a sign of mental illness: "Mrs. Hooker was laboring under a monomania superinduced by over-excitement," and "Mrs. Woodhull had exercised a controlling influence over a too susceptible mind" (*O*, 358). An ally of Hooker's ensured his own ostracism when he criticized the family's treatment of her: "She was not a crazy woman but a bolder Beecher than he.…[Mrs. Hooker] has been placarded as insane because she advised him to make a clear and full confession…" (*O*, 415).

Even Henry Ward Beecher came under suspicion of evincing a degree of insanity. Hooker was not alone in imagining that the Beecher–Tilton scandal unveiled the preacher as a secret free lover. The diarist George Templeton Strong observed:

> Verily they are a peculiar people. They call each other by their first names and perpetually kiss one another. The Rev. Beecher seduces Mrs. Tilton and then kisses her husband, and he seems to acquiesce in the osculation.… They all seem, on their own shewing, to have been behaving like bedlamites and to have been afflicted with both moral and mental insanity.   (*O*, 414)

To Strong, at least, this "osculation" hardly seemed political—or sane. In fact, the reported kissing between the Beechers and the Tiltons refers to testimony on a pre-scandal moment, when jealously had not yet led to accusations of infidelity and the couples had experimented with a free-love lifestyle. "Moral insanity" was ironically leveled at the group for the portion of the affair that was motivated by a conscious, self-reflective attempt to reconsider the possible configurations of intimate domestic life. Beecher was ultimately acquitted of this insanity, while Woodhull was tried and found guilty for publicizing the "obscene" details. Hooker alone bore the continued stigma of madness.

Given the insistence with which the Beecher scandal focused on these scenes of "political osculation," the implications of a surprising scene of kissing in the court-room in *The Gilded Age* are more readily apparent. By 1873, Twain had distilled several years' worth of free-love scandal and high-profile murder trials into one tableau of passionate osculation. Near the end of *The Gilded Age*, the authors report:

> And now occurred one of those beautiful incidents which no fiction-writer would dare to imagine, a scene of touching pathos, creditable to our fallen humanity. In the eyes of the women of the audience Mr. Braham was the hero of the occa-sion; he had saved the life of the prisoner; and besides he was such a handsome man. The women could not restrain their long pent-up emotions. They threw themselves upon Mr. Braham in a transport of gratitude; they kissed him again and again, the young as well as the advanced in years, the married as well as the ardent single women;…in the words of a newspaper of the day they "lavished him with kisses."…This beautiful scene is still known in New York as "the kissing of Braham" (*G*, 410).[57]

While in his earlier story "The New Crime," the community at large is on the side of common-sense justice, by the time Twain revisits the theme of insanity in *The Gilded Age,* the public's response to an insane murderer is a kind of insanity of its own.

Tracing this history makes clear that the kissing of Braham, the kissing of Woodhull, the kissing of Beecher, and the kissing of Laura in *The Gilded Age* all would have resonated for Twain's readers as scenes of what Hooker calls "political osculation," a fortuitous phrase aiming to name a kind of physical contact that, in the domain of the nineteenth-century public sphere, is not properly possible. "Free love" as a social program inevitably was interpreted as "free lust" (and was often renamed as such by its opponents), and "political" kissing was "sickening" even to the nation's leading suffragists.[58] While Twain most often used "insanity" to decry forms of public enthusiasm that looked like self-defeating abdications of political power, his text helped shape the discursive context in which emotional insanity could pathologize any counterhegemonic political movement.

Afterword: Mobs, Masses, and Multitudes

Throughout this chapter I have shown how Twain's initial critique of plutocratic power lapses with alarming regularity into sweeping assaults on the emotionality of the masses, and how Stowe's defense of love comes to entail an assault on the nascent political energies of "free love." Twain's and Stowe's anxious assessment of political emotion focuses insistently on three aspects of group behavior: first, the irrationality, impulsiveness, and contagion of the crowd; second, the crowd's susceptibility to manipulation by public figures who are themselves rational but make cynical use of the mob's susceptibility; and lastly, how the excesses of popular emotion threaten to dismantle institutions, eroding frameworks for generating democratic consensus (politics) or assigning blame and assessing punishment (the law). While Twain returns again and again to scenes of mass emotion in rearticulating these central concerns, Stowe condenses a similar set of beliefs into a brusque dismissal of those "crack-brained" reformers eager to overturn centuries of order. In so doing, Twain and Stowe anticipate the nervous accounts of mob emotion that took shape at the turn of the century, as Gustave Le Bon, Sigmund Freud, Gabriel Tarde, and others outlined the pathologies of crowd behavior, or what Freud would call mass psychology.

Le Bon, in particular, set the baseline diagnosis from which most later accounts begin, wherein participation in a crowd is seen as a fundamentally regressive act: "isolated, [a man] may be a cultivated individual; in a crowd he is a barbarian... acting by instinct."[59] As William McDougal summarized the general clinical outlook by 1920, a crowd is:

> [E]xcessively emotional, impulsive, violent, fickle, inconsistent, irresolute and extreme in action, displaying only the coarser emotions and the less refined sentiments; extremely suggestible, careless in deliberation, hasty in judgment, incapable of any but the simpler and imperfect forms of reasoning; easily swayed and led, lacking in self-consciousness, devoid of self-respect and of sense of responsibility, and apt to be carried away by the consciousness of its own force, so that it tends to produce all the manifestations we have learnt to expect of any irresponsible and absolute power.[60]

In McDougal's account, the crowd expresses an innate tyranny of its own through unthinking acts of force but, even more disturbingly, its power can be harnessed by what Le Bon calls the despotism of a ringleader or agitator.[61]

As William Mazzarella has noted, crowd theory's implicit and explicit assault on popular governance led to a range of later efforts to rehabilitate the crowd, either depicting such groups as civic assemblies that produce rather than undermine the liberal subject, or displacing autonomy from the individual to the group by celebrating the "emergent integrity of collectivities."[62] The problem, however (which Mazarrella locates most prominently in Hardt and Negri's concept of "multitudes"), is that these theories replace the autonomous, rational individual as the agent of liberal fantasy with an equally impossible counterpart: the pure vitality of unmediated collectives. Thus, while the theory of the multitude rescues the masses from crowd theory's disdain, Mazarella argues that only crowd theory, especially the mid-twentieth-century work of Elias Canetti, offers models for asking if or how a crowd's power might lie precisely in its mediation: "social institutions...are not abstractions imposed on the vital energy of their adherents but rather mechanisms through which the creatively mimetic energy of groups can be harnessed and in that way realized while being regulated."[63]

I end by sketching these later debates about group psychology not because they lend Stowe and Twain the dubious honor of anticipating a later century's anti-popular and anti-emotional bias. Instead, the tensions to which Mazzarella draws our focus provide a way to see why *The Gilded Age* and *My Wife and I*, which I have described as deeply problematic, are also surprisingly compelling. Stowe tried desperately to yoke love to existing institutions of marriage and property while courting just enough of love's irrationality to challenge the most brutally instrumental forms of possession and exploitation that marriage could authorize. Twain, on the other hand, depicts so many scenes of crowd emotion, it's hard not to detect a reluctant fascination with its power, even as his crowds invariably are linked to a degraded submission to wealthy elites (a problem for democratic sovereignty) or to the insanity of unrestrained love (a problem for legal reason). Put another way, Twain is fascinated by the mediation of crowd emotion but sees it as always and necessarily expressive of unlawful tyranny. Stowe is fascinated by institutional mediation but only as a buttress to inherited forms. Together, however, they provide a glimpse of the free love movement that speaks to Mazzarella's desire to "find a way to talk about the emergent potentials of group energy that is at the same time a theory of social mediation"; that, is, "a theory that would not pit 'order against desire' but would rather be able to track their dialectical co-constitution."[64]

After all, Woodhull's sudden visibility occasioned a crisis within competing branches of the suffrage movement, as she was embraced by the Stanton–Anthony liberal wing of suffragists (or the National Woman Suffrage Association, to which Isabella Hooker allied herself), while Stowe shifted toward the more cautious American Woman's Suffrage Association. Contra Stowe, free love evidently was not pure unreason awaiting co-optation but was itself an effort to capitalize on the movement's mimetic energies, driving various efforts to rethink existing political and social institutions. Twain had something to learn about love's institutions, as well. It's worth noting that the boisterous crowds cheering the real-life Laura Fair were the intended result of protests by the California Woman Suffrage Association and the Pacific Slope Suffrage Association.[65] And despite Twain and Warner's lament about women "besieging" Congress, Woodhull's famous essay was hardly an anarchic assault, as she "would most respectfully petition your Honorable Bodies to make such laws as in the wisdom of Congress shall be necessary and proper for carrying into execution the right vested by the Constitution in the citizens of the United States to vote, without regard to sex."[66] Love could be destructive and constructive, opposed to outmoded institutions—but sometimes in the mode of repair.

That said, Twain and Warner's mischaracterization of "free love" isn't surprising, and not only because Twain's commitment to a self-consciously masculine form of sober reason made him suspicious of "sentimental" crowds. Woodhull pitched the power of desire's self-dispossession to a public already dispossessed by the occult workings of speculative capital; she offered a vision of radical forms of communal dependence at a moment when a commitment to individual accountability looked like a solution to corporate irresponsibility; and she offered "love" as a transformative experience of suspended sovereignty to citizens for whom democratic sovereignty was threatened by politicians' greed and desire. In this context, Stowe's affirmation of property and self-possession was canny, if problematic. Already primed to diagnose multiple versions of suspended agency as madness, few could join the anonymous reader who, ridiculing public charges of free love's insanity, suggested that the Gilded Age public sphere needed more political emotion, not less; more eruptions of unruly public desire; and riskier forms of social relations and political action: "It would be a great benefit to the world if more of our women had half Victoria C. Woodhull's craziness."[67]

Repulsion

{2}

Desire, Disgust, *Democracy*

OR, AVERSIVE ATTACHMENTS

Romancing Conservatism

Henry Adams's 1880 political satire, *Democracy: An American Novel* appears so rife with disdain for American politics its title must be a cruel joke. In Sandra Gustafson's recent overview of the nineteenth-century American novel's demo-cratic ambitions, for example, *Democracy* looks uncomfortably out of place alongside an earlier canon of "self-consciously democratic literature."[1] These works by authors including James Fenimore Cooper, Harriet Beecher Stowe, and Mark Twain give voice to the lowly, and dramatize—however imperfectly—the nation's ideals of equality, liberty, dialogue, and consent. But can we see Adams's *Democracy* as more than a foil? If American literature's abiding thematic concern with "democracy," and the democratic aspirations of the novel form itself, express at least a degree of idealism, must we understand Adams's ambivalent, pessimistic, and cynical narrative as necessarily anti-democratic? Tracking another subset of the American canon (including Herman Melville, Walt Whitman, and Henry David Thoreau) that grappled with the nation's democratic aims, Stanley Cavell has described their affective tenor as a "mood at once of absolute hope and yet of absolute defeat."[2] How might we read a novel entitled *Democracy* that skips the first part, starting *and* ending with bitter resignation? Could such a text teach us anything about practices or habits of democratic life?

I will argue that teasing out the novel's lessons requires conceptualizing the political work of an aversive affect, disgust, that is related to but distinct from the "pessimism" that has most provoked critical suspicion. But asking questions about *Democracy*'s democratic imagination first requires grappling with the problem of conservatism in American literary history since many of the novel's primary features—its elitism and nostalgia, and its interest in the perpetuation of institutions—are the hallmarks of conservative ideology in the US. These are also the qualities that, in Gustafson's account, distinguish Adams's novel from the "dem-ocratic political and esthetic ideals articulated by an earlier generation of American novelists" (33), which form the antebellum canon she dubs "Democratic Fictions."

As I noted in the Introduction to this book, critics have tended to prize this earlier body of work's radical, anti-institutional imaginaries, favoring texts that pay homage to democratic ideals while offering a critical take on the hegemony of official politics and history. In this context, Adams's romance of DC life looks compromised from the start by its institutional setting—a futile search for democracy in all the wrong places, from which its pessimism naturally follows.

Yet the notion of the "romance," especially as defined by Nathaniel Hawthorne, helps us unpack the competing allures of anti-institutional romanticism and conservatism within the nineteenth-century canon, and sheds light on *Democracy*'s awkward fit alongside earlier democratic literature. Hawthorne identified a commitment to institutions as conservatism's core, but in an ambivalent light. In the well-known ending of *The House of the Seven Gables*, the reformer Holgrave renounces his radical views in favor of the serenity of marriage and home ownership: " 'Ah, Phoebe, I told you how it would be!' said the artist, with a half-melancholy laugh. 'You find me a conservative already!' "[3] Holgrave's radicalism previously consisted in a fundamental aversion to "the moss-grown and rotten Past" embodied in "lifeless institutions."[4] With only a morose chuckle marking the occasion, Hawthorne abruptly transforms his zealous radical into a reluctant conservative— a cautious caretaker of inherited institutions.

As in Hawthorne's usage, definitions of "radical" and "conservative" that focus on each position's relative orientation toward institutions build on American readings of Edmund Burke's counter-revolutionary writing. Burke insisted, "we owe an implicit reverence to all the institutions of our ancestors."[5] In an American context where the justness of the Revolutionary War was an article of faith, Burke's conservatism could still be valued in a moderated form. An excerpt from a March 1843 lecture called "The Philosophy of Reform" by E.H. Chapin, reproduced in the *Democratic Review* among many other venues, warns against a "conservatism" that "loves existing institutions because they happen to exist" but also a radicalism whose footsoldiers "wag[e] war with all existing institutions."[6] Holgrave's sudden shift from one extreme to the other is particularly perverse in that his reversal threatens to undermine the work of literature as Hawthorne himself taught us to understand it. In his prefaces, he identifies romance with an airy space of imagination apart from and critical of institutions, a dynamic echoed in Michael Davitt Bell's influential opposition of the "freedom of the romance" to the "conservatism of the novel."[7] A fundamental tension thus emerges between conservatism and literature; if the conservative's deference to tradition and hierarchy defines a managerial disposition devoted to nurturing institutions, and institutions stifle creativity, then "conservative literature" seems oxymoronic.

It is no wonder, then, that Christopher Hitchens identified the dullness of institutional politics as a major reason for *Democracy*'s artistic failure and for the lack, in his estimation, of any great Washington Novels: "Washington is and always has been irretrievably bogged down in process. And process doesn't…make for electrifying prose."[8] In this chapter I argue that Adams interrogates what he is sometimes said to merely represent: our sometimes-debilitating attachments to the institutional workings of democracy. This may be a propitious moment to examine this aspect of Adams's so-called conservatism without needing to anxiously disown it, since I'm writing at a time when US conservatives have largely abandoned the institutional reverence once taken to be conservatism's hallmark.[9] Self-described conservative columnist David Brooks, for example, seeks to return the party to its putatively Burkean roots: "a belief in steady, incremental change…a respect for hierarchy, precedence, balance and order, and a tone of voice that is prudent, measured and responsible."[10] Brooks admits "conservatives of this disposition can be dull, but they know how to nurture and run institutions."[11] That institutional "dullness" has emerged as object of desire is just one way that current political contexts might push us to re-examine a novel like *Democracy*, given that its famed pessimism expresses a lament about the fate of democratic institutions, and its awkward fit in the canon of American fiction has everything to do with its fascination with the conventions, rituals, character types—and even "process"—of Washington, DC.

But before undertaking this reappraisal one last prefatory question remains, to which I hinted above: why consider *Democracy's* apparent conservatism through this book's lens of "political emotion"? As it happens, when readers have identified elements of Adams's novel as especially troubling or worth celebrating, they have almost always pertained to the text's tone. Teddy Roosevelt famously denounced *Democracy* for its cynicism, while grudgingly acknowledging the appeal of its bitter satire:

> The other day I was reading *Democracy*, that novel which made a great furor among the educated incompetents and the pessimists.…It had a superficial and rotten cleverness, but it was essentially false, essentially mean and base, and it is amusing to read it now and see how completely events have given it the lie.[12]

Roosevelt saw the novel's despondency as contradicted by progressive-era reforms. By 1953, however, Russell Kirk was happy to claim Adams's despair as a central feature of the "conservative mind." Kirk sought to trace a lineage from Burke through American federalism to twentieth-century conservatism, a genealogy that hinged on the late-nineteenth-century contributions of Henry Adams. Kirk declared that "Adams' conservatism is the view of a man who sees before him a steep and terrible declivity," leading to "a pessimism deep and unsparing as Schopenhauer's."[13] Commentators have continued to build on Kirk's account as recently as 2014, praising the affective tenor of Adams's frustrated conservatism: "When a conservative fails at politics, his temptation is to become a Declinist…sighing wistfully at the civilization that is moldering around him. Henry Adams is America's greatest Declinist, and proof that this particular form of despair has its charms, even its own genius."[14] As in its Burkean form, Adams's conservatism registers affectively as pessimism, and performs its political work by reinforcing a disbelief in utopian schemes and a distrust of government.[15]

This chapter takes its cue from these efforts to take seriously the politics of Adams's tone, though I argue that his affective politics are more complicated and interesting than mere conservative pessimism. Building this case begins with the seemingly modest claim that Adams is not merely pessimistic about democracy; he is disgusted with it. For Adams and his ilk, the era of Grant was synonymous with shady deals facilitated by immoral lobbyists preying on the ambitions and appetites of debased leaders. This understanding of Washington as a cesspool—a repugnant, malarial swamp—hyperbolized legitimate concerns about corruption. As in the twenty-first century, however, such rhetoric also threatened to produce apathy, suspicion, and fantasies of a more efficient politics, which could only be secured by extra-democratic means.[16] Adams, an exemplar of the "mugwump type," yearned for civil service reform and similar efforts to insulate government from the passions of the mob and the appetites of the party boss or plutocrat.[17] As with the "measured tone" that defines Brooks's nostalgic conservatism, the mugwump worldview was characterized by a rejection of emotion that was nonetheless defined by affective norms. High-minded disgust is one feeling allowed to the mugwump, who otherwise stakes his authority on a neutered, anesthetic form of republican virtue immune to passion.

It will be the task of this chapter to explore the vicissitudes of Adams's disgust, drawing on a range of theorists who have helped to make visible repulsion's status as an unstable but surprisingly nuanced political feeling: a gesture of refusal that requires proximity; the opposite of both beauty and desire and yet fundamental to experiences of both; a "low" bodily feeling yet one linked to strong moral judgments; an emotional response that is by definition exclusionary (and has been called irredeemably antidemocratic or even anti-political) yet remains oddly social.[18] I show how Adams sometimes falls prey to disgust's anti-democratic seductions, but elsewhere plays on its constitutive tensions, using disgust to guard against a total commitment to "radical" anti-institutional romanticism and against the bureaucratic allure of institutional "conservatism."[19] I ultimately contend that Adams helps us see disgust's defining dynamic of repulsion and attraction as a potential resource for combating an apathetic acceptance of democracy's failings— a dynamic of aversive attachment whereby disgust has the complex capacity to squelch or express a desire for the political.

Comfortably Numb

"For reasons which many persons thought ridiculous, Mrs. Lightfoot Lee decided to pass the winter in Washington."[20] This sentence opens *Democracy*, and it cites the motivation for Madeleine Lightfoot Lee's sudden migration from New York to Washington as one of the persistent questions the text proposes to elucidate. The actual events of her relocation, and thus the novel's basic plot, are easier to summarize: Madeleine, a member of New York's high society, has just returned from a disappointing shopping trip abroad, through which she sought distraction from an as-yet unspecified personal tragedy. "Frankly avow[ing] that she was American to the tips of her fingers" (D, 5), she next turns her attention to Washington DC, hoping to find solace closer to home. But it soon becomes clear that Madeleine has also set her sights higher than mere domestic tourism: She wanted "to see with her own eyes the action of primary forces; to touch with her own hand the massive machinery of society....She was bent upon getting to the heart of the great American mystery of democracy and government" (D, 7). Indeed, as she puts it, "What she wanted was POWER" (8). "Power," for Madeleine, is akin to ambition, but her quest is soon revealed to be geared more toward finding and studying power than wielding it.

Madeleine ultimately finds the power she seeks embodied in Silas P. Ratcliffe, an ambitious senator with long-term designs on the presidency. Despite her more abstract interest in power, she also begins a flirtation with him, and the talk of the town quickly focuses on their seemingly inevitable marriage. Madeleine is troubled by the uneasy relationship between the civics lesson she sought and the marriage plot she found, and the novel is largely devoted to her ambivalent attraction to the defiantly ambitious and self-interested Ratcliffe. Ultimately, Ratcliffe is revealed to have participated in a corrupt scheme to pocket federal dollars. The novel ends with Madeleine breaking off their informal engagement, and fleeing to Europe, disappointed.

I began by suggesting that *Democracy* offers a complex and anxious rumination on the effects of a range of aversive political emotions. Initially, however, Madeleine proclaims little interest in emotion of any sort. That is, if the language of fingertips, hands, and eyes suggests a high degree of aesthetic sensitivity, Adams quickly reveals that Madeleine understands a kind of post-traumatic *numbness* to be her most valuable political asset: " 'To lose a husband and a baby,' said she, 'and keep one's courage and reason, one must become very hard or very soft. I am now pure steel' " (D, 8). Having "exhausted at least two lives, and being fairly hardened to insensibility in the process" (D, 7–8), Madeleine travels to Washington to finalize this metamorphosis from softness to hardness and from personal weakness to public agency. While Madeleine understands the loss of her spouse and child to have depleted "all the ordinary feminine resources," the allegorical space of the capital promises to turn her intimate enervation into public toughness.[21] Put another way, the loss of particularity that has been called the price of ascension to the category of citizen is, to Madeleine's mind, no sacrifice at all.[22]

Madeleine's take on the deadened disposition required for politics offers an early sign of her status as a complex authorial surrogate. While Jacksonian democrats deemed high-minded notions of republican virtue elitist, Adams and his peers revived the idea that a disinterested professional class was essential to democracy. This notion was given classic expression by Alexander Hamilton, when he opined that "the man of the learned profession...will feel a neutrality to the rivalships between the different branches of industry," and thus "be likely to prove an impartial arbiter between them, ready to promote either, so far as it shall appear to him conducive to the general interests of the society."[23] Brooks Simpson points to Adams's 1879 biography of Secretary of the Treasury Albert Gallatin, for example, as a particularly clear expression of Adams's endorsement of this ideal of the "public-spirited, disinterested man of intellect."[24] But what's striking in *Democracy*, then, is that disinterest and impartiality are rendered with such intensity. Madeline's quest for sourcing the center of power in Washington as the seat of official politics, insofar as it demands a loss of the particularity of affective life, will, she hopes, transform her insensitivity from the mark of an emotional wound into a political asset, a sharpened rational-critical faculty.[25] While Adams is sometimes dismissed as an out-of-touch elitist, *Democracy* hints early on that, at the very least, the mugwump ideal of nonpartisan, expert judgment will be subjected to acute pressure within the test space of the novel.

Take, for example, Adams's narration of the quite precise negotiations by which Madeleine positions herself as simultaneously an aesthete, and a passionless political observer. If Madeleine's oddly aesthetic language of seeing and touching might cast doubt on her ability to so thoroughly cordon off sensuous experience, Adams suggests she manages this feat in part by permitting herself some feeling, but only in the highly circumscribed space of the home. Upon arriving in Washington, Madeleine's first task is to establish her newly rented house on Lafayette Square: "She shrugged her shoulders with a mingled expression of contempt and grief at the curious barbarism of the curtains and the wall-papers, and her next two days were occupied with a life-and-death struggle to get the mastery over her surroundings" (*D*, 9). While Madeleine's "contempt" and "grief" might already appear to contradict her claim to "insensibility," the narrator's wry hyperbole suggests that this form of aesthetic experience offers little threat to her posture of calm self-possession. Indeed, given that I have already forecast the role that disgust will play in Madeleine's—and Adams's—political phenomenology, it's worth noting that some accounts of disgust speak of contempt as a related form of distaste, but one that has little of the former's corporeal intensity. One theorist, for example, describes contempt as "less immediate and bodily,... more intellectual and, above all, more ironic than disgust."[26] What's more, "contempt" as an aesthetic judgment suggests a specifically classed form of disdainful unconcern: "The upper classes... could look down upon the lower classes with self-assured contempt. At the same time, they ran no danger of feeling any disgust; for such contempt essentially went along with indifference."[27] With a shrug of her shoulders, Madeleine exudes composed distaste.

For all the noisy show of her decorating, then, Madeleine's contempt is largely consistent with her anesthetic aims. She experiences a weak repulsion toward DC's bad taste but seems—at least initially—fully capable of remaining aloof from its uncouth excess, a fact Adams underscores in an extended vignette of mock-heroic ornamentation:

> [T]he interior of the doomed house suffered as though a demon were in it; not a chair, not a mirror, not a carpet, was left untouched, and in the midst of the worst confusion the new mistress sat, calm as the statue of Andrew Jackson in the square under her eyes, and issued her orders with as much decision as that hero had ever shown. Towards the close of the second day, victory crowned her forehead. A new era, a nobler conception of duty and existence, had dawned upon that benighted and heathen residence. The wealth of Syria and Persia was poured out upon the melancholy Wilton carpets; embroidered comets and woven gold from Japan and Teheran depended from and covered over every sad stuff-curtain.... The setting sun streamed softly in at the windows, and peace reigned in that redeemed house and in the heart of its mistress.   (D, 9)[28]

In a dynamic that highlights Madeleine's eagerness to precisely manage her DC sojourn, over-the-top decorative excess leads, unexpectedly, to "calmness" and inner "peace." This highly orchestrated emotional experience in private is the direct counterpart to her steely reserve and tough-minded reason in public.

To some extent, the defensive or anesthetic aspirations of Madeleine's taste align her with the Gilded Age's "aesthetic style," the mode of aestheticism that, in the years following the Civil War, was typified by an increased interest in interior decorating, amateur artistic production, and the collecting of fine arts and bric-a-brac.[29] However, if devotees of this decorative mode have been said to cultivate spaces of "aesthetic sedation" and a "refuge from...public scrutiny," Adams challenges this version of the interior's (non-)relation to the public sphere.[30] He does this most notably by invoking the martial image of Andrew Jackson, an element of unrest that directly contradicts an easy application of historians' understanding of the escapist or anesthetic tendency in Gilded Age aestheticism.[31] What's more, Madeleine's parlor expresses with parodic intensity the rhetorical gestures that Amy Kaplan has designated "manifest domesticity."[32] As in Kaplan's analysis of the simultaneous contraction and expansion of the nineteenth-century domestic sphere, the parlor functions as a private refuge, but it also appears deeply implicated in national projects of territorial acquisition. Evoking the nation's encroachment on western borderlands, Adams goes so far as to reimagine Andrew Jackson's massacre of the Red Stick Creeks at the Battle of Horseshoe Bend as an epic act of interior decorating, with Madeleine taming the wilds of uncultivated Washington using the trinkets of empire.

I begin with this account of Madeleine's aestheticism, and the elements of unease that undercut its paradoxically anesthetic aspirations, because it establishes early on a key tension within the novel. On the one hand, Madeleine sets up a clear opposition between the realms of privacy and publicity. Politics is cast as a realm of abstract power and institutional forms, where her post-traumatic anesthesia lends support to a posture of critical distance and quasi-scientific reason.

The privacy of the parlor, on the other hand, is a regimented space of feeling, where a small measure of sensuous sensitivity can be safely indulged.[33] Oscar Wilde famously declared, "into the secure and sacred house of Beauty the true artist will admit nothing that is harsh or disturbing, nothing that gives pain, nothing that is debatable, nothing about which men argue."[34] Given Madeleine's stated interest in immersing herself in the things "about which men argue," and her already fragile emotional state, her parlor looks all the more important as a space of emotional rejuvenation.[35] If historians have identified a proprietary, sedative, and escapist component to the Gilded Age's decorative arts, Adams undercuts Madeleine's desire for such a space from the get-go. Contempt shapes her affective transactions with a world of aesthetic objects that are inextricably connected to a wider world of politics and history.

One sign of how complexly Adams troubles these boundaries is that the question of gender—supposedly sidelined by Madeleine's tragic estrangement from the role of wife and mother—returns so insistently. Madeleine has been called Adams's "surrogate heroine," though little attention has been paid to the dynamics of that surrogacy.[36] The novel's focus on DC social life and its female protagonist led many to assume the anonymous author was a woman. Adams's own wife was a common suspect. But *Democracy* makes clear that Madeleine is no easy stand-in for a male or female author, given that she is positioned as something like a republican version of the imperial eunuch. While the eunuch's passivity and loyalty is ensured by castration, Madeleine's mournful numbness (and "grief and contempt") is central to the ways she navigates, without being caught up in, the feminized space of the salon and the masculine theaters of war. It is as though Madeleine, as Adams's complex stand-in, dramatizes a neutered gender that models a specifically political form of detachment.

In this, she anticipates Adams's later and better-known *The Education of Henry Adams*, the preface of which famously positions the author as a mere "manikin on which the toilet of education is to be draped." That is, the manikin announces an autobiography with a radically effaced ego at its center.[37] Martha Banta has examined Adams's complex relation to gender norms, which was highlighted by Adams's adoption of Senator Timothy Howe's insulting epithet for him, "begonia," as a mark of distinction.[38] Adams implies that he isn't bothered by the imputation of being "showy" with "no useful purpose," yet Banta demonstrates that Adams was indeed troubled by—in John Carlos Rowe's paraphrase—"his own sense of inadequacy regarding the questionable 'work' of Harvard Professors of History, dilettante writers, and 'brilliant' conversationalists in the 'salons' of power."[39] Like a "begonia," the feminized or neutered anatomy of a tailor's manikin must have offered a fraught self-image for a man who so often depicts himself as impotent in comparison to the vigor of Gilded Age captains of industry. But, like Madeleine herself, the manikin turns out to be a complex representation of a feeling body under erasure, an odd but effective icon for the chastened passions required for impartial governance.

From Parlor to Lobby

It may be true, as one critic has it, that Madeleine has "lost her hold on the private sphere" and doesn't know "how to proceed with a career in the public sphere";[40] but the immediate collapse of the borders delimiting Madeleine's aesthetic parlor reveals that the real question is whether she can maintain a separation between these imaginary zones. Most importantly, Madeleine's uncertain connection to her own publicity is soon indexed throughout the novel by a growing public association between her "parlor," or space of retreat, and the relatively new notion of the "lobby" and its denizen, the "lobbyist."[41] The *Oxford English Dictionary* shows the term "lobbyist" emerging near the end of the nineteenth century and defines it as "one who frequents the lobbies of the House of Representatives in order to influence members in the exercise of their legislative functions."[42] As though morphing into a lobby, Madeleine's salon becomes "the favorite haunt" of prominent foreign ministers, senators, and financiers. Even worse, Madeleine is soon the preferred guest at any party held to curry favor with Ratcliffe, provoking her first twinge of conscience: "Me! at a lobby dinner! Is that proper?" (*D*, 29).

The notion of the "lobby dinner" achieved notoriety during this period through the real-world gustatory exploits of Sam Ward, the famous "King of the Lobby," who was renowned for wining and dining his political targets into submission.[43] The *National Police Gazette* delighted in recalling this aspect of Ward's career in his obituary: "He always believed and acted upon the belief that the way to gain men's support was to tickle their palates. His dinners became famous, and the most eminent statesmen were not averse to sitting down to them."[44] In 1872 the author Fanny Fern helped spread the still-popular adage that "The way to a man's heart is through his stomach";[45] the *Gazette*'s language reworks this piece of romantic advice in a political context, underscoring how, for Gilded Age Americans, the "lobby" as the space surrounding the halls of Congress was fantasmatically extended to the restaurants, ballrooms, and private residences where realpolitik took place. The lobbyist thus expanded the real estate of official politics, even as women were negotiating new routes of access into public life: The spaces in which the lobbyist conducted business often coincided with the realms of domesticity and genteel culture in which women already exercised greater influence.[46] It was almost inevitable, then, that these two figures would converge in the popular imagination, constructing the "female lobbyist" as a monstrous threat to the purity of political reason.

Regarding this new political menace, one periodical of the time explained, "[Y]outh and beauty, tact and elegant dress, are the great aids of the female lobbyist."[47] Such a transgressive politicization of the female body provoked elaborate fantasies of anti-democratic seductions. A cartoon from an 1880 issue of the *Police Gazette* might well have served as an illustration for Adams's *Democracy*; it depicts a series of tableaux in which the "Queen of the Lobby" works her feminine wiles. In an inset frame, the "Queen" marks her senatorial target, gazing at him through binoculars.

A fragment of a handwritten note lying in the lower left hints at sexual impropriety: "My Dear Senator, I would like to see you for a few moments before leaving Albany." The proposed meeting is depicted in the main frame, in which the lobbyist leans seductively towards the senator, exposing the flesh that operates "In the interest of a certain railroad company [at a] salary [of] $400 per month" (Fig. 2.1).

Linking Madeleine Lee with such sexualized images of "feminine blandishments," the term "lobbyist" persistently trails her. In particular, her parlor-as-lobby

FIG. 2.1. *"Queens of the Lobby." Illustration by unknown artist accompanying an article of the same title by Didymus,* The National Police Gazette *35, no. 125 (February 14, 1880): 1. This reprint is from an image which originally appeared as part of ProQuest® American Periodicals product. Reprinted with permission from digital images produced by ProQuest LLC. www.proquest.com.*

threatens to connect her with the novel's own grotesque figuration of the "Queen of the Lobby," Mrs. Sam Baker, widow and former partner of the novel's Sam Ward stand-in. The Bakers play an important role at the end of the novel, when the reader learns that Madeleine's friend John Carrington served as executor to Baker's will and thus had access to papers documenting a particularly brazen case of Ratcliffe's bribe taking. Madeleine's initial contact with Mrs. Baker is significant in its own right, insofar as the latter's tales of Washington intrigue "initiated [Madeleine] into the mysteries of the lobby" (D, 116).[48] Adams's description of Mrs. Baker emphasizes the epicurean charms of the lobby, reporting, "There was a geniality in her address, savouring of easy Washington ways, a fruitiness of smile, and a rich southern accent, that explained on the spot her success in the lobby" (D, 113). Melding Sam Ward's specifically culinary seductions with standard modes of rhetorical suasion and sexual allure, Mrs. Baker deftly appeals to all of her target's senses. Madeleine is fascinated and horrified by Mrs. Baker as a distorted mirror of her own southern charm, and Mrs. Baker reawakens Madeleine's concerns about the "propriety" of her involvement in lobby dinners. Madeleine overcomes revulsion for the sake of her political education, however, and interrogates Mrs. Baker on the workings of the lobby:

> "Do you mean that you could get them all to vote as you pleased?" asked Madeleine.
>
> "Well! we got our bills through," replied Mrs. Baker.
>
> "But how did you do it? Did they take bribes?"
>
> "Some of them did. Some of them liked suppers and cards and theatres and all sorts of things. Some of them could be led, and some had to be driven like Paddy's pig who thought he was going the other way. Some of them had wives who could talk to them, and some—hadn't," said Mrs. Baker, with a queer intonation in her abrupt ending.   (D, 115)

The abrupt ending implies a sexual manipulation that might stop at flirtation or extend to prostitution; these "Paddy's pigs," with or without wives, could be led by playing on their most unrestrained appetites, be they gustatory or sexual.[49]

In this passage's slippery evocation of the lobbyist's persuasive tactics, Adams dramatically confronts norms of rational political debate, reasoned consent, and virtuous leadership with images of sex, bribery, and appetitive excess. The more Madeleine is initiated into the lobby the more she is worn down by her newfound knowledge—and the more Ratcliffe's frank admissions of democracy's failings start to seem laughably understated: "There is much in politics that disgusts and disheartens; much that is corrupt and bad" (D, 60). While Madeleine is hardly an idealistic reformer, her journey in Washington initially has an air of sober gravitas thanks to its echoes of Alexis de Tocqueville's famous tour of America's fledgling democracy. Like Tocqueville (and Adams for that matter), Madeleine admires elements of the political process, is skeptical about others, and remains at all events curious about its operation. Yet before the novel has so much as fully narrated her arrival in DC and her initial housekeeping, Madeleine is surrounded by and implicated in the grotesque intimacies of political pig driving and palette tickling.

Democracy's Atmospheres

This overview of the unexpected collapse of "parlor" into "lobby," and Madeleine's descent from a quest for republican virtue—or, at the very least, critical detachment—to her complicity in Ratcliffe's corruption brings me back to my core questions: What does it mean for Madeleine's democratic ideals, and for the readers', to be roped by the narrative into what the text repeatedly refers to as a disheartening and repulsive political "atmosphere"? Is the pessimism expressed by the novel's sketch of democracy's degraded milieu necessarily "conservative?" Sianne Ngai has described a text's "tone" as "its global or organizing affect, its general disposition or orientation toward its audience and the world."[50] *Democracy* evokes its tone of bitterness and repulsion by self-consciously focusing on the very phenomena of a diffuse, global affect: Congress is described as "reek[ing] with the atmosphere of bargain and sale" (*D*, 65); Madeleine "felt an atmosphere of bargain and intrigue, but she could only imagine how far it extended" (*D*, 90); and this "disgusted and depressed Madeleine's mind" (*D*, 96). Madeleine's first inklings that she may not be able to maintain her longed-for detachment likewise take shape as a visceral sense of dispersed unease: "She [was] conscious in a thousand ways that the atmosphere became more and more dense under the shadow of the Secretary of the Treasury. In spite of herself she sometimes felt uneasy, as though there were conspiracy in the air" (*D*, 113). Even Ratcliffe mobilizes a similar language to depict his own immersion in corruption as a kind of noble sacrifice: "In politics we cannot keep our hands clean. I have done many things in my political career that are not defensible. To act with entire honesty and self-respect, one should always live in a pure atmosphere, and the atmosphere of politics is impure" (*D*, 168). It's clear that this atmosphere is understood spatially as the juxtapolitical domains of the parlor, the salon, and the lobby, but also more generally as an affective ambience that contaminates character and reader alike.[51]

Teresa Brennan began her seminal work of affect theory, *The Transmission of Affect*, with the question: "Is there anyone who has not, at least once, walked into a room and 'felt the atmosphere'?"[52] This question launches a consideration of how affect undermines fantasies of autonomy and self-containment. In Brennan's terms, "the transmission of affect means that we are not self-contained in terms of our energies. There is no secure distinction between the individual and the 'environment' "; "this is why [affects] can enhance or deplete."[53] In *Democracy*, once the barrier between parlor and lobby has broken down, the repeated figuration of a polluted emotional atmosphere casts affective transmission as a grave threat to political agency. That this "atmosphere" is specifically one of disgust makes it even more threatening to Madeleine's democratic experiment. As Madeleine listens to

Mrs. Baker's inside account of the lobbyist's wiles, for example, her desire to understand the workings of democracy is confronted with an instinctive aversion:

> Thus Mrs. Baker rippled on, while Mrs. Lee listened with more and more doubt and disgust. The woman was showy, handsome in a coarse style, and perfectly presentable. Mrs. Lee had seen Duchesses as vulgar. She knew more about the practical working of government than Mrs. Lee could ever expect or hope to know. Why then draw back from this interesting lobbyist with such babyish repulsion? (D, 116)

Madeleine presents her interest in Mrs. Baker as cognitive—a desire to know and understand the mechanisms of power. Her disgust, on the other hand, is immature, bodily, and irresistible.

If pessimism and disgust underscore the novel's unflattering portrait of American democracy, and these feelings might well threaten to produce something of Madeleine's instinctive recoil in readers, it's also clear that her repulsion is reassuring. The reader has watched with concern as Madeleine becomes increasingly intimate with Ratcliffe, often seeming on the verge of becoming a lobbyist herself. In this light, Madeleine's instinctive disgust assures us that she still has her moral bearings, however much she may rationalize her interest in Mrs. Baker's backroom dealings. The novel's language of reeking odors, dense or impure air, and vulgar appetites might thus be said to mobilize what William Miller has described as disgust's capacity to yoke visceral aversion to moral judgment. Miller's analysis casts disgust as a recoil from boundary violations between the pure and the impure, the clean and the contaminated.[54] If Sam Ward was renowned for his immoral palate tickling, disgust withdraws from this kind of political impurity with the visceral force of a spitting out or a spitting up. And if the border between private and public is repeatedly threatened by the parlor's transformation into a lobby, repulsion reasserts the necessity of re-establishing that boundary. Madeleine's initial foray into politics was built on what looked like naïve optimism that institutional politics could be a mechanism for positive social change. Disgust operates on Madeleine's political faith much as Freud saw it function for sexual desire: it works as a "reaction formation," a force that inhibits the expression of a dangerous desire by prompting retreat at the very moment when the drive urges forward.

Adams thus presents disgust in an ambivalent light, as both a crucial moral sentiment and a threat to Madeleine's political agency. Yet the net result might well reinforce a view of the novel as conservative in its anti-reform disposition. Contemporary critics, however, were less charmed with this conservative pessimism than later commentators like Russell Kirk. These early readers focused on the novel's dangers for a democratic readership. In August of 1883, a reader of the journal *The Literary World* vented his scorn for the novel that, in his account, inaugurated the debased genre of the "Washington Novel": "There never was a more untrue and impossible book than *Democracy*.... Its libelous falsity secured its flattering reception in England, the reecho of which gave much buoyancy to the later cheap editions here."[55] Offering a unique image of transatlantic reverberation, this letter writer imagines a British audience delighting in a novel that exposes the corrupt underbelly of America's political system and an American audience, licensed by this foreign curiosity, indulging in the genre's tawdry and unpatriotic pleasures. If *Democracy* ropes its readers into a depressing and disgusting political atmosphere, it seemed to some as though its only possible pleasures were for foreign aristocrats or cynical democrats.

Indeed, this *Literary World* reader was not the first to sense that the evocation of something foul in the air might be the defining gesture of the Gilded Age Washington novel. Henry James, mostly admiring John De Forest's ear for political satire in the latter's 1875 novel *Honest John Vane*, still recoiled from its tone: "Whether accidentally or intentionally we hardly know, 'Honest John Vane' exhales a penetrating aroma of what in plain English one must call vulgarity. Every note the author strikes reverberates with a peculiarly vulgar tone; vulgarity pervades the suggestions, the atmosphere of his volume."[56] For James, De Forest's critique— like Adams's, focused in part on the corrupting influence of the lobbyist—might be fully justified, yet exposure to this rank atmosphere seemed likely to provoke a total abandonment of democratic ideals. In this, James intuits what has been called disgust's "weak intentionality." Unlike strong emotions that spur one to action, disgust leads to confusion and paralysis. And unlike emotions such as sympathy or love that bind a subject to an object, disgust is largely prophylactic, "constituted by the vehement rejection or exclusion of its object."[57] An "atmosphere" of disgust would thus be doubly anxiogenic as it intensifies a confused relationship to political agency, and creates a profound sense of inter-subjective permeability. What's more, disgust can be quite specific about the repulsive objects from which one must detach but all-too vague about the attachments—whether to individuals, institutions, ideologies, etc.—that might take their place.

To better understand this dynamic we might return, for example, to the passage cited above. For Madeleine Lee, the lobbyist Mrs. Baker is both "interesting" and disgusting. Sianne Ngai has argued that "interesting" is an unexpectedly tricky term of valuation: "The most characteristic thing about the interesting is thus its lack of distinguishing characteristics."[58] Yet if the label "interesting" appears to make a somewhat vague, underwhelming, and intuitive claim about an object that has caught our attention, Ngai argues that we must also consider the extended temporality of the interesting as an aesthetic category—"not just the spontaneous, feeling-based act of judgment but that judgment's discursive and narrative aftermath."[59] To call something interesting is to announce an intention to further justify its worthiness of critical attention. In the above passage from the novel, however, the critical judgments that might follow in the wake of finding a lobbyist "interesting" seem very much in abeyance. Adams leaves the reader greatly in doubt about what exactly Madeleine hopes to gain from spending time with such curious but unsavory characters. Her disgust, on the other hand, is immediate and unambiguous—she recoils before she can even fully account for her own repulsion. In the space of one passage, then, Adams presents disgust as a resource and a trap, a powerful moral sentiment and an obstacle to a more sustained critical engagement with democracy. Meanwhile, for many critics, the novel itself seemed like a repulsive threat to the purity of American literature's properly democratic commitments.

Civil Service Reform

Clearly some readers felt that *Democracy* and other novels of its ilk had either concocted the corruption they claimed to observe, or wallowed unnecessarily in the depravity they pretended to condemn. The disgust Adams evokes threatened to leave readers of his novel worse off than when they started: equally subject to a corrupt political system, but now robbed of the emotional resources to effect democracy's repair. In fact, Adams explicitly explores the ways giving in to disgust may be to suspend one's own agency or to delegate it to another, as when Ratcliffe intentionally dwells on the disgusting details of politics in order to make his successful navigation of such a system seem like a virtuous sacrifice:

> Even this half revelation of the meanness which distorted politics; this one-sided view of human nature in its naked deformity playing pranks with the interests of forty million people, disgusted and depressed Madeleine's mind. Ratcliffe spared her nothing except the exposure of his own moral sores. He carefully called her attention to every leprous taint upon his neighbours' persons, to every rag in their foul clothing, to every slimy and fetid pool that lay beside their path.... He meant that she should go hand in hand with him through the brimstone lake, and the more repulsive it seemed to her, the more overwhelming would his superiority become.   (*D*, 96–7)

In passages such as this Adams complicates his own disgust, suggesting that an aversion to democracy is not an unavoidable or even proper judgment, but one reflective of Ratcliffe's own cynical worldview. While the novel itself was blamed for a dark view of democracy, at times Adams projects this pessimism onto the novel's villain, suggesting that it is the corrupt senator who is "filled with disgust and cynical contempt for every form of politics" (*D*, 85).

Of course for those who celebrate the novel's "conservatism," its depiction of the impossibility of reform might be seen as a powerful argument—reinforced affectively by disgust and pessimism—for the sanctity of existing institutions, hierarchies, and traditions. Yet this notion that the novel is "conservative" by virtue of its challenge to a fantasy of democracy's redemption is complicated by the novel's overt reform aspirations. Contemporary readers easily recognized that the novel was directly engaged in a debate relating to a very specific reform program, even if this program was referenced primarily as a lost opportunity. One 1880 review of the novel, for example, proposed that the still anonymous author's "attitude is that of a disappointed Civil Service Reformer, who has ceased to look for any improvement in the system and believes that things are steadily going from bad to worse."[60] Adams was indeed increasingly disappointed by the failed promise of the civil service reform movement, yet he remained dedicated to it as an ideal, and its central concerns permeate the novel.

Civil service reform was part of a broader pattern in which, as Warren Susman notes, " 'Leadership' became one of the key words at the end of the [nineteenth] century. Schools began to offer courses in it, and Presidents of the United States indulged in learned lectures about it."[61] Civil service reform hoped to rationalize politics by placing greater emphasis on quantifiable expertise, arguing for rational and transparent appointments with a resulting suspicion of forms of non-reified personal value. Emily S. Rosenberg similarly notes that nearly all "people who adopted the 'progressive' label . . . shared a fundamental faith in professional exper-tise," a proclivity that expressed an elitist desire for "expert and efficient people" to regulate the "social disorders of the late nineteenth century."[62] Adams and his mugwump cohort adopted this approach, prefiguring the Progressive movement of the early twentieth century and advocating civil service reform as a key front in the battle against industrial wealth and the rise of an American plutocracy. Limiting the capacity of the powerful to trade favors or spoils was, for Adams and his allies, a fundamental attack on the power of the political party and the financial monopoly.

Adams was an avid reader of and occasional contributor to *The Nation*, which, under E.L. Godkin's editorship, had called loudly for reform of the Johnson ad-ministration and for support of the civil service reform "Jenckes Bill," the precursor to the better-known "Pendleton Bill," then under debate in the mid-1860s.[63] Adams does not seem to have become consistently dedicated to the cause until after the election of Ulysses S. Grant in 1868. While many reform minded Republicans were initially optimistic that the Grant administration would mark the end of an era of patronage and spoils, Adams has been credited with early skepticism—which, after the announcement of Grant's cabinet appointees, turned to nearly universal outrage and a sense of betrayal in the reform camp. Even so, Adams described his brother and himself, both engaged in reform, as "up to the ears in politics and public affairs" and predicted hopefully, "we shall perhaps make our little mark."[64]

Adams's clearest effort to make that mark came the year following Grant's election, with the publication of his essay "Civil Service Reform" in the *North American Review*. In this essay, Adams initially adopts a somewhat sympathetic pose toward the new president, highlighting the need for clear guidelines regard-ing the selection of civil servants and citing the ease with which such decisions are contaminated by private concerns:

> To act upon the new rule [regulating appointments] without suitable notice was unfair to his friends; for however just the reform might be in the abstract, in practice it would be considered a refusal of confidence to individuals, and would

tend to discredit them in the eyes of their constituents. A friendly appeal of this sort was difficult to resist. The applicant was perhaps a soldier, a comrade of the President, a man who had suffered in the national cause.[65]

In the wake of the passions of the Civil War, nothing could be more natural, Adams suggests, than for a man to have a legitimate claim of friendship and honor on another man, yet such claims had to be differentiated from a rational system that would benefit the public good through qualified, capable applicants. Thus Adams urged Grant to "extend a network of [competitive examinations] over every office, down to the Treasury porters, and establish his reforms so firmly in the minds of the people that the Republic would never again be in danger on this score."[66] Exams, a crucial part of the reform movement since the Jenckes Bill, not only would provide a clear standard of expertise and capability but also would free the president from the wearying demands of dispensing patronage.[67]

In many ways the novel's "atmosphere of bargain and intrigue" appears per-fectly suited to advance Adams's civil service reform program. Adams makes clear that Madeleine approaches politics with something like the reformer's interest in subjecting applicants to exams, though the "tests" in question are here compared to chemical manipulation: "She wanted to learn . . . what was the quality of the men who controlled [government]. One by one, she . . . tested them by acids and by fire. A few survived her tests and came out alive, though more or less disfigured, where she had found impurities" (D, 12). This faith in clinical distance initially under-girds Madeleine's confidence that she can manipulate senator Ratcliffe without becoming implicated in his quest for power. In a crucial scene, she imagines graphically that she can cut through the image of Ratcliffe's hulking frame to locate the pure political power he represents:

> Through him she hoped to sound the depths of statesmanship and to bring up from its oozy bed that pearl of which she was in search; the mysterious gem which must lie hidden somewhere in politics. She wanted to understand this man; to turn him inside out; to experiment on him and use him as young physiologists use frogs and kittens. If there was good or bad in him, she meant to find its meaning. (D, 20–1)

Madeleine's language of physiological taxonomy asserts her perceptual mastery of the political field. Adams frequently proclaimed his many intellectual debts to Alexis de Tocqueville, who famously called for a "new political science." Madeleine's vivisection metaphor links her democratic inquiry to empirical methods, under-scoring a wish that new sciences of the social could equal the natural sciences in their positivist pretensions.[68] This aura of clinical detachment is crucial to her efforts to manage each new encounter with Washington power brokers so as to ensure in advance that she will remain safely unmoved by their charms.

What's more, the dissection metaphor directly links Madeleine's political science to an overtly anti-sentimental program to advocate for the scientific necessity and ethics of vivisection. In 1881, the year following Democracy's publication, a meeting took place in London to address a debate that had been raging for years about the morality of the practice. Even more striking, a later editorial in the *North American Review* advocated for vivisection specifically in terms of the necessity of suppressing disgust:

> We cannot decide the right or wrong of vivisection by the abhorrence it naturally excites. The butcher's trade is revolting, but we pay him well. We shudder and turn sick when we pass by the anatomical dissecting-room, but it is now licensed.... [T]he horrorized sentimentalists must stand aside if they will not listen to reason....It cannot be too strongly said that feeling is no guide for judgment.... Questions of morals require calm, cold reasoning.[69]

Democracy anticipates this argument by proposing that rational detachment begins with the suppression of the gag reflex. Adams's overdetermined image of Madeleine's political physiology plays on the unexpected common ground shared by the physiologist and the civil service reformer: a shared desire to insulate judgment from feeling and to overcome disgust in favor of taxonomic precision and rational order.

Adams underscores this taxonomic impulse by describing nearly all of Madeleine's encounters with Washingtonians as structured by the idea of "types": objects, like both physiognomic specimens and bureaucratic applicants, of rationalist encounter that are divorced from particularity. Of her friend and admirer, the southern lawyer John Carrington, for example, Madeleine declares admiringly, "[H]e is a type!" (*D*, 13). Adams catalogs other specimens in Madeleine's collection: "A very different visitor was Mr. C.C. French, a young member of congress from Connecticut...Quite another sort of person was Mr. Hartbeest Schneidekoupon, a citizen of Philadelphia...A much higher type of character was Mr. Nathan Gore, of Massachusetts..." (*D*, 24–5). As Susan Mizruchi has shown, the notion of "types" was central to the rationalistic ambitions of late nineteenth-century social science, which made a "distinction between the rational clarity of science and the bewildering particularities of aesthetics."[70] Madeleine anticipates the importance "types" would hold in these new sciences of social behavior. If disgust threatens to sap the reformer's energy and undermine democratic confidence, new bureaucratic taxonomies of merit could offer one route to bypass democracy's most grotesque intimacies.

However, this language of types also hints at anxieties within Madeleine's rationalistic confidence. In Adams's autobiography, *The Education of Henry Adams*, young Henry similarly comes to view senators taxonomically: "What struck boys most was their type. Senators were a species."[71] Watching a man become a "species" of senator is one of the many ways Adams describes his education as a string of experiences in which private, intimate bonds—his friendship with Senator Charles Sumner, for example—are transformed (and often destroyed) by their transposition into the realm of the political.[72] If such a transformation is marked with regret in *The Education*, for Madeleine, the reduction of men to species is designed precisely to inoculate her against the possibility of an intimate bond or any tie structured by desire rather than detached, scientific contemplation. But typology carries other emotional risks. Madeleine's scientific rhetoric locks her into a reading in which evidence of Ratcliffe's corruption must, via the "type's" logic of exemplarity, influence her assessment of democracy itself: "If I throw him overboard, everything must go, for he is only a specimen" (*D*, 44). To encounter Ratcliffe in his embodied particularity is to risk an emotional attachment that might cloud judgment, or a disgust that might weaken reformist zeal. But generalizing Ratcliffe and his ilk as specimens and species threatens to incite a rationalistic paralysis that parallels disgust's dispirited recoil.

The Friend Zone

I have argued that Adams narrates Madeleine's experience of DC life as a series of competing attractions and repulsions: she is "interested" in lobbyists but also retreats from them; she wants to examine Ratcliffe but only if he can be safely dissected without desire and without disgust. But perhaps no affective relation more dramatically illustrates the importance of this dynamic of alternating attraction and withdrawal to Adams's thinking than his treatment of friendship, an emotional relation that has long been theorized as both essential to democracy, and as a profound threat to it. Recent critical valorizations of friendship have taken many forms, from Derrida's reappraisal of friendship as an alternative to logocentric notions of universality, reciprocity, and equality, to work in the Foucauldian domain of gender and sexuality, where "friendship" maintains a space of uncertainty that postpones the classification and normalization of female–female, male–male, and male–female relations and identities.[73] For critics of nineteenth-century American literary history, friendship is often seen as the cornerstone of Walt Whitman's emotional democracy. His neologism "camerado" is said to "emphasize the need of friendship, especially among men, for a democratic society"[74] and Whitman's lyric intimacies with lovers, pupils, patients, and comrades are prized as "a means to social tolerance and empathetic cohesion."[75]

Yet this celebration of camaraderie bumps up against worries about friendship's role in contemporary politics. Peter Goodrich, for example, warns of the "new casuistry," with its "casus pro amico, its nepotism, its hiding of politics behind the declared but inscrutable beliefs of the heart."[76] Earlier I noted that Adams's essay on Civil Service reform emphasizes a familiar, understandable scenario, in which the President must resist a "friendly appeal" from a "comrade." As the argument develops, it becomes clear that Civil Service Reform is expressly addressed to protecting democracy from friendship: "[Even] if the President held firm against reasoning [in requests for appointments], there remained the earnest appeal to personal friendship, far more difficult to resist or evade than any weapon in the whole army of logic."[77] For Adams, friendship is a form of intimacy so powerful as to require governmental intervention to combat its persuasive allure. In *Democracy*, friendship is similarly presented as a problem. "Friends" and friendship are discussed largely in terms of Ratcliffe's political alliances and backroom scheming, as a condensed overview makes clear: There are the "daily draughts [of flattery] from political friends" (*D*, 18) that enlarge Ratcliffe's ego. These flattering friends demand a return on their investment and become the "friends [who] expected him to do something when, in fact nothing could be done" (*D*, 66). There is also the problem of "the President's opposition to Ratcliffe's declared friends," which makes it "impossible to force any of them into office," and Ratcliffe's counter strategy of "manipulate[ing] with the utmost care" the President's own "few personal friends" (*D*, 92). Ratcliffe's great strategic success is to "convert one of [the President's] personal, confidential friends" (*D*, 93) to his own side, disrupting an intimate tie that is implicitly posited as a force resistant to manipulation. Of course these kinds of office seekers and spoilsmen are more or less what we might call "frienemies," a "choice company of friends and admirers, who had beguiled their leisure hours... cursing him in every variety of profane language" (*D*, 83). Nonetheless, these friends have their (im)patience rewarded, as one great political truth in the novel is that "Ratcliffe's friends did come into their fair share of the public money" (*D*, 105).

Madeleine occasionally is recognized as a special friend of Ratcliffe's and so implicated in this web of friendly favors. Crucially, however, friendship for Madeleine more commonly represents a strategy not of obligation but of distancing. Again, much as I suggested that Adams explores modes of interest or attachment in tension with the desire to recoil, his focus on what looks like the novel's only positive or binding emotional register turns out to once again center on a mode of disgust. That is, for Madeleine, "friendship" names a kind of relation that is not love or marriage. It is a crucial, *defensive* posture in a novel in which nearly everyone she encounters in Washington is ready to make her his bride. Old Baron Jacobi, the Bulgarian minister, "would have married both sisters at once" (*D*, 23), and the young reform journalist Nathan Gore is forgiven his presumption in warning Madeleine of Ratcliffe's corruption, since she "half thought that it had depended only on herself to make of Mr. Gore something more than a friend" (*D*, 111). John Carrington is one of the few characters in the novel who legitimately seems able to claim a kind of intimacy with Madeleine, having found her "a warm friend... full of sympathy where sympathy was more than money, and full of resource and suggestion where money and sympathy failed" (*D*, 56–7). But when he comes to press his suit, Madeleine rejects him on the grounds of this friendship: "Mr. Carrington, I am the best friend you have on earth. One of these days you will thank me with your whole soul for refusing to listen to you now" (*D*, 143). Finally, in the dire closing moments of the novel, when Ratcliffe demands that Madeleine make good on her "coquettish" flirtation, she employs a rhetoric of friendship in articulating her refusal: "Since I am forced to give you pain, was it not fairer and more respectful to you to speak at once? We have been friends....I sincerely want to avoid saying or doing anything that would change our relations" (D, 188). Throughout *Democracy*, the marriage plot and the seduction story have menaced Madeleine's preferred, scientific relationship to politics. In this context, friendship emerges not as a resource for fluid political intimacies but as a mechanism for managing proximity and distance, a means to produce a form of intimacy that is also detached and critical.

It's worth stressing this aloofness that Adams makes fundamental to friendship. The imbrication of intimacy and distance is, after all, precisely that which Derrida excavates in his discussion of friendship:

> Let us note in passing that these two words, respect and responsibility which are linked and constantly provoke each other, appear to refer, in the first case to distance, to space, and to the look [regard], and in the second case to time, to the voice, and to listening. Their co-implication can be sensed at the heart of friendship, one of whose enigmas comes from this distance or this respectful separation which distinguishes it, as feeling, from love.[78]

Here Derrida is building on Kant's account of friendship, which describes moral friendship as a delicate balance between attraction and disgust.[79] As one commentator notes, Kant's "proposal to distinguish friendship from love by defining the former in terms of repulsion emphasizes to an unprecedented degree the distance of friends with respect to one other."[80] Again, scholars of nineteenth-century American literature may be predisposed to read "friendship" through the lens of a homosocial vision of loving comrades—a community of intimate strangers whose emotional bonds offer an implicit rebuke to superficial forms of institutional politics. It's all the more striking then that *Democracy*—which might look, finally, to explore a binding affect in contradistinction to its otherwise-pervasive negativity— ends up accentuating a vision of friendship that locates disgust at its heart.

Excavating an element of "repulsion" within friendship makes it all the more suited, as a concept, to help negotiate a space between intimate subjection and apathetic withdrawal, as it offers a form of attachment that is always predicated on distance. In casual speech, to be "just friends" is to emphasize a lack of sexual intimacy. A related joke speaks of one who is rebuffed in their efforts to escalate a friendship to a romantic and sexual relationship as being caught in the "friend zone." For Madeleine, the "friend zone" suspends the counterpoised threats of wholesale implication in Ratcliffe's ambitious schemes and complete disgusted withdrawal. Adams riffs on this dynamic of suspended attachment-without-seduction, of proximity and recoil, as a mode of ambivalent political investment. Madeleine, modeling Adams's anxious style of political involvement, is always simultaneously approaching and withdrawing from the stink of democracy's polluted atmosphere.

Conclusion: Aversive Attachments

I began this chapter by suggesting that, despite its title, *Democracy: an American Novel* does not seem, at first blush, to live up to the demands of "democratic fiction." The novel does not elevate the thoughts and deeds of common folk, nor foster sympathy for the downtrodden, nor does it explore vernacular narrative as a counterpoint to official history. Its scenes never focus on warm bonds between citizens as a model for national belonging. At best, as I argued in the previous sections, Adams was drawn to a scientific view that makes room for some interest in politics, or a discourse of friendship that walks the line between cold withdrawal and passionate attachment. "Interest" and "friendship" offer two lukewarm forms of political desire. But one might object that it is yet more damning evidence against the novel's democratic credentials that this interest is so easily corrupted, and friendship—the novel's one positive affective relation—arrives under a cloud of suspicion, and does its most powerful political work by rejecting, not fostering, political intimacies.

And of course the most striking way the novel fails to achieve what Whitman called "emotional democracy" is what I have described as its persistent "atmosphere" of disgust. Whitman is often seen as the quintessential poetic embodiment of democracy precisely because of his immunity to disgust. In *Leaves of Grass,* he famously takes everything in: "All this I swallow and it tastes good...I like it well, and it becomes mine."[81] Indeed, William Miller posits the suppression of disgust as a defining gesture of democracy. While repulsion itself may be an anti-democratic affect, its overcoming is a uniquely democratic disposition.[82] And Martha Nussbaum has called for a renewed commitment to Whitman's suspension of disgust: "We might, with Walt Whitman, go still farther: the really civilized nation must make a strenuous effort to counter the power of disgust, as a barrier to the full equality and mutual respect of all citizens."[83]

Late-nineteenth-century readers anticipated these concerns about the anti-democratic effects of the novel's intensely negative affects. Surely "democratic fiction" must have as a minimal condition a more forceful attachment to or investment in democracy. Not only does political disgust refuse this attachment, its defensive repulsion has a serious cost. Disgust, after all, has a "style of negativeness, a depressed and depressing style that makes us uncomfortable....Indignation gives us reasons for living. Disgust gives us reasons for withdrawing. Disgust does its moral work but leaves us feeling polluted."[84] In fact, whatever subtle modulations of political emotion have characterized her time in the capital, by the novel's close Madeleine appears to have succumbed to her repulsion. After learning of Ratcliffe's history of bribery and subsequently rejecting him, she is on the verge of collapse: "Worn out by long-continued anxiety...[her] strain could only end in a nervous crisis, and at length it came: 'Oh, what a vile thing life is!' she cried, throwing up her arms with a gesture of helpless rage and despair. 'Oh, how I wish I were dead!'"

(*D*, 183). Madeleine retreats from "vile" Washington and returns to New York with her sister, Sibyl, with plans to depart for Europe the following month. The novel ends with a letter from Sibyl to Madeleine's friend John Carrington informing him of their itinerary, avoiding mention of Madeleine's somewhat scandalous departure.

Madeleine adds her own postscript, however, in the form of a strip of paper inserted into the envelope for Carrington's eyes only, which reads, "The bitterest part of all this horrid story is that nine out of ten of our countrymen would say I had made a mistake" (*D*, 202). Her language is uncertain, but Madeleine implies that an American populace resigned to the stink of corruption would have encouraged her to marry Ratcliffe, a presidential hopeful, and become the future first lady. In the absence of virtue, why not gratify ambition? For a novel called *Democracy*, this language of a quantifiable percentage of "countrymen" is one of the strikingly few appearances of anything like "the people," and it confirms Ratcliffe's claim that the failings of democracy can be laid at their door: ninety percent of them vote, as it were, for corruption and compromise.

Madeleine's casual estimation of popular sentiment echoes her realization that she herself has been cast as a metaphor and metonym for the electorate at the moment of Ratcliffe's marriage proposal: "Ratcliffe's offer must have been seen by half Washington, and her reply was awaited by an immense audience, as though she were a political returning-board. Her disgust was intense..." (*D*, 174). With her fluctuating emotions scrutinized like a commission announcing election returns, Madeleine is driven to confess, "Democracy has shaken my nerves to pieces" (*D*, 200). The reader's disgust and nervous exhaustion, like Madeleine's, is intense. Yet just as the extremity of Madeleine's response demands that we question her own self-description of anesthetic detachment, I have argued that the very intensity of the novel's "atmosphere" may require a more nuanced account of Adams's investment in democracy.

And of course, thus far, I've left out a flip side to disgust's aversive energies— which is to say the strange intimacy between repulsion and fascination, disgust and attraction. For Freud, reaction formations lead to the repression of desire, but also to desire's intensification. As he writes in *Three Essays on Sexuality*, "The sexual instinct in its strength enjoys overriding this disgust."[85] Adams hints at a similar dynamic. Following Mrs. Baker's revelations of the sordid details of the lobby, Madeleine specifically frames her newfound knowledge in terms of clinical curiosity, a form of fascination that counters disgust:

> Not until this moment had she really felt as though she had got to the heart of politics, so that she could, like a physician with his stethoscope, measure the organic disease. Now at last she knew why the pulse beat with such unhealthy irregularity, and why men felt an anxiety which they could not or would not explain. Her interest in the disease overcame her disgust at the foulness of the revelation. To say that the discovery gave her actual pleasure would be doing her injustice; but the excitement of the moment swept away every other sensation. (*D*, 191)

Earlier "the interesting" was easily displaced by repulsion. Here, however, clinical detachment has its own emotional dimension: an interest that now has enough intensity to sweep away aversion. Adams is no Freudian provocateur: he reassures us that Madeleine's desire for the political does not "enjoy" overriding disgust. It would, indeed, be an "injustice" to call this interest "pleasure." But it's clear that Adams wants to highlight the diffuse affective registers of withdrawal *and* attachment. Disgust, nervousness, fascination, pain, and near-pleasure emerge as an idiosyncratic emotional scale for tracking Madeleine's attraction to and withdrawal from Gilded Age democracy, an ongoing process of managing the rewards and penalties of political involvement.

It is in fact the link between desire and disgust that leads Nussbaum, otherwise unwavering in her condemnation of disgust, to admit some unease in her call for a disgust-free democracy: "[T]he disgusting and the attractive are interwoven in a complex manner. Would a sexuality free of all sense of the disgusting be feasible and imaginable?...[W]e need to ask whether the disgust-free attitude does not remove too much."[86] And Sianne Ngai has wondered if disgust might be more social than we often credit: "[Disgust] seeks to include or draw others into its exclusion of its object, enabling a strange kind of sociability."[87] Disgust refuses both pity and "contempt" as weak affective postures of toleration. What's more, disgust reminds us that some forms of political judgment require the capacity to differentiate, to deny, and to exclude. Ngai argues that "The hegemonic pluralism of both the academy and the larger society...conscripts the appealing rhetoric of inclusivity to *exclude critical discourses of exclusion.*"[88] Ngai positions disgust against a "pluralistic desire," which she argues is too-casually imagined to be equivalent with democracy.

Taking a cue from Ngai's account, might we make a bid for disgust in Adams's text as itself a democratic affective posture, but from the opposite end of the emotional spectrum from Whitman's exuberant inclusivity? As tempting as this is, we may still hesitate to claim that the novel's disgust and disdain for popular sovereignty so easily routes us back to a desire for the political, back to an attachment to American democracy. After all, Ngai's concern is with literary texts that make themselves repulsive to refuse a form of benign toleration that nullifies art's impact. To provoke "disgust" at the political itself is a more troubling proposition.[89] But I'd argue it's a gambit worth pursuing. Critics have been interested in the democratic effects of democratic affects relating to sympathy, compassion, and the cultivation of attachments to the nation, to fellow citizens, and to common ideals. My larger claim in this book is that by rethinking the seeming equivalence between "democratic literature" on the one hand and narratives of sympathy, identification, fellow-feeling, and attachment, on the other, and by broadening our sense of the affects—especially negative or seemingly unsociable affects—that count as democratic, we gain a richer understanding of the everyday political emotions that both constrain and enable political activity.

In this context, I would propose that *Democracy: An American Novel*'s primary provocation is its depiction of the affective work of remaining in proximity to political desire, despite the strain of democracy's nerve-wracking and disgust-inducing atmosphere. To be optimistic about democracy, to be attached to the political, including institutional politics, as a site for transformation, is to be vulnerable to nerve-shattering disappointments. Disgust protects us from this desire, but also intensifies it. I began this chapter by noting an anxiety on both the contemporary US left and right about the proper posture toward political institutions. Like the "half-melancholy" conservatism that Hawthorne attributes to his reformer Holgrave, Adams explores a variety of in-between affective states that define an ambivalent relationship to political institutions. In this way, we might riff on John F. Kennedy's famous gesture of respiratory inclusivity to say that Adams's frustrated and frustrating narrative of political desire, for all of its repulsive odors and unclean sights, keeps us all breathing the same foul air of democracy.[90]

Depression

Strange Apathy

SENTIMENT AND SOVEREIGNTY IN *RAMONA*

Barely Living

In a personal letter dated November 18, 1879, the popular poet, columnist, and novelist Helen Hunt Jackson appealed to editor and author Charles Dudley Warner, pleading with him to put pen to paper on behalf of the Ponca, a tribe of Native Americans who had been forcibly displaced from their Nebraska homeland. "I wish you would write something about them, as you did about the Doe in the Adirondacks!" Jackson implored Warner in one of the earliest records of her taking up the so-called Indian question. "There is no telling what you might accomplish by it. You might even prick through to [Secretary of the Interior] Carl Schurz's heart."[1] Four years later, when embarking on the novel to be called *In the Name of the Law*, later retitled *Ramona* (1884), Jackson returned to the idea of just such a pointed allegory in a missive to her friend the poet Thomas Bailey Aldrich:

> Do you remember, of course you do, Warners [*sic*] story of the Doe?—do you think the story of two human beings, husband and wife, fleeing from place to place, to place, seeking a chance of life, and a home, and never finding it, could be told as simply and unsupportedly as that was, and be effective?—I think so. That is what I am going to try to do. (*L*, 300)

The Warner tale in question, "A-Hunting of the Deer" (1878), follows a doe and her foal as they are tracked through the Adirondack woods. The story devotes most of its space to humanizing the deer and celebrating her maternal instinct, physical grace, and resilience—which collectively make the story's conclusion all the more unsettling. Driven in desperation to swim toward freedom, the doe is trapped midlake by a "gentleman" hunter and his ill-mannered guide. When the first man hesitates to dispatch the deer, the guide is more decisive: "He slung [her] round, whipped out his hunting-knife, and made a pass that severed her jugular. And the gentleman ate that night of the venison."[2] Warner transitions from anthropomorphizing the doe to describing her as "venison," dramatizing a sudden reduction from quasi-personhood to mere animal flesh.

In this book's first chapter I discussed the novel Warner co-authored with Mark Twain, *The Gilded Age* (1873), a biting political satire that might have served as a model for Jackson's exposé of the corruption and cruelty enabled by US Indian policy. Yet it was Warner's later, seemingly minor story of outdoor life that caught Jackson's attention as a template for her narrative of native suffering.[3] In this chapter, I ask what it would mean to reread *Ramona*, a historical romance tracking persecuted and beleaguered Indians, as modeled on a tale of animal life and death—that is, as an alternative to the popular, and continued, critical inclination toward interpreting the novel as the "*Uncle Tom's Cabin* of the Indian."[4] Harriet Beecher Stowe's seminal abolition novel is generally understood to have fostered an emotional bond between her white readers and her black protagonists, encouraging the attribution of personhood to slaves who, under the law, were considered things or possessions.[5] Jackson famously announced her intention to write a novel that would induce the same paradigm-shifting effect attributed to Stowe's work, inviting readers to presume a cognate effort on Jackson's part to elevate indigenous characters to the status of "persons" invested with dignity and agency. Yet Jackson's linking of *Ramona* to *Uncle Tom's Cabin* has also predisposed critics sensitive to the limitations of Stowe's rhetoric to find the same shortcomings in Jackson's novel. As critics of literary sentimentality have argued, texts like *Uncle Tom's Cabin* threaten to swap private emotion for public action and mass-mediated consumption for structural transformation.[6] Further, sentimentality's universalizing impulse may elide the gender, racial, and economic differences that underlie the suffering in need of amelioration.[7] In the case of *Ramona*, critics have seen these faults in the flatness and passivity of its indigenous characters, as well as in the novel's later role in developing and marketing a southern California tourist aesthetic.[8]

I will argue, however, that in light of this alternate authorial account of the novel's origins, that is, Jackson's stated interest in linking human and animal life, *Ramona* can be seen more accurately as a version of what Lauren Berlant has called a "countersentimental" text that, like most works grappling with *Uncle Tom's Cabin*'s legacy, is deeply committed to developing literature's transformative potential even as it explores the cost of pursuing change on sentimentality's terms.[9] Rather than present a blandly universal "person" with whom we might empathize, *Ramona* peels back the signs of indigenous personhood to reveal a kind of animal life underneath—a life, I will argue, that evokes Giorgio Agamben's notion of "bare life," a biological remainder stripped of political existence and kinship. In *Ramona*, however, we might more accurately speak of "barely living," as Jackson translates Warner's tale of animal desperation into a human idiom by highlighting the *ongoing* emotional strain of life under federal management, which kept native peoples suspended in a persistent state of uncertainty, depression, and exhaustion.[10] Against critics who lament Jackson's failure to attribute sufficient agency to her Indian protagonists, I claim that her troubling but powerful evocation of animal-like desperation reveals the critical potential latent in Agamben's account of the interdependencies between national sovereignty and bare life, an account that is sometimes said to fail to address "the problem of resistance."[11] Further, Jackson's work helps to link biopolitical discourses about bare life with a critical focus on processes of racialization: two strains of political theory that are sometimes said to be in tension, or even opposed.[12]

To pursue this theoretical interest in Jackson's countersentimental interrogation of bare life, my account looks historically to the 1879 trial of *Standing Bear v. Crook*. This trial stands as a transitional case between two landmark developments: the 1871 congressional act ending formal treaty-making with indigenous tribes and the 1887 General Allotment Act, which solidified the government's strategy of dissolving tribal affiliations by transferring tribal land titles to individual Indians and nonindigenous Americans. Jackson's countersentimentality comprises two distinct yet closely related strategies, both shaped by the pressures of this particular moment in the history of US–Indian relations. First, *Ramona* takes as a primary theme the unpredictability of sympathy's political effects, offering a preemptive defense against the hostility of Indian Agency officials toward overtly emotional rhetoric, which they denigrated as feminine irrationalism. Second, in evoking an indigenous "life" reduced to a quasi-animal existence, Jackson dramatizes the personal effects of structural injustice in affective terms, without pursuing the narrative (or institutional) production of "persons." This latter point is of particular importance because, as critics within the field of Native American studies have shown, the decades surrounding the novel's publication mark a shift in US strategy, from dealing with Indians as tribes and nations to policies designed to individuate and (to varying degrees) assimilate the native subject.[13] I propose that Jackson seeks to avoid participating in this state-sanctioned attribution of personhood by offering a nuanced exploration of native suffering, focusing specifically on the traumatic effects of the United States' bureaucratic shuffling of the boundaries, both literal and figurative, of indigenous sovereignty.[14]

In Chapter 2 I argued that "disgust" is a charged feeling in the context of democratic politics. In this current chapter, I explore "depression" as an equally fraught political emotion. Like disgust, depression, can look a- or even antipolitical. In the twenty-first century depression is likely to be thought of as a biochemical, not a social, problem.[15] And depression, often characterized by feelings of isolation, can appear to be defined by an essential unsociability.[16] Recently, however, critics have attended to depression as a political condition. Depression may register the dissonance of subjects called on to embody impossible forms of autonomy, agency, and self-care amid social contexts that are fundamentally limiting and damaging.[17] Depression thereby offers a powerful rubric for studying a transitional nineteenth-century moment in US–Indian relations. Sara Ahmed warns, "The civilizing mission can be redescribed as a happiness mission. For happiness to become a mission, the colonized other must first be deemed unhappy."[18] In my reading, Jackson ultimately refuses to turn frowns upside down, and rejects an administrative view of the Indians' stripped-down existence as something like the chrysalis stage of a more beautiful, unfurling American personhood.

Nonetheless, as I will show, Jackson's efforts to dramatize animal-like desperation as a sign of structural injustice must also be seen as a risky strategy within the wider context of the expanding administrative state, which had its own frameworks for linking observations about emotion to political outcomes more suitable to the Bureau's vision for the dawn of the "era of assimilation."[19] This may be surprising, given that we think of bureaucracies as opposed to emotion, and late nineteenth-century Indian policy had a particularly rationalistic tenor. As historian Mark S. Weiner, notes:

> [T]he reforms of the assimilationist period...brought into being a series of federal programs designed to restructure the most intimate elements of native life.... These programs...relied on an increasingly professional civil service that was...increasingly guided by social scientific expertise. Forged in the midst of a movement to create a professional managerial class that would place federal administration on a scientific foundation, assimilationist policy bore the imprint of this historical origin.[20]

Jackson's antagonist in the Ponca affair, Carl Schurz, was viewed as a chief ally in the crusade for new managerial ideals to shape Indian policy and law. For Schurz, the Indian problem required an unsentimental willingness to come to terms with the inevitable erosion of tribal life. An enlightened bureaucracy could bestow a truncated set of civil rights on Indians by the judicious management of populations and of territory.[21]

But an analysis of *Ramona* in the context of the Ponca case reveals that Jackson and Schurz in fact shared a central concern with political emotion in general and depression in particular. In earlier chapters I have explored how an opposition between "official" and "emotional" democracy (and the valorization of the latter as literature's purview) breaks down when one attends to the Gilded Age novel's exploration of institutional politics as a site of intense investments and aversions. Grant-era Indian policy offers a glimpse of a different, darker form of institutional feeling, as Schurz and his agents looked for signs of Indian sadness as confirmation of this populations' need for incorporation into US law. Jackson, who would herself later serve as an Indian agent, sometimes echoes this form of bureaucratic sentimentality. But I propose that her novel ultimately refuses the Agency view that legal personhood based on tribal disbanding could be both cause and solution to Indian depression. Colleen Boggs has cautioned, "biopolitics thrives on the mutability of the line between human beings and animals."[22] Jackson explores this troublesome boundary to imagine forms of life not organized by impoverished juridical frameworks. *Ramona* keeps the sadness and suffering of the Indians' worn-down life in view, postponing the triumphant individuation of the Indian, animating instead an uncanny form of animal life as the novel's unacknowledged protagonist.

Ramona, Hot and Cold

Early in its pages, *Ramona* offers a condensed account of its eponymous heroine's lineage. Angus Phail, a Scottish sailor, was engaged to the aristocratic Ramona Ortegna, who married another man while Phail was at sea. The betrayal propels Phail into a life of debauchery, including a drunken union that produces his half-Indian daughter, Ramona. Desiring a better life for his mixed-blood child, Phail removes Ramona from her Indian mother and delivers her to his former fiancée, the Señora Ortegna, who remains childless in her marriage to an abusive Mexican landowner. Ramona is raised for a time by Ortegna but changes hands once again when, on her deathbed, Ortegna gives the child to her sister, Señora Gonzaga Moreno, who reluctantly agrees to serve as Ramona's guardian, despite an aversion to racial "crosses." The Señora Moreno, widow of an esteemed Mexican general and fiercely proud of her noble heritage, is contemptuous of the American settlers encroaching upon her property's borders and haughty toward the Indians who work her ranch. Ramona is raised in ignorance of her mixed heritage and thus remains unaware that the Señora's persistent coldness toward her—underscored by the Señora's passionate devotion to her birth son, Felipe—is motivated by a disdain for the Indians. Yet Ramona and Felipe care deeply for one another, and the Moreno family maintains a strained peace until Felipe is injured during the yearly sheep shearing. Felipe's injury puts Ramona in close contact with Alessandro, the head of a band of Luiseño Indians from the town of Temecula that is called in to provide brute labor. Alessandro quickly becomes indispensable, both in overseeing ranch activities and in providing loyal care to the ailing Felipe. When Ramona and Alessandro are caught in what looks to be an illicit embrace (in fact, a tender moment following the couple's engagement) the Señora begins to make arrangements to send Ramona to a convent. The remainder of the narrative traces Ramona and Alessandro's elopement and the tragedies that befall the lovers as their lives further entwine with the scattered bands of Native tribes who have been chased off their own land by violent settlers, unjust laws, and a corrupt Indian Agency.

In the novel, Ramona's liminal cultural status allows her to function as both an object of sympathy—a racially neutral stand-in for the displaced tribes—and the reader's own proxy, as an observer of Indian suffering. She simultaneously extends and elicits sympathy. By creating a clear object and vehicle of compassion, the novel seems to reproduce a central feature of the aesthetic-political mode of the sentimental: a reassuring certainty about sentiment's ability to humanize victims of social violence.[23] Before proceeding with the work of detailing the novel's complex affective strategies, however, it's important to note the lengths to which Jackson goes to flag, and guard against, the vicissitudes of sentimentality. This emerges especially in the novel's persistent concern with the Señora's persuasive power, which relies precisely on the instability of emotion. Indeed, the Señora's capacity to manipulate others' feelings to her own ends is in many ways the narrative's prime engine.

The Señora's suasive dexterity first comes into play when she convinces Felipe, whose feelings for Ramona are more matrimonial than brotherly, to expel the woman he loves from his home, despite his own self-sacrificing desire to have Ramona and Alessandro stay on the ranch as husband and wife. The Señora counters Felipe's wishes that Ramona and Alessandro might receive the family's blessing by recalling her promise to her dying sister to care for Ramona as a family member and questioning whether Felipe would countenance a match with an Indian laborer for his own blood sister:

> [Felipe] saw the meshes closing around him. He felt that there was a flaw some-where in his mother's reasoning, but he could not point it out....His brain was confused. Only one thing he saw clearly, and that was, that after all had been said and done, Ramona would still marry Alessandro... [without] his mother's consent. "Nor with mine either, openly, the way she puts it.... I wish he had never set foot on the place!" said Felipe in his heart, growing unreasonable, and tired with the perplexity.[24]

The Señora pre-emptively shutters potential conflicts before they erupt into open antagonism, repositioning difficult ethical questions as nondebatable administra-tive procedures. This tactic notably turns Felipe's "heart" into a site of unreason, weariness, and confusion rather than a seat of moral sentiment. Felipe ultimately is forced to confess: "Truth is, this miserable business has so distraught my senses, I can't seem to see anything as it is. Dear mother, it is very hard for you. I wish it were done with" (*R*, 145). The Señora thanks Felipe for his "precious sympathy," although one lesson for Jackson's reader is that sympathy comes cheap and is easily dispelled and that the emotional resources required for its extension are easily depleted.[25]

Even more crucial is Jackson's depiction of an administrative hostility to emotion as itself a style of affective influence. This was a potentially consequential observation. Questions about the proper intensity of political disagreement, and the emotional costs of political involvement, were central to the public debates that shaped Jackson's earliest interest in the Indian question. In the margins of a December 9, 1879, letter from Helen Hunt, who was not yet married to her second husband, William Sharpless Jackson, the *New York Tribune* editor Whitelaw Reid scrawled a note to one of his reporters: "This is from Helen Hunt who is a little crazy, I am afraid, on the Ponca question" (*L*, 31). Much of the country was growing incensed over recently revealed details concerning the forced relocation of the Ponca, to the Indian Territory in present-day Oklahoma, following treaty negotiations in which the tribe's Nebraska and Dakota homelands were transferred to Lakota ownership. Many Ponca died on the initial forced march south, and many more suffered and succumbed to disease as they struggled to adapt to the significant change in climate. In response to these hardships, a band led by Chief Standing Bear fled the reservation in order to return to native soil. En route, Standing Bear's group sought refuge with the Omaha, a friendly tribe with whom they had widely intermarried. Secretary of the Interior Carl Schurz considered this exodus to be a violation of the federal mandate relocating the Ponca and authorized an order for General George Crook to arrest the band and return its members to the Oklahoma reservation. Encouraged by the *Omaha Herald* assistant editor Thomas Henry Tibbles, the Ponca sued for a writ of habeas corpus, which the presiding judge, Justice Dundy, granted, declaring the Ponca's detention unlawful. Following the trial, Tibbles organized a national speaking tour to publicize the Ponca's mistreatment. The case captured Jackson's imagination, and she, along with other Boston reformers, joined Tibbles in championing the right of the remaining Ponca to return to their homeland and lobbied to have Dundy's landmark recognition of Indians as "persons" brought to the Supreme Court and made federal law.[26]

Jackson embarked on a furious letter-writing crusade to the nation's leading newspapers, exposing Schurz's unwillingness to rectify what she saw as the blatant wrongs suffered by the Ponca and to address the extraordinary series of treaty violations that led to the Ponca's expulsion. Almost from the start, opponents of reform attacked Jackson and her cohort's efforts as sentimental rhetoric, discounting her advocacy, in particular, as feminine gush. Jackson was appalled when even her husband chimed in with warnings to refrain from appearing too impassioned. Jackson responded: "You say 'keep cool! keep cool'—right my darling—that is just what I do keep, my brain. Mr. Hale—Gen. Armstrong, Mr. Goddard—all said I had not written a word a 'cool headed man might not have written'!" (*L*, 62). The question of "coolness" mattered significantly, since Schurz was in the midst of a campaign to paint any interest in the case as exaggerated and over-emotional.

Like Henry Adams, discussed in Chapter 2, Schurz was an early advocate of civil service reform. For Schurz, a sanitized bureaucracy promised to administer difficult social problems in the light of scientific principles and a commitment to impersonal, abstract reason.[27] In his view, any challenge to the justness of federal Indian policy could only be a misguided and nostalgic importation of feelings into a rationalistic political realm where affect no longer had a legitimate role. He thus responded to reports of the Ponca's mistreatment by claiming that "the highly-colored stories which are told about the brutal military force employed in compelling their removal from Dakota to the Indian Territory are sensational fabrications."[28] As Jackson noted, however, the military servicemen who had executed their orders were charged with no special brutality; indeed, General Crook himself, who was tasked with finding and returning the rogue Ponca, was an outspoken critic of the government's policy and was essentially in favor of the plaintiffs in the case in which he was named defendant.[29] For Jackson, the forced removal itself was sufficiently horrible to require no sentimental dressing-up. To make her case, she pointed to the report filed by the agent who oversaw the Ponca's removal. Listing the agent's entries from the record for June 2 through July 9, 1877, with its details of starvation, death, and disease, Jackson remarked bitterly that the document offered "a 'highly-colored' story, indeed!…What 'sensational fabrication' could compete with this?"[30]

Despite the apparent integrity of Jackson's account, historians have widely endorsed the *Tribune* editor Reid's diagnosis that she was over-emotional to the point of insanity. As one prominent telling has it, "Reform movements became more practical during the eighties largely because Schurz exposed the evils of over-enthusiasm."[31] Such accounts subscribe to the view that bureaucratic rationality offers an important corrective to the excesses of political emotion. One of the first critical accounts of Jackson's involvement in the Ponca case explicitly lamented that Jackson appealed "solely to the emotions whereas these problems can be solved only by cold, careful, sustained use of the intellect."[32]

What these readings miss, however, is that if political issues were cast as problems of feeling during the debate over the Ponca, it was not due to Jackson, the so-called sentimental reformer. Indeed, it is remarkable how frequently *opponents* of reform focused on questions of emotion throughout Standing Bear's trial. Commissioner of Indian Affairs E.A. Hayt, for example, claimed that he "visited these Indians during the month of October last, and found their condition very much improved, both as to their outward circumstances and their feelings... [though] It is true that during the first four months of their residence in the Indian Territory they lost a large number by death."[33] Even beyond the chilling flatness of Hayt's assessment of Ponca fatalities, his degree of nonchalance is notable on two accounts. First, it shows how sentimental political judgment was a fundamental feature of the state bureaucracy: observations about Native "feelings" or moods convert effortlessly into an assessment of the population's material conditions. Second, Hayt uses his observation to legitimize the state's Indian policy: the tribe's good feeling demonstrates a federal commitment to justice.

This insistence on the improved disposition of the tribe was emphatically contradicted by Standing Bear's evident fury during the trial, as he testified to the Ponca's continued suffering, prompting even the largely sympathetic court to express discomfort at his intensity:

> [Standing Bear—] What have I done? I am brought here, but what have I done? I don't know. It seems as though I haven't a place in the world, no place to go, and no home to go to, but when I see your faces here, I think some of you are trying to help me, so that I can get a place sometime to live in, and when it comes my time to die, to die peacefully and happy. (This was spoken in a loud voice, and with much emphasis.)
> The Court—Tell the witness to keep cool.   (*P*, 82)

The court cast Standing Bear's hot anger as a failure to maintain a cool composure, and he, like Jackson, was urged to rein in his passion for his own benefit and for the benefit of his cause. Yet in doing so, he was perversely called on to maintain sovereign control of his own body and to discipline himself to conform to juridical affective norms, even as he appeared in court to protest the law's violation of his tribal sovereignty and legal standing.

This examination of the affective tenor of the Ponca question allows us to return to the question of the Señora's role in defining Jackson's relation to the sentimental novel. With remarkable frequency, critics have pointed to the Señora's persuasive prowess as a model for Jackson's own efforts at emotional suasion, seeing the Señora's behind-the-scenes power brokering as an allegory for the work of the sentimental novel itself.[34] Yet in light of Carl Schurz's expert manipulation of emotion in the government's handling of the Ponca tribe, it is more likely that Jackson looked to the secretary of the interior, who cast himself as both an icon of cool-headed reason and as the victim in a melodrama of beset manhood, as her model for the Señora's tyrannical manipulation.

Indeed, Jackon emphasizes that the Señora's approach to feeling is more managerial than indulgent. The Señora is called a master at defusing "discussions which would have been hot and angry ones in any other hands than [hers]." By adopting an "exquisite gentleness of tone," the Señora has a "genius" for never "appear[ing] as a factor in the situation...[for] wield[ing] other men, as instruments, with the same direct and implicit response to will that one gets from a hand or foot" (R, 14). While the Señora herself is described on the novel's first page as often "brimful of storm," her managerial style is decidedly bureaucratic.

Jackson's portrait of the Señora focuses on her managerial disposition, a posture of clear-headed analysis that takes its "tone" as a sign of uncontestable objectivity. She thus helps us see how Schurz's insistence that hot-headed reformers and imprisoned Indians maintain their composure was ironic twice over, given his own passionate rhetoric and the limitations he placed on Native self-governance. What's more, by making good feelings (both the Indians' and their own) an indicator of good intentions and administrative efficiency, Indian Agency bureaucrats positioned all disagreement and debate as an affront to the senses, a distracting and wearying excess that threatened to derail an orderly judicial process. Jackson's countersentimental novel thus dramatizes her own ambivalence toward sympathetic feeling as a reliable goad to social justice. In this way, it responds to a key moment in the Indian reform debate, during which sentimentality was politically declawed by a bureaucratic discourse that denigrated *and* deployed sentimental rhetoric.

Habeas Corpus: "You Will Have to Have a Body to Show"

Thus far I have suggested that we must read *Ramona* as a novel deeply anxious about the suspension of political agency as a result of excessive emotion, *and* the regulation of affect by enlightened administrators. Jackson's countersentimentality was thus partially self-policing. But her portrait of the Señora's "cool" form of emotional manipulation ultimately reveals more about Indian Office bureaucrats, who were outraged by any bad feelings disruptive to their self-serving sangfroid. Examining the legal notion of habeas corpus, or a writ suing for release from unlawful detention, I will now build on this account, showing a flip side to the nexus of sentimental and bureaucratic reasoning by which the administrator's good feelings serve as the guarantor of good law. Signs of indigenous depression and suffering were equally necessary for Indian Agency officials, who were eagerly documenting evidence of tribal dissolution and the putatively inevitable disappearance of the Indian.[35]

After all, even as Standing Bear was chastised during his trial for being too surly and impassioned, the court's interest in another cluster of *negative* affects displayed by the once-powerful chief was central to the federal government's efforts to dismantle tribal structures of self-governance. While the Indian Agency representatives presented their good feelings as bestowing personhood on the native, becoming a person in the eyes of the law demanded an equal demonstration of vulnerability, suffering, and dependence—that is, bad feelings—on the part of the Indians themselves. After tracking this component of the trial's affective dimension, I will show how *Ramona* undertakes a sometimes confused but ultimately powerful critique of the Indian Agency's efforts to reduce and administer the precarious lives of indigenous peoples. Unpacking *Ramona*'s unstable narration of optimism and despair reveals how the novel mirrors the court in presenting a hopeless, exhausted "bare life" as an object of philanthropic interest but, in so doing, also reveals the darker underside of the court's much-celebrated recognition of Indian "personhood."

In Standing Bear's opening remarks to the court in the case of *Standing Bear v. Crook*, he placed himself at the mercy of US law: "For many years we have been chased about as a dog chases a wild beast.... [A]ll [the Ponca] ask [now] is that they may have a chance to make a living for themselves" (*P*, 116). For Jackson, Warner's "Story of the Doe" concerned a desperate plea for a "chance at life," and Standing Bear offers an eerie echo of that tale, casting his persecution as that of a hunted animal, pleading only for a place "sometime to live and... die" (*P*, 116). Standing Bear's rhetoric was canny in its docility; he performs a distinction between the Indian chief as military antagonist and the Indian ward as supplicant. But his strategic humility also provides a window into one of the most disturbing aspects of the habeas corpus prosecutorial strategy, which was predicated on just how little had to be claimed on behalf of the Ponca in order for the court to declare their arrest and detention unjust.

The *Omaha Herald* assistant editor Thomas Henry Tibbles's 1880 account of the case, *Standing Bear and the Ponca Chiefs*, presents an early published analysis of that strategy, courtesy of A.J. Poppleton, a well-regarded lawyer whose aid Tibbles enlisted in the Ponca's cause. Poppleton was optimistic that he could help the Ponca precisely because habeas corpus provided protection for those who enjoyed only imperfect access to the law:

> I think we can make the writ hold. It is true that these Indians have been held by the courts as "wards of the nation," but this writ was intended for the weak and helpless—for wards and minors. A ward cannot make a contract, but it does not follow from that, that the guardian can imprison, starve or practise [*sic*] inhuman cruelty upon the ward.   (*P*, 35)

Tibbles was greatly encouraged and felt the notion of unlawful detention would gain mainstream support, appealing to Americans' powerful commitment to individual freedom. In an earlier novel, Tibbles protested Schurz's use of a law designed to detain white settlers caught peddling alcohol on Indian reservations to instead arrest those who ventured on Indian land to help tribes organize politically. Tibbles dramatizes this abuse when his protagonist, a lawyer working on behalf of a tribe falsely accused of attacking a village, is arrested by a reservation agent. Shackled to a fellow prisoner, the lawyer voices his—and Tibbles's—exasperation with Indian Office tyranny: "What an infernal thing this Indian system is.... Think of it! Here we are, two American citizens, chained together in a miserable dungeon.... Is the Secretary of the Interior an absolute monarch? Can he arrest and put in chains any man he sees fit?"[36] Tibbles's implicit reference to habeas corpus law was meant to present the Indian system as an uncomfortable anomaly within a democracy, producing a peculiar space in which a kind of "monarch" exercised his power without the check of law. The soft-spoken Schurz made an unlikely dictator, but in the minds of his opponents, he was the very picture of lawless tyranny, exercising limitless extrajudicial power over all who entered his domain.

For Tibbles, then, false imprisonment and the need for a writ of habeas corpus revealed the extraordinary status of the reservation as an exception to the rules of law, democracy, and justice. The Indians were included in the law as an anomaly, independent enough to warrant the appellation "nation" yet specifically designated as dependent: subject to the law yet with no rights under it.[37] While Tibbles imagined this tyranny as a foreign element within the American democracy, the political theorist Giorgio Agamben's account of modern power describes such a "state of exception" as constitutive of sovereign power, including democratic power, more generally.[38] In fact, it is habeas corpus that offers a particularly concise expression of the logic by which sovereign power is extended, via a seeming paradox, using a law that is associated with the liberties and rights of the individual citizen. For Agamben, habeas corpus reveals the processes by which "unqualified life," or zoe, becomes political:

> Consider instead the formula of the writ that the act of 1679 generalizes and makes into law: "We command that you have before us to show, at Westminster, that body.... which is held in your custody... as well as the cause of the arrest and the detention."... It is not the free man and his statutes and prerogatives, nor even simply homo, but rather corpus that is the new subject of politics. And democracy is born precisely as the assertion and presentation of this "body": habeas corpus ad subjiciendum, "you will have to have a body to show."[39]

In other words, while habeas corpus is commonly understood as a law by which the falsely imprisoned can be released, following the letter of its law, it is in fact a demand for the presence of one subject to the law, and that presence is simply the living body, subtracted from any fuller sense of a "citizen" or a social human being. For Agamben, the danger is that when bare life becomes political—when mere biological life is taken to be the proper object of biopolitical management—a richer or more complex sense of political life recedes into the background.

What is especially notable along these lines about *Standing Bear v. Crook* is how much attention was paid to the minimal life with which the court and the Indian Bureau were concerned. For the defense, Standing Bear was "not entitled to the writ of habeas corpus, not being a person or citizen under the law." The defense pointed to the Dred Scott case, which made citizenship and legal recognition as a person preconditions for receiving the protection of the law. By disqualifying Standing Bear from the category of person, individual, or citizen, the defense also disqualified the Ponca's legal standing as a nation, willfully misreading the afore-mentioned statute that forbade further treaty-making with tribes as annulling all former treaties, a reading specifically denied by a provision in that same document. For the defense, an Indian was a "ward," and to forcibly remove the Ponca was only to literalize their status as being more akin to political prisoners than citizens.

In the court's ruling in favor of the Ponca, however, Justice Dundy found that the law did not require the one suing for a writ of habeas corpus to be a citizen. Instead, the law made reference only to "persons or parties." Dundy then explained, with some evident sarcasm, that "Webster describes a person as 'a living soul; a self conscious being; a moral agent; especially a living human being; a man, woman or child; an individual of the human race.' This is comprehensive enough, it would seem, to include even an 'Indian' " (*P*, 100). Ignoring this irony, accounts of the trial have typically celebrated the law's recognition of the "personhood" of the Indian; take the titles of two such recent retellings: *Standing Bear Is a Person: The True Story of a Native American's Quest for Justice* and *"I Am a Man": Chief Standing Bear's Journey for Justice*.[40] Yet Dundy's ruling shows that even during the trial there was an embarrassed acknowledgement of how little the court needed to recognize in order to deem Standing Bear a "person" or a "man." Put another way, "person" was the only term capacious enough to bring into the law a minimal living being: one unable to make contracts; incapable of political affiliation; unsuited to "civilized" life; stripped of familial ties; sick, moody, dying, and mourning; and yet able to function as the "body" whose presence was demanded by the writ.[41]

In fact, much of the trial was spent trying to prove that Standing Bear was suf-ficiently reduced to appear before the law as a mere "life," stripped to its barest biological existence, rather than a political being. To this end, the prosecution em-ployed a series of strange questions: " 'Ask [Standing Bear] whether, after the time they left the Indian Territory, he intended to continue to exercise his powers as chief, or whether they simply acted together as friends?' [Objected to by counsel for the government as leading. Overruled.] ... 'Ask him whether, when [the other members of the band] advised with him, it was simply in a social way, because of his having been chief, or whether they recognized any authority in him' " (*P*, 84–5). An editor's note to the University of Nebraska Press's reissue of Tibbles's *Standing Bear and the Ponca Chiefs* helpfully explains:

> Webster had preempted the defense's possible recourse to an 1870 report of the Senate Judiciary Committee which concluded that the Fourteenth Amendment had no effect on Indian tribes by pointing to its exemption of those Indians who

had dissolved their tribal relations. Thus Standing Bear's relationship to his tribe was an important point in the case.   (*P*, 93)

The prosecution labored to assure the court that Standing Bear had no political authority, that he had dissolved all political relations, and that the members of the tribe he just led through unspeakable trials were, improbably, more like casual acquaintances. Institutional personhood is here defined by the absence of feelings of kinship.

In Chapter 2, I argued that Henry Adams explored "friendship" not as a relation defined by closeness but as a distancing strategy. To remain "just friends" is to disavow a romantic connection, and to ensure that one's political judgments are not clouded by the seductive powers of an intimate. Putting a similar logic to very different ends, the prosecution described Standing Bear's family and tribe as "simply" friends, and their bonds as "simply" social, stressing that Standing Bear appeared before the court stripped of any meaningful political authority or complex social ties. The appeal to habeas corpus meant that Standing Bear's legal status as a "person" required a measure of proof that he was sufficiently reduced to little more than a living body. In this context, Standing Bear's self-description of being hunted "like a wild beast" looks like a desperate but effective strategy; one perfectly adapted to a legal and bureaucratic framework that would only acknowledge isolated and weakened Indians as potential applicants for a putatively liberating but heavily burdened personhood.[42]

Strange Apathy

As this essay's opening consideration of emotional incoherence suggests, reform opponents' demands that Jackson remain cool-headed in her arguments on behalf of the Indians lent a countersentimental tenor to her own thinking and writing about suffering and "hot" responses to it. The novel's chronic instability of feeling, as explored most powerfully through the Señora's perplexity-inducing persuasion, suggests that while Jackson was fascinated with emotion in general, and at times optimistic about affect's political effects, she was most interested in understanding how feelings fall prey to misdirection, manipulation, and confusion. Her concerns were well-founded: in the court case of *Standing Bear v. Crook*, the instability of feelings regarding Native suffering supported the legal positioning of Standing Bear as occupying a zone of indistinction, producing an atmosphere of emotional confusion that offered phenomenological confirmation of his status as both inside and outside the law. Standing Bear was at once called on to manifest his self-control and gratitude *and* expected to appear as a kind of bare life, a living being whom the law registered as human yet would not recognize politically.

With Standing Bear's uncertain status—balanced somewhere between sovereign personhood and bare life—in mind, I want to return to *Ramona*, which we are now in a position to see as a narrative exploration of this zone of indistinction, in which "life" appears as the material upon which a sovereign power relies for its own confirmation. If the text in part reproduces a logic by which feeling is fantasized to work as a measure of injustice, Jackson also uses an emotional vocabulary to plot her characters as shifting points within this indeterminate zone, narrating "bare life" as a field in which her characters move in proximity to and from the law. Jackson tracks this movement in terms of optimism and pessimism, hope and depression: Ramona increasingly maintains a hopeful, life-building focus on the couple's future existence, while Alessandro's pessimism and bad feeling mark his decline toward a state resembling animal life. Critics have often worried about the failure of Jackson's Native protagonists to evince forward-looking political agency, appearing instead as passive victims. While these critics are correct in seeing the characters' agency as circumscribed, such a reading must take into account that Jackson's goal was precisely not to establish Native sovereignty in this sense but to dramatize the bare life that was on display both in Warner's tale and in the case of Standing Bear. This was a type, she rightly intuited, that was better suited than a fully realized "person" to attract the philanthropic attention of her readers. Such a tactic has potential risks and rewards. Jackson highlights the traumatic effects of the federal government's assault on tribal life, but also threatens to endorse the biopolitical logic by which a quasi-animal life of depression and illness is cast as a transitional step toward legal personhood. She sees individual depression as a symptom of the loss of tribal sovereignty, but struggles to find narrative strategies for representing Indian agency that wouldn't play into the hands of the Indian Agency.

The oscillation between a desire for political agency and the reality of political depression is thus at the novel's core, not simply a symptom of its false consciousness. That said, it's easy to see how readers and critics could be uncomfortable with Alessandro's failure to take decisive action. Early in the couple's escape from the Señora, Ramona and Alessandro stop at a trading post where Alessandro hopes to pick up his father's prized violin, one of his few remaining assets. While waiting for the store owner to return, Alessandro's thoughts turn to his father's recent death during the expulsion of the Temecula tribe: "Alessandro sat still by the fire. A strange apathy seemed to have seized him; at last he said wearily: 'I must be going now. I wanted to see Mr. Hartsel a minute, but he seems to be busy in the store'" (*R*, 213). In abruptly deserting his plan to acquire the funds crucial for his and Ramona's escape, Alessandro displays a distressing failure to steer his own fate. This is one of the earliest signs foreboding the couple's difficult future following their seemingly triumphant departure from the Moreno estate.

The only check on Alessandro's fading will is his desire to protect and provide for Ramona. For a time, this instinct produces in him a sort of minimal attachment to the present on behalf of his new bride's immediate needs: "'And these are the men that have stolen our lands, and killed my father, and Jose, and Carmena's baby!' thought Alessandro. . . . But [his] heart was too full of other thoughts, now, to dwell long on past wrongs, however bitter. The present called him too loudly"

(*R*, 215). After Alessandro loses his home to a squatter following a period of relative calm, however, darker feelings take hold:

> From this day Alessandro was a changed man. Hope had died in his bosom. In all the village councils—and they were many and long now, for the little community had been plunged into great anxiety and distress—Alessandro sat dumb and gloomy. To whatever was proposed, he had but one reply: "It is of no use. We can do nothing."   (*R*, 249)

Depression is often characterized by the very paralysis Jackson diagnoses in Alessandro: "The depressed individual, caught in a moment with no tomorrow, is left without drive, bogged down in a 'nothing is possible.' "[43] Alessandro's paralyzing melancholy is likewise cast as a disease of deficient futurity, but Jackson hints that his failure to imagine a "tomorrow" cannot be understood without placing it in the context of a history that is flagged only as "past wrongs." That minimal memorial obliquely evokes Jackson's *A Century of Dishonor* (1881), in which Jackson documented in great detail the longue durée of one hundred years' worth of colonial conquest, violated treaties, and the slaughter of Indian civilians. While some have worried that Jackson was unable to imagine vigorous forms of indigenous agency, she appears to struggle precisely with how to make a space for forward-looking activity and optimism in a historical context defined by radical constraints on Indian sovereignty.

   We can track Jackson's struggle with the question of indigenous agency by attending to her idiosyncratic emotional vocabulary. In Sianne Ngai's account, social conditions of "suspended agency" demand that we "attend to the aesthetics of the ugly feelings that index these suspensions."[44] Jackson anticipates Ngai by generating new affective categories when a traditional taxonomy fails. For example, the text is so attuned to Alessandro's shifting moods that Jackson is careful to distinguish even his most future-oriented moments as merely a variety of qualified optimism:

> Majella [Alessandro's name for Ramona] had found friends. Something, not quite hope, but akin to it, began to stir in Alessandro's heart. He would build a house; Majella should no longer live in this mud hut. But to his surprise, when he spoke of it, Ramona said no; they had all they needed, now. Was not Alessandro comfortable? She was. It would be wise to wait longer before building.   (*R*, 280)

To begin—even tentatively—to think that things might get better, and to work toward that improved future, would seem to fall safely under the rubric of "hope." Hope's "not-quite-ness," then, does not announce an affective failure on Alessandro's part. Instead, Jackson implies that structuring conditions have so radically shaped and constrained the meaning of "hope" that they demand new emotional vocabularies. So too Jackson's earlier description of Alessandro's "strange apathy," which can hardly be supposed to mean his sadness is surprising or inexplicable. Rather, like "not quite hope," "strange apathy" names an ongoing effort to muster the resources for living under conditions of radical precarity.

The instability and opacity of Alessandro's feeling should lead us to doubt claims that Jackson presents Alessandro as an "exotic victim...deprived of agency who may be 'inhabited' by Anglo readers."[45] What's more, critics who have chastised Jackson for denying Alessandro a fully realized political voice have missed how closely they echo Ramona's own attempts to call Alessandro back from the abyss of despair and to instill in him a sense of the importance of future-oriented activity.[46] That is, this call for greater optimism and agency that critics so wish to see often appears in the novel as an almost ruthless refusal of Alessandro's ugly feelings.[47] In a rare scene in which a note of open discord enters the young lovers' relationship, Ramona expresses a wistful nostalgia for the "olden time...when the men like Father Salvierderra had all the country. Then there would be work for all, at the missions" (*R*, 222). Yet Alessandro is privy to a darker side of mission history and warns her that the absolute power of the priests was sometimes corrupting. He relates the account of a Franciscan father's Indian underling, who, having been sent to retrieve a band of fleeing Natives, returns with pieces of each of the disobedient runaways' ears. Musing on this cruelty, Alessandro remarks, "It was stupid of them to stay and be like beasts, and not know anything; but do you not think they had the right?"

Ramona, horrified by the story, nonetheless insists on the absolute sanctity of the father's mandate to spread the gospel: "It is the command to preach...to every creature....I think they ought to have made the Indians listen. But that was dreadful about the ears, Alessandro. Do you believe it?" (*R*, 223). Ramona, fully committed to the benevolent influence of Christian teaching, cannot hear the violent pun or see the relation between the compulsory listening she calls for and the practice of cutting off the ears of disobedient Natives. Able to imagine "mak[ing] them listen" only as a loving compulsion, Ramona cordons off the realities of the missionary past from her nostalgic view of the olden days, which remains crucial to her vision of future happiness.

This scene finds its mirror soon thereafter in a moment when it is Alessandro, rather than Ramona, who willfully mishears a story about the Franciscan fathers in order to effect a subtle emotional revision. Ramona, recalling the Catholic training she has just defended, enjoins Alessandro to practice an ascetic optimism: " 'Dear Alessandro,' said Ramona, 'it is a sin to always mourn. Father Salvierderra said if we repined under our crosses, then a heavier cross would be laid on us. Worse things would come.' " Alessandro misconstrues the adage, perhaps willfully: " 'Yes,' he said. 'That is true. Worse things will come.' And he walked away, with his head sunk deep on his breast" (*R*, 301). Recasting conditional optimism as declarative pessimism, Alessandro refuses the nominal hope Ramona offers. Ramona's allusion to the lessons of her missionary upbringing also suggests something the text ultimately bears out: that Ramona's future is indeed brighter than Alessandro's, due to her agility in moving between the fading Indian culture and high-born Spanish American society, as well as her ability to temper her Indian-ness with European Catholicism.

While both characters appear allied in their uncertain status outside the protection of the law, Ramona is in fact subtly aligned with the biopolitical mandate to imagine a good life on the horizon of each fresh misfortune. Indeed, the fact that the mixed-blood Ramona appears well-suited to adapt to white standards of domesticity and labor serves as the primary evidence for those critics who see the novel as directly anticipating or even contributing to the Dawes Act's new focus on allotment, individuation, and assimilation.[48] However, the juxtaposition of this rosy vision of compulsory domestic bliss with Alessandro's powerful negativity suggests, at the very least, a deep ambivalence on Jackson's part about the cost of assimilative policies.[49] On the one hand, Alessandro's pessimism and apathy dramatize the deep effects of sustained suffering and anxiety, with Ramona's counterfactual optimism looking like a crucial emotional resource, and perhaps a route to assimilation. On the other hand, her willful amnesia exposes her alignment with a missionary system of care that was also a regime of tender violence.[50] This in turn suggests profound continuities with a later system of bureaucratic management, which shares with the area's missionary past a precise regulation of indigenous affect.

In the aforementioned scene in which Alessandro declares his utter lack of hope, he punctuates his declaration by comparing his plight to that of an animal: "It is of no use. We can do nothing, any more than the wild beasts. They are better than we" (R, 249). The language here directly recalls Standing Bear's lament that his people had been "chased about as a dog chases a wild beast," and it similarly dramatizes an extreme form of dehumanizing persecution. But in the context of the novel's ambivalent treatment of Ramona's compulsory hope, this imagery takes on a new force. Alessandro's language reveals a dawning awareness of Native rights, even as the only "right" he claims is a choice between coming under the tutelary and disciplinary control of the Franciscans or of remaining in a state of animal life, to "stay and be like beasts." Faced with the supposed utopia of the missionary education that stakes a claim to "every creature," an animal life outside the law emerges as a surprisingly attractive alternative.

This opposition of the animal to the juridical is another face of what I have described as Jackson's countersentimental politics. Lauren Berlant has tracked how sentimentality presumes that "identification with pain, a universal true feeling, then leads to structural social change."[51] But this transaction "reauthorize[s] universalist notions of citizenship in the national Utopia, which involves believing in a redemptive notion of law as the guardian of public good."[52] When Jackson has Alessandro choose depression over optimism, and choose bare life over personhood, we can see a provisional resistance to this sentimental affirmation of the state and the law.[53]

Lingering Doubts

As forecast, "depression" offers a troubling but potent rubric for analyzing the novel's political interventions. Jackson uses despair to index how policies promoting

Indian personhood were dehumanizing in their effects. In one of sociologist Alain Ehrenberg's key formulations, depression is said to proliferate in a social context in which, "instead of being acted upon by an external force (or complying to the law), persons base their actions on an internal drive or mental capacities."[54] Under such a regime, "notions like 'projects,' 'motivation,' and 'communication' are…the norm. They [enter] our social hierarchy and inhabit it from top to bottom…we [learn] to adapt ourselves to them."[55] In *Ramona*, however, Alessandro embraces hopelessness to place the overt violence of the Franciscan's bloody discipline on a continuum with the missionary mandate to perform hopeful productivity, and the bureaucratic mandate to put the tribal past behind him.

But if this reading suggests that *Ramona* is smarter about political emotion than critics have credited, I want to caution against hyperbolizing the power of its critique, or papering over the ways the novel potentially reinforces the law and bureaucratic norms. For example, it is tempting, but ultimately problematic, to align Jackson's challenge to the pathologization of negative Indian affect with an ongoing project within contemporary indigenous studies. This work has framed affects of bitterness, anger, and resentment as a "politics of refusal" and a step toward critical consciousness.[56] Similarly, finding a space within political discourse for Indian anger and sadness is sometimes positioned as an alternative to a politics of "recognition" and "reconciliation," which may sustain a framework in which native peoples request to be "acknowledged" by a nation-state whose power such a request confirms. Glen Coulthard, for example, has made a provocative call to differentiate backward-looking Nietzschean *ressentiment* from a more necessary and active political resentment that could fuel indigenous critique.[57] But Jackson's narration of native depression is not fully recuperable along these lines. Even as her efforts to make native suffering visible seem necessary and important, the novel affords few opportunities to redescribe depression as critique, or apathy as refusal.

In part, this is because the novel's stripping down of Alessandro to a state bordering on animal life ultimately might not depict an alternative to citizenship, including those lying outside the realm of personhood and autonomy, but rather a crucial step toward his potential incorporation into US law. After all, in the case of Standing Bear, which, as I've argued, shaped so much of Jackson's thinking on the Indian question, it was the Ponca chief's reduction through the logic of habeas corpus that ultimately led to his theatricalized reincorporation into a juridical framework. In the trial's famous conclusion, after Justice Dundy had granted the writ, Standing Bear addressed one of his lawyers, John Lee Webster, in a speech that was widely reported and reproduced:

> Hitherto, when we have been wronged we went to war to assert our rights.…We had no law…so we took our tomahawks and went to kill.…But you have found a better way. You have gone into the court for us, and I find our wrongs can be righted there. Now I have no more use for the tomahawk. I want to lay it down forever. (*P,* 114)

In dramatically staging his submission to the law, Standing Bear effectively passes through the zone of indistinction, emerging on the other side with a questionable level of personhood but with the sovereignty of the law spectacularly confirmed.

If Standing Bear's famous speech suggests one way in which the stripping back of the Indian's life is meant to return him to the arms of the law, Jackson reveals her ambivalence toward this process by focusing on how the law, when confronted with the spectacle of bare Native life, fails to uphold its end of the bargain. Slowly drifting into abject melancholy, Ramona and Alessandro are driven to appeal to the government when their child, christened Eyes of the Sky, falls ill. The couple's white friend Aunt Ri explains to Alessandro that there is an Indian Agency doctor whose job is to care for all the Indians of the region. Upon visiting the doctor, Alessandro is overwhelmed by the power and largesse of the government:

> Alessandro looked at the bottle of medicine like one in a dream. Would it make the baby well? Had it indeed been given to him by that great Government in Washington? Was he to be protected now? Could this man, who had been sent out to take care of Indians, get back his San Pasquale farm for him? Alessandro's brain was in a whirl.   (R, 285)

Alessandro soon learns, however, that in order to benefit from the agency's generosity he must write his name in the doctor's book, becoming in effect one of "his Indians." Assured that this entails no real sacrifice of autonomy, a reluctant Alessandro is coaxed into signing for the sake of his child, in order to formalize the government's obligation to help him: "Alessandro's name was in the Agency books. It was for this he had written it,—for this and nothing else,—to save the baby's life. Having thus enrolled himself as one of the Agency Indians, he had a claim on this the Agency doctor" (R, 287).

The medicine only exacerbates the infant's sickness, and the doctor refuses all entreaties, including payment in gold, to make a follow-up house call. The child soon dies, and Alessandro and Ramona find that their registration with the government has brought them no closer to legal or political equality with their white neighbors. For Jackson, who no doubt had Standing Bear in mind, the reduction to bare life brought on by suffering, illness, and death primes the Native subject to yearn for incorporation into the white man's law. In this dynamic, the Indian reduced to bare life affirms, rather than poses a threat to, the sovereign power of the federal government. Yet this logic, of grounding the sovereignty of the US government in the bare life of the Indian, short circuits if the law ultimately fails to lay claim to that life. In such a reading, the wrong done by Alessandro's coerced contract would not be that it brings him under the yoke of the law but rather that it stages his continued status as both inside and outside that law as a transformation, as though he were entering a new, formal agreement that would change his indeterminate standing.

Seen in this light, Jackson's critique is pointed but remains constrained by the terms of the Dawes Act's assimilationist logic. But if Standing Bear was reduced to a minimal "person" in order to confirm the sovereignty of the law, the government's failure to incorporate Alessandro in his animal-like state produces an uncanny return in the novel's closing chapters of something similar to a "bare life." After enduring the death of his child, Alessandro ultimately succumbs to constant duress, his mind unable to grasp even the basic concept of ownership. In a delirium, he mistakenly rides off on another man's horse and subsequently is shot dead by the horse's owner. Jackson based the murder of Alessandro on a real-life case, intending to dramatize the injustice of a system in which Indians were constantly backed into a corner by white aggression and could be killed with no legal recourse. Jackson paints the scene using matter-of-fact prose:

> In a moment more Ramona followed—only a moment, hardly a moment; but when she reached the threshold, it was to hear a gun-shot, to see Alessandro fall to the ground, to see, in the same second, a ruffianly man leap from his horse, and standing over Alessandro's body, fire his pistol again, once, twice, into the forehead, cheek.   (R, 305)

The scene calls to mind the concluding image of Warner's "Story of the Doe," in which the deer is summarily executed after a lengthy chase. Strengthening the connection, Jackson draws a direct line to another story from the same collection, "How I Killed a Bear," in which Warner details his encounter with a bear in plain language:

> I slipped in a charge, keeping my eyes on the bear. He never stirred.... Still he might be shamming: bears often sham. To make sure, I approached, and put a ball into his head. He didn't mind it now: he minded nothing. Death had come to him with a merciful suddenness. He was calm in death. In order that he might remain so, I blew his brains out, and then started for home.[58]

The text makes light of the killing, its blunt details producing a darkly humorous contrast with Warner's self-parodic account of his peaceful domestic life, in which violence is completely omitted. Yet a later reader of *Ramona* returning to Warner's story would find an eerie premonition of Alessandro's murder.[59] With a nonchalance similar to that of Warner's hunter in "How I Killed a Bear," Jackson narrates the repeated gunshots to Alessandro's head and face. In modeling the flight and death of Alessandro on Warner's tales of animal cruelty, Jackson appears intent on evoking what Agamben calls bare life, stripped of its value, existing within the law as an exception to the law, a life that can be ended with impunity. If such bare life was, in the trial of Standing Bear, a precursor to the pageant of Indian agency willfully surrendered in deference to the justness of US law, the violence of bare life in *Ramona* lingers as an image of extrajudicial violence, rendering palpable the threat of death that polices the ill-defined borders of indigenous sovereignty.

Conclusion: Fleshing Out Bare Life

I have been arguing that seeing Alessandro's descent into depression and madness as a sustained meditation on everyday suffering partially redeems the novel from what some critics have seen as its failure to imagine scenes of effective political agency. Such criticisms serve as a precursor to an even more common and substantive attack on the novel's politics: that the characters' lack of volition anticipates the novel's ultimate inability to envision the multiethnic America that such a subaltern resistance could bring into being. In this analysis, Alessandro's madness and death and Ramona's subsequent departure for Mexico are persistently cast as the novel's greatest obstacles to achieving its political potential.[60] John Gonzalez argues that Ramona's relocation is meant to "keep the nation free from the insidious atavistic influence of mixed blood," while Carl Gutiérrez-Jones claims that Ramona and Felipe's eventual marriage at the novel's close suggests a retreat from a public political story to a private romance, and that these "insulating tendencies suggest the denial of an entire historical period representing mestizaje (the mixing of racial heritages) itself."[61] A reader of these analyses unfamiliar with the novel might assume that the text treats the marriage of Ramona and Felipe with a sense of exuberant joy and promise for the future, perhaps tinged with a respectful tear for the death of Alessandro. Both Gutiérrrez-Jones and Gonzalez imply a sort of fetish operation, whereby a falsely coherent image of matrimonial bliss displaces and masks the history and details of racial antagonism. Yet Jackson's text links Ramona's fate to Alessandro's far more insistently than that. Even in her marriage to Felipe, Ramona continues a pattern of pursuit, suffering, and death that characterizes the novel as a whole rather than transcends it.

After all, much as Alessandro's "brain gives way" to a state of insensitivity that "mercifully" keeps him from fully experiencing his demise, Ramona also enters a state of anaesthetized awe in the moment of Alessandro's death: "Nature sends merciful anaesthetics in the shocks which almost kill us. . . . It would be long before Ramona would fully realize that Alessandro was dead. Her worst anguish was yet to come" (R, 341). Cruelly echoing Alessandro's melancholy insistence that "worse things will come," the narrator predicts with total certainty that Ramona's suffering will only increase as she comes to terms with her loss. The novel then accelerates to its close, narrating Felipe's arrival, the pair's return to the Moreno ranch, Felipe's confession of his longstanding love for Ramona, and the forming of their plans to depart for Mexico. While this arrangement offers the barest hope for a future free from persecution, Ramona receives Felipe's declaration of love not with passionate joy but instead with an outcry "of terror and of pain":

> Ramona drew nearer to him, still with her hands clasped. "I have always loved you," she said. "I love no other living man; but, Felipe,"—her voice sank to a solemn whisper—"do you not know, Felipe, that part of me is dead—dead? can

never live again? You could not want me for your wife, Felipe, when part of me is dead!" (*R*, 348)

What Ramona offers Felipe is not a triumphant love but what she calls a "broken fragment of a life" (*R*, 349). She explicitly contrasts her active, passionate, impetuous decision to run away with Alessandro with her current "weighing [of Felipe's] words, not in the light of passion, but of calmest, most unselfish affection" (*R*, 349). In what improbably has been described as a "stock sentimental ending," Ramona reaffirms that "part of her was dead" but agrees to marry Felipe, and the pair set a course for Mexico.[62]

The novel thus closes with a border crossing, albeit one undertaken by a heroine stripped down to a state of numbness and defeat, a "fragment of a life," a living human being at the threshold of death. Ironically, it is here that critics have found an expression of something like an active political will, although one expressing Jackson's fearful rejection of the mestizaje culture, which the novel—almost—had appeared able to imagine. Yet in a reverse of the same logic, the depiction of Ramona and Felipe's future life as a continuation of Alessandro's slow death offers little purchase for critics who articulate another prominent strain of response to the novel: that its concluding border crossing celebrates and affirms a Creole culture, or even a trans-American cosmopolitanism.

Instead, it might be helpful to consider this minimally hopeful vision as anticipating one of Agamben's preferred figures for bare life, the refugee:

> If refugees...represent such a disquieting element in the order of the modern nation-state, this is above all because...they put the originary fiction of modern sovereignty in crisis. Bringing to light the difference between birth and nation, the refugee causes the secret presupposition of the political domain—bare life—to appear for an instant within that domain. In this sense, the refugee is...the first and only real appearance of rights outside the fiction of the citizen that always covers them over.[63]

To some extent, the refugee illustrates bare life: his is a life traumatically divorced from the rights of the citizen, whether displaced by war, expatriation, or exile. On the other hand, the bare life of the refugee makes him appear as a strange actor on the political stage, whereas bare life usually operates as the unseen and unacknowledged baseline foundation of sovereign power.

The bare life of the refugee, and the "fragment of a life" that Jackson sends across the border into Mexico for refuge, might be seen as assonant creatures of modern politics. Jackson explicitly stages Ramona's departure as a flight from persecution, explaining that Ramona's motivation for leaving the United States was "that she would spare her daughter the burden she had gladly, heroically borne herself, in the bond of race" (*R*, 347). Jackson's text is meant to shame readers, making America seem like a place from which Ramona must escape and presenting Mexico as a surer refuge for the persecuted than her own birth country.

More importantly, though, Ramona's insistence that "part of her" is dead implies that part of her lives on: not yet cloaked in the form of American or Mexican citizenship, her greatly reduced "life" nonetheless appears invested with an eerie liberty and serves as the undead protagonist of the novel's closing pages.[64] At a moment when sympathizing with Indians as "persons" could appear to facilitate tribal dissolution and relocation, Jackson's countersentimental conclusion makes visible the weariness, depression, uncertainty, and anxiety that characterize the Indian's legal and political half-life, without proposing better feeling as a solution. At the same time, the pageantry of Standing Bear's release reminds us that the spectacle of native suffering and the fragmented subject it reveals always threatens to reinforce the inscription of life within a juridical frame, buttressing the same sovereign power from which Ramona and Alessandro flee.

However, if bare life is seen as a remainder of the state's assault on Indian political communities (forms of life that do not place the "autonomous individual" front and center, and do not root their visions of happiness in US law), then a different possibility emerges. What we might call Ramona's "fleshing out" of bare life lends these lives a corporeal, affective visibility that refuses to be papered over, occluded by bureaucratic visions of efficiently managed populations and incrementally improved feelings. Ann Cvetkovich has argued that there may be value in letting "depression linger" and refusing "pastoralizing or redemptive accounts of negative feeling."[65] Lingering with Alessandro's animal-like desperation and depression would thus be to stay with the political, attached to the hope—if not quite hopeful—for a political life before and after personhood.

Suspicion

On the Hatred of Hypocrites

DONNELLY, DU BOIS, RACE, AND REPRESENTATION

"We cannot let up on hypocrisy. It bothers us all the time."
—JUDITH SHKLAR

Suspicious Objects

In his bestselling 2005 book, *What's the Matter with Kansas?*, Thomas Frank argues that conservatives' "systematic erasure of economics" has disguised citizens' real interests with a misleading cultural veneer. Conservatives, Frank claims, insist "class is about what one drives and where one shops and how one prays, and only secondarily about the work one does or the income one makes."[1] In this account, the Right's pseudo-populism is characterized by a fundamental hypocrisy, a deceitful exterior. In his 2007 *The Trouble With Diversity*, however, Walter Benn Michaels suggests that liberals are equally guilty of displacing class from public discourse. For Michaels, the valorization of racial and ethnic "diversity" constitutes its own form of hypocrisy: elites' high-minded tolerance of cultural difference masks a self-serving willingness to tolerate widening economic inequality.[2] Of course, a common claim leveled against economic populists—think labor leader Eugene Debs in the twentieth century or Bernie Sanders in the twenty-first—is that the apparent universality of class masks a white worldview unresponsive (or even hostile) to racial minorities.[3] A focus on class might be the antidote to hypocrisy; it might be the symptom.

An accusation of hypocrisy is clearly a powerful, if imprecise, way of calling out political dishonesty and disguised self-interest. But how does hypocrisy—and, specifically, a putatively hypocritical racial- or class-based political rhetoric—relate to this book's concerns with Gilded Age literature and affect? Unlike the exhaustion, disgust, and depression I have explored thus far, I will show that "hypocrisy" is not itself an affective orientation toward the political, but rather the target of some of our most intense political emotions. We hate the hypocrite. We are suspicious of him. As Judith Shklar notes in the passage that serves as my epigraph, he "bothers us all the time."[4] Sara Ahmed has described the family as the "happy object" par excellence; those "affect aliens" who do not "reproduce its form" are cast "as the cause of unhappiness."[5] I propose to evoke a related, inverse dynamic and call the hypocrite a "suspicious object." He is the target of such disdain, frustration, and mistrust that he appears to contain within him the negative political feelings he evokes. As a result, the hypocrite perpetually reconfirms the bad feelings we associate with politics, and perpetually re-energizes a hermeneutics of suspicion.

For example, in 1871, two years before Mark Twain and Charles Dudley Warner would describe their age as "Gilded" with a false finish, Walt Whitman identified hypocrisy as the defining feature of postbellum politics: "What penetrating eye does not everywhere see through the mask? We live in an atmosphere of hypocrisy throughout."[6] Predictably, this rampant hypocrisy evoked disgust with a political bureaucracy "saturated in corruption," a "tainted" judiciary, and cities "reek[ing]" with "scoundrelism."[7] While Whitman's language is uniquely impassioned, I have already shown that other major political novels in the period made similar links between politicians' duplicity and a wearying "atmosphere" of disgust.

This chapter takes a different track, however, by focusing on two figures whose works develop an alternate approach to, and set of feelings about, hypocrisy. First, I examine the work of Ignatius Donnelly, lieutenant governor of Minnesota (1860–3), congressman (1863–9), state senator (1874–8; 1891–3), best-selling author, leading founder of the American People's Party, and the author of that party's much-cited Omaha Platform (1892).[8] I focus on Donnelly's under-studied political novel *Doctor Huguet* (1891), a work that strives to imagine how a black–white alliance might take shape under a populist banner of economic equality, but in so doing is forced to confront the problem of political hypocrisy. Donnelly's novel, I claim, is shaped throughout by a question it only obliquely acknowledges: How does one distinguish between mutually beneficial alliances and the hypocrite's ruse of disguised self-interest?

Second, I turn to W.E.B. Du Bois, whose work offers a way of theorizing the hypocrisy that Donnelly's novel anxiously dramatizes. I examine texts including his best-known work, *The Souls of Black Folk* (1903), his first novel, *The Quest of the Silver Fleece* (1911), and his sweeping history of the place of African Americans in the Civil War and postbellum political life, *Black Reconstruction* (1935). In these twentieth-century texts' retrospective look at Reconstruction and the corruption of the Gilded Age, Du Bois returns repeatedly to the figure of the hypocrite but of an idiosyncratic sort: a damaged political subject whose apparently internal contradictions index institutional racism.

Throughout Donnelly's and Du Bois's writing, alliances are formed and dissolved, interests are disguised and misrecognized, politicians betray the people, some people betray their race, others are disloyal to their class, and many are false to their own beliefs. These melodramas of hypocrisy and deceit generate a familiar cluster of negative political emotions. These feelings in turn spark a desire for less complicated, less intense, less mystified forms of politics. On the other hand, the very fact of these authors' turn to literature attests to a view of politics as inescapably emotional, aesthetic, and produced through complex acts of representation.[9] Sometimes both Donnelly and Du Bois yearn for "class" to re-align voters according to "interests" that were presumed to be self-evident. At other times, these authors' writings can be seen to search for forms and figures that could mediate between, but not therefore dissolve or equate to, imperfectly aligned and even conflicting interests. Donnelly monumentalizes hypocrisy and its consequences while Du Bois tends to de-dramatize it. But between them the hypocrite emerges less as an individual moral failing or act of betrayal and more as a structural position that describes a subject rent by the untenable positions offered by a circumscribed political landscape.

Bruno Latour has argued that "doubts on politics have no other origin: the worthy figures of autonomy and liberty mask the dreadful labour of composition, betrayal, transmutation and metamorphosis."[10] I propose that *Doctor Huguet*—a novel that recounts the magical metamporphosis of a white man into a black body and a key strain of Du Bois's work which uses a language of hypocrisy to focus on citizen-subjects caught between irreconcilable political positions—juxtaposes a range of related but distinct forms of political "transmutation." These instances of apparent hypocrisy include the politician's deceitful mask, but also the inevitable distortions of representative politics and the everyday labor of alliance. Hypocrisy always names a relation to social or political institutions, which provide the norms to which the hypocrite feigns adherence.[11] But if hatred of hypocrisy can fuel powerful critiques of bad norms or expose false devotion to good ones, it can also lapse into a hatred of the political as such, a distaste for the grubby work of bargaining and revision.

It is because of hypocrisy's anti-political tendencies that both Donnelly and Du Bois can be seen to offer an importantly counterintuitive approach to this much maligned vice. Both authors, in decidedly different ways, seek to re-align the range of affective responses to the hypocrite, rendering him a figure of fascination and pathos whose structuring contradictions are not a private moral failing but an index of a social world that is itself out of whack. At a moment when "hypocrisy" was becoming a simple synonym for Gilded Age fraud, these authors help us see the intense suspicion of hypocrisy during Reconstruction and its aftermaths as a symptom of the tension between race and class—analytic frameworks and social determinants that were actually and historically, though not necessarily, opposed.[12]

True Interests

Doctor Huguet, published in 1891, was Donnelly's first novel in the wake of his best-selling dystopian novel from the prior year, *Caesar's Column* (1890). Donnelly wrote *Doctor Huguet* during his second (nonconsecutive) term in the Minnesota senate, not long after a meeting of the National Alliance Union in Cincinnati where he made the decisive speech that led to the foundation of a national populist movement and earned him the moniker of the "father of the People's Party."[13] Donnelly thus wrote *Doctor Huguet* in the thick of the daily political struggles of an elected official, and it offers a unique and, at times, bewildering mix of antiracist social protest with meditations on the nature and function of political power in general.

An allegory, the novel follows a wealthy, educated white southern gentleman who, at his fiancée's urging, masks his radical views about enfranchising and educating southern black people in order to avoid jeopardizing his political career. Huguet is then divinely punished for what the text calls his hypocrisy by being "metempsychotically" transposed into the body of a black chicken thief, Sam Johnsing. Huguet, unable to convince his friends of his true identity, rises to prominence as a black preacher and schoolteacher but ultimately is lynched, an act that returns him to his white (living) body. With firsthand knowledge of the suffering endured even by educated black people, Huguet finally pledges to uphold the principles of political equality, despite the force of white southern prejudice.

Doctor Huguet thus places an educated and eloquent white man in a black body to see, in the test space of the novel, whether his virtues will be perceived behind the mask of the racialized body. Donnelly's most recent biographer records a number of admiring letters from black readers astounded that an established white politician would be willing to embark on a literary venture so certain to alienate white readers and voters—and even more surprised that he was capable of the imaginative exercise of living as a black man in postbellum America.[14] Most recent readers of the novel have been less impressed. Critics question the extent to which Donnelly managed to offer a genuinely radical critique of racial prejudice, and whether his rhetoric reveals racist elements to his own understanding of black/white difference.[15] In light of this debate between those who see the novel as anti-racist, and those who question its progressive credentials, the novel's other dominant themes have seemed less worthy of critical attention. Yet as much as *Doctor Huguet* is clearly concerned with racial questions and provocative in its approach, understanding the novel requires that we take seriously the parallel problem of political hypocrisy as such. That is, while the divinely punished act of hypocrisy provides the conceit that permits the novel's exploration of racial prejudice, the racial split serves as a mechanism to dramatize the ethics of political representation. Put more simply: sometimes it looks like hypocrisy is a subset of the problem of racism—a type of racist behavior that afflicts even those who appear to oppose racism. But at other times race is the occasion for political hypocrisy to reveal itself as a problem in its own right.

Indeed, as already hinted, the novel's most spectacular transformation—that of the white Huguet's re-embodiment in black form—is linked throughout to a more mundane kind of false exterior, that of everyday political hypocrisy. Before Huguet's transformation, the novel's primary drama comes from the conflict between

Huguet and his fiancée, Mary, who first urges him to pursue a political career, and later insists that he suppress his radical views to ensure his electability. To make her case, Mary offers a seductive portrayal of the fame and admiration to be won on the public stage:

> I began to think...that the world was, indeed, really longing and waiting for me to serve and save it; and that it would be a crime against my race and my country...to longer delay the revelation of my greatness.... [Mary argued that] I must pave the way to enter, in a few years, the Senate of the United States.... [S]he drew a vivid picture of herself sitting in the gallery, listening to me pouring forth the eloquence that would delight and enthrall the world. I was fool enough to believe it all.[16]

Mary tempts Huguet to hypocrisy through brazen blandishment. As one overview of hypocrisy in the Western philosophical tradition notes, flattery and hypocrisy often go hand in hand: "Hypocrisy and self-conceit are thus two sides of the same coin: they are both the result of a gap between appearance and reality."[17] The conceited politician who believes he is better than he is has already taken one step closer to pretending he is what he isn't. Mary's rhetoric cleverly inflates Huguet's ego by eroticizing his eloquence—dramatizing her eager reception of his "pouring forth" in "vivid" terms—while also sanitizing it as a noble act of self-sacrifice.

Even as he warms to the idea of seeking election, however, Huguet continues to express displeasure at the idea of adopting any expedient masks: "Surely you do not advise me to encourage my fellow citizens in a course which I know to be most destructive of their true interests. Now, if I went out, and talked these things upon the platform, I might overcome the unreasoning bigotry to which you allude" (D, 73). In Huguet's sanguine political fantasy, facts clearly presented and openly debated are an efficient remedy for southern white prejudice.[18] In this view, a more liberal approach to the South's black population would in fact serve black and white "interests" alike, a fact that only needs a fair hearing. Despite his resistance, however, Huguet soon confesses that Mary "almost...persuadest [him] to be a hypocrite!" (D, 75). He soon begins plotting to disguise his radical views, committing the odd offense of what the text calls being "false to the black man in [his] thoughts" (D, 94). This formulation casts his hypocrisy as an intimate betrayal, even as the text hyperbolizes the consequences of his political infidelity in its magical racial transformation.

Given the convoluted plot, it's worth stating the apparent lesson of this parable as simply as possible. Ideally, Huguet would be able to acknowledge his sympathy for African Americans. He would speak openly of his belief that the working classes of both races share the same economic interests, and the validity of these ideas would, when debated openly, win the day by virtue of their superior logic. Instead, Huguet has hidden his real beliefs in order to sustain the support of southern Democrats, embracing a notion that politics is necessarily a game of pretense. In this more deceitful approach, one wins power then attempts to alter society.

This embrace of hypocrisy as a tactic is punished by a materialization of his hypocritical ruse. He loses the exterior appearance (literally: he's turned black) he was all-too-ready to give up (figuratively: he planned to hypocritically disavow his earlier public pronouncements of his true beliefs).

It's worth noting that, despite the text's overt identification of Huguet's stratagem as a form of "hypocrisy," the nature of his political infidelity barely meets the term's minimal definition. Hypocrisy is defined broadly as "the assuming of a false appearance of virtue or goodness, with dissimulation of real character or inclinations."[19] Noting that the concept thereby embraces a wide range of social customs and rituals, David Runciman has examined efforts to guard against the temptation to obsess indiscriminately about even minor forms of dissimulation by ordering hypocritical acts according to their relative severity. Considering eighteenth-century philosopher Bernard Mandeville's distinction between "fashionable" and "malicious" hypocrisy—which insists that fully conscious deception is worse than everyday social masquerade—Runciman wonders:

> Would it not be *better* if our politicians were fully conscious of what they are doing, rather than simply being slaves to the fashions that they are endeavouring to regulate? But if they are fully conscious of what they are doing, does it not follow that their own hypocrisy, which is unavoidable in any social setting, will be of the malicious or designing kind?[20]

Runciman pinpoints the difficulty of evaluating the moral standing of hypocritical acts. Unlike other transgressions, it is not clear how intention would mitigate or exacerbate the crime of hypocrisy, especially when committed by a public figure. Is it better or worse to know that one is acting a part? If, in La Rochefoucauld's famous formulation, "hypocrisy is a tribute vice pays to virtue," is it better or worse to know that we fall short of the standards we promote? What's striking for my purposes here, however, is simply that Huguet's hypocrisy is so minor it would not even register on Mandeville's scale. Huguet does not subtly disguise his vices by unconsciously adopting the customs of polite society, nor does he consciously set out to deceive. Instead, he fails to fully express a praiseworthy belief. Or to be more precise, Huguet merely *thinks* about failing to fully own his radical commitment to racial equality. He is untrue to himself, and "to the black man," in his thoughts.

To be sure, then, Donnelly's novel attributes remarkably—perhaps laughably—high stakes to an ambiguous form of political hypocrisy. In the world of *Doctor Huguet*, Jesus Christ intercedes in southern politics because a local candidate for office fails to embrace the tenets of radical Reconstruction. Yet given Donnelly's centrality to progressive agrarian politics, and the important counterpoint he offers to accounts of "populism" that see it as synonymous with racism and nativism, the extraordinary weight this novel places on this form of political "hypocrisy" demands attention—even more so, given the links the novel draws between hypocrisy and Huguet's desire to transcend race via class, a fantasy that remains so powerful today.[21]

Equality? As If!

In order to begin to understand why *Doctor Huguet* places so much emphasis on an ambiguous form of mental hypocrisy, a seemingly trivial variant of this so-called "minor" vice, we need to understand the ways the novel ventriloquizes a set of beliefs about populist agrarian politics to which Donnelly wholeheartedly subscribed. In the novel, the crux of Huguet's radical ideas, which lead his southern neighbors to suspect him of being a "Republican in disguise," can be reduced to two essential points. First, Huguet de-essentializes biological difference by arguing that the white man is "but a bleached negro" (*D*, 54), that both races share common ancestors, and that ultimately minor differences of complexion arise from differences in climate. Second, the novel asserts that if there are these physical differences as well as educational differences resulting from the deprivations of black life under slavery, to educate and protect African Americans is not to deny these differences or to assert complete social equality but rather to act in accordance with the principle of *political* equality.[22] As Huguet argues in the novel:

> Political equality does not imply social equality, or physical equality, or moral equality, or race equality. When you go to the ballot-box to vote you find a group assembled of white men, originally of different nationalities Yankee, French, German, Irish, Scotch of different complexions, conditions, mental power, education and knowledge.   (*D*, 61)

Huguet subscribes to a form of counterfactual equality that later would come to be associated with Habermasian formulations of the ideals of a rational public sphere. In Nancy Fraser's paraphrase, for example, the ideal public sphere rests on "the assumption that it is possible for interlocutors in a public sphere to bracket status differentials and to deliberate *as if* they were social equals; the assumption, therefore, that societal equality is not a necessary condition for political democracy."[23] It is understood that this "as-if" equality does not describe an objective state of affairs, but rather a governing ideal. Before his transformation, Huguet evinces an abiding faith in the as-if public sphere, arguing that the norms of political equality can operate even if everyday life is, in actual fact, saturated by irrational prejudice and structured by widespread inequality. Unfortunately for Huguet, he repeatedly discovers that his arguments against discrimination fail to produce a rational discourse about race, and fall well short of persuading his southern neighbors. Despite making some headway, Huguet's interlocutors always fall back on their settled beliefs. As one of his sparring partners confesses, "you must excuse an old man like me if I cannot overcome in an hour the prejudices of a lifetime" (*D*, 69).

Mary, recognizing the persistence of intolerance, scolds Huguet for recklessly speaking his mind on the topic of race, especially when it has so little effect: "[Y]our radical and liberal views, as to the negroes...have offended our neighbors, and the more they think over them the more they dislike them" (*D*, 70). Significantly, Huguet's neighbors do not reject his reasoned arguments for black equality by seeking to counter or undermine them; rather, the rationality of Huguet's ideas simply cannot survive the transition from the scene of their public enunciation to the social contexts in which settled prejudices are reconfirmed:

> They take your reasoning, upon scientific probabilities, as a bare statement of fact, that the whites were originally black. And when they think it all over, at home, away from the magnetism of your voice and presence, they will, I fear, pardon me, they will regard it as ridiculous, or worse as high-treason against our Caucasian blood and lineage.   (D, 72)

For all of Donnelly's faith in public debate as a space of counterfactual, disembodied rationality, Huguet's experiences reveal the extent to which reason requires an embodied supplement. Without the seductive force of his speech, carriage, and appearance, logic slowly gives way to prejudice.

This tension between the public sphere ideal of bracketed social difference and the actual import of embodiment and affect prefigures the exaggerated problem Huguet experiences when the white body that formerly buttressed his persuasive reason suddenly turns black. The transformation is preceded by a shocking dream: "The Christ [appeared] surrounded by millions of dark hands. Why *dark* hands? Where were the hands of my own race? What had *I* to do with the negroes? Could it mean that I had been false, in my heart, to God and my fellow-men?" (D, 87). Huguet awakens to a "strong, *negro-like* smell," and the sensation of touching his face with its "flat nose and a pair of swollen lips" (D, 89). Critics have rightly balked at the racism of the passage's description, suggesting that Donnelly simply could not overcome his deep-rooted bigotry despite his best intentions.[24] However, there is reason to suspect that, in the context of Donnelly's larger reflections on political persuasion, he narrates this reaction in part due to his desire to emphasize that Huguet awakes to a body quite different from the one that exerted such a magnetic force on even his staunchest opponents, and one that triggers a phobic response even in one committed to overcoming prejudice. Not only does Huguet suddenly have a black body, it is the first time this eminently rational and eloquent gentleman has had to contemplate his body—or anyone else's—at all.

The stakes of Huguet's corporeal transposition are clarified by the ways Donnelly builds on and departs from an important literary predecessor: Robert Montgomery Bird's *Sheppard Lee* (1836). The novel's titular protagonist can occupy the body of any recently deceased person. In Bird's conceit, Sheppard Lee uses this power to seek "happiness" but finds that all people—rich and poor, black and white, pious and debauched—suffer from their own unique ailments and discontents. Perversely, it is Sheppard Lee's time in a black body as Tom, a former slave, which offers him a brief glimpse of happiness, since in Bird's account Tom's ignorance and dependence afford a certain peace. Until an abolitionist pamphlet incites discontent among the slaves, Tom and his black brethren are content; free of the care of self-management, they are spared the nervous and physical diseases of the market and civilization.

Sheppard Lee is thus the direct antecedent to *Doctor Huguet*: a white man is "metempsychotically" transposed into a black body. *Sheppard Lee* and *Doctor Huguet* both explore the relation between the mind and the body. In *Sheppard Lee*, however, the apparent similarity of plot masks a fundamentally different logic. As Christopher Looby has shown, Bird was a great reader of David Hume, who argued that the "self" was merely the fictive unity of a succession of perceptions and sensations.[25] In *Sheppard Lee*, Bird lends a unique inflection to these theories, making an even stronger case for the centrality of the body to selfhood: "the associations of the mind, as well as many of its other qualities, are more dependent on causes in the body than metaphysicians are disposed to allow."[26] If different bodies perceive the world with a slightly different perceptual apparatus, then a consciousness transplanted to a different body is not really, in any meaningful sense, the same person. Thus, each time Sheppard Lee shifts physical form his personality changes; he takes on the temperaments and habits of his host. While it's not clear whether Bird means to endorse or parody a racist notion of the happy slave, when Sheppard is Tom he actually feels happier and more carefree. He is not simply the white Sheppard Lee trapped in a black body; he is a version of Sheppard Lee whose mind now reflects the influences of black embodiment.

Edgar Allan Poe was an admirer of Bird's work, but noted in a review that the story would have had greater power if Bird had not relied on this conceit whereby Sheppard takes on much of the character of his host.[27] To render Sheppard–Tom as bearing only faint traces of Sheppard's original personality was, in Poe's eyes, to miss much of the delicious narrative potential in describing a relatively consistent point of view as it experienced new corporeal prisons. As Bird tells it, Sheppard–Tom's story is basically Tom's story: it is what happens to Tom as he behaves mostly as Tom always has. Far more interesting, according to Poe, would have been to have a stable narrative point of view that could describe the unique experience of serial re-embodiment. Donnelly was a great fan of Poe's, and he follows Poe's advice to Bird in labeling this form of transmutation "metempsychosis," a term Poe uses in "Metzengerstein" and other stories. He further flags his debt by using a stanza from Poe's "The Conqueror Worm" as *Doctor Huguet*'s epigraph. So it's no surprise that Donnelly fully follows Poe's advice to Bird in narrating the uncanny experience of a self-contained consciousness trapped in a foreign body: Huguet is still Huguet, though now in Sam Johnsing's skin.

The comparison between *Doctor Huguet* and *Sheppard Lee* helps us see that while both narrators' metempsychotic transformation shows that—in Donnelly's words—"the body is the man," this means entirely different things for the two authors. For Bird, the body shapes, even determines, personality. For Donnelly, the body is completely inconsequential to the mind, personality, temperament, and experience of the person in question. However, for Donnelly, the superfluity of the body to the mind is ultimately irrelevant, since race is revealed to be a super-ficial biological fact that nonetheless entirely determines social standing.[28] For Bird, a white mind in a black body (or a diseased body, or a fat body) is more or less a different mind. For Donnelly, a white mind in a black body is the same mind, but it might as well be different given the power of the color line.

The notion that a white mind in a black body loses its social influence is, then, the fundamental logic of the novel's anti-racist message: even intelligence and eloquence are unjustly devalued if the speaker is black.[29] But—and this is the point I want to stress—this idea is very much a problem for the novel's anti-hypocrisy polemic. Huguet is divinely punished for not speaking plainly. But a major implication of the book's metempsychotic plot is that plain speech is never plain; its force as political speech is always determined by extra-rational forces ranging from the benign or inevitable (one attends more closely to the speech of a loved one, respected friend, or admired public figure) to the pernicious (the same words spoken by a white man and a black man are given vastly different weight). Suddenly we are far from a fantasy of a rational-critical public sphere and closer to Jacques Rancière's conception of politics as fundamentally aesthetic: "Political activity is whatever shifts a body from the place assigned to it.... It makes visible what had no business being seen, and makes heard a discourse where once there was only place for noise."[30] As the novel makes clear, plain speech may be treated as senseless din once the public sphere's as-if counter-facts meet the brute facts of the existing regime of racial domination. Even as the novel makes such an impassioned call for open and overt radicalism, it struggles with its own account of the limits of putatively transparent facts. Sincerity, openness, and transparency turn out to be the privilege of white men alone.

The Hypocritical Public Sphere: Or, Bacon's Mask

In the next part of this chapter I want to flesh out some of the conceptual implications of Donnelly's complicated narrative of racial passing. I'll then show how one of Donnelly's earlier texts, *The Great Cryptogram*—a work that made him both famous and infamous—provides an important counterpoint to *Doctor Huguet's* apparently unwavering denunciation of the figure of the hypocrite. In the process I will consider how contemporary political theory helps us think about the dangers of Donnelly's dreams of transparency; and conversely, how Donnelly dramatizes a fraught moment in American politics that anticipates key concerns of twentieth- and twenty-first- century political theory.

First, as already suggested, Huguet's disappointment that his voice and mind no longer garner respect after his transmutation vents—with near-parodic intensity— a proto-Habermasian ideal of the rational-critical public sphere. Huguet, much to his dismay, finds that citizenship and public discourse are not as abstract or disembodied as an idealized conception of these spheres would suppose. Jodi Dean has argued that the Habermasian ideal posits an exemplary subject whose own self-transparency models the longed-for clarity of the public sphere: "Rather than irrevocably opaque and unspeakable, the subjectivity Habermas theorizes strives

WILLIAM SHAKSPERE.

FRANCIS BACON'S MASK.

Fac-simile of the Frontispiece in the Folio of 1623.

Facing this portrait in the Folio are presented Ben Jonson's famous lines:

This Figure, that thou here seest put	O, could he but have drawn his wit
It was for gentle Shakespeare cut;	As well in brasse, as he hath hit
Wherein the Graver had a strife	His face, the Print would then surpass.
With nature, to out-doo the life:	All that was ever wr:t in brasse.
But since he cannot, Reader, looke	
Not on his Picture, but his Booke	

FIG. 4.1. *"William Shakspere. Francis Bacon's Mask." Image reproduced from*
The Great Cryptogram's first US edition published in Chicago by R.S. Peale & Co. (1888).
Author's personal collection. The portrait of William Shakespeare engraved by Martin
Droeshout is from the frontispiece to the First Folio collection of Shakespeare's plays (1623).
Digital images of the complete Folio are hosted by the Folger Shakespeare Library, under a
creative commons license, at www.folger.edu.

for transparency. It is fundamentally open and ready for discussion."[31] Huguet,
proud of his logical faculties and oratorical prowess, is very much ready—even
eager—for discussion, but southern white prejudice blocks the ears of a population that is not ready for discussion with him.

The novel thus suggests that the main problem Huguet encounters is an
emotional public sphere that fails to meet Huguet's rational-critical subjectivity on
its own terms. Dean, however, worries that there is an antidemocratic risk inherent
to critiques of democracy undertaken in the name of transparency and "the
public." That is, it is not simply a problem if the public sphere fails to live up to
ideals of transparency; rather, there is a problem with the ideals themselves:

> When based on the notion of the public, democratic political theory is likely to
> focus mistakenly on revealing, outing, and uncovering what has been con-
> cealed or withheld.... [T]hese restrictions narrow the range of thinking about
> politics, distracting us from fundamental social and economic antagonisms

and deflecting attention from questions of biopolitics, transnational alliance, and the place of fantasy, to mention just a few.[32]

In Dean's account, a "politics" undertaken in the name of the public may distract from "fundamental...antagonisms," which is, in essence, to say that fantasies of a transparent public sphere may distract from anything that might properly count as "politics" at all.

And in fact, it turns out that, in *Doctor Huguet*, Donnelly offers repeated and seemingly involuntary confirmation of how easily an intense suspicion of ideological mystification lapses into a wholesale rejection of politics. The novel drips with anti-political disgust: Huguet denigrates political activity as a "sordid and debased struggle of little creatures" (*D*, 11); and he laments abandoning his cherished ideals in order to "wrangle and wrestle in the mud of politics, for the temporary honors or the vile spoils of public life" (*D*, 35). Lamenting his fall into the hypocrisies of politics in language awkwardly evocative of the violence of the slave catcher, Huguet goes so far as to say that he "felt like setting the dogs on the men who called upon me to tempt me into the dirty puddle of this unclean strife" (*D*, 35). Donnelly's limited fame as the founder of a third political party would suggest that his vitriol is, more precisely, for partisan politics. Conforming to the southern Democrat's institutional racism might win a ready-made constituency, but only at the cost of unbearable moral contortions. But Huguet's expression of disgust with "public life" more broadly seems to confirm Dean's fears. In a fantasy of political transparency, all strategizing can only be registered as putridity, corruption, and filth.[33]

A fuller picture thus emerges of how and why an act of mental hypocrisy is the unexpected point on which the whole plot hinges. Donnelly's concern with exploring the gap between real interests and political representation in the idiom of hypocrisy anticipates Hannah Arendt's critique of the revolutionary hatred of the hypocrite, which, in her account, fueled the violence of the Reign of Terror. For Arendt:

> [T]he demand that everybody display in public his innermost motivation, since it actually demands the impossible, transforms all actors into hypocrites....In politics, more than anywhere else, we have no possibility of distinguishing between being and appearance. In the realm of human affairs, being and appearance are indeed one and the same.[34]

The hatred of the hypocrite is fueled by an aversion to public artifice, but, for Arendt, there is no such thing as politics, or indeed any form of human social life, without representational forms. Judith Shklar's aforementioned *Minor Vices* picked up on Arendt's concerns, claiming that charges of hypocrisy confuse substantive disagreement over political principles with the inevitable fact of inconsistency. Further, charges of hypocrisy miss the ways American equality is not founded on sincerity but, precisely, pretense: "The democracy of everyday life, which is rightly admired by egalitarian visitors to America, does not arise from sincerity. It is based on the pretense that we must speak to each other as if social standings were a matter of indifference in our views of each other. That is, of course, not true."[35]

Donnelly's novel very much wants it to be true that social standing does not matter. He wants to believe that political ideas grounded in rational interest can win the day, with no need for rhetoric or pretense—and certainly not "hypocrisy." While Shklar explicitly links the celebrated principle of counterfactual equality with the maligned sin of hypocrisy as two related forms of pretense, Donnelly is anxious to keep them separate. As I have shown thus far, however, the experience of being in a black body undermines his confidence in the power of the rational-critical public sphere. But if the persistence of the *desire* for transparency traps *Doctor Huguet* in an over-rigid insistence on sincerity (either virtue reigns, or all politics is tainted), Donnelly's earlier work offers a characteristically bizarre but rich meditation on the question of what we might call, following Shklar, necessary pretense.

To recover this alternate imagination of political hypocrisy we need only look to the image that begins this section (Fig. 4.1), which served as the frontispiece to Donnelly's *The Great Cryptogram: Francis Bacon's Cipher in the So-Called Shakespeare Plays* (1887).[36] *The Great Cryptogram* claimed to prove that Shakespeare's works were, in fact, authored by Francis Bacon by deciphering a series of hidden messages within Shakespeare's plays. The image constitutes a cringe-worthy clipping from the least-respectable work of Donnelly's unconventional literary career.[37] While Donnelly's advocacy for Bacon's authorship has continued to earn him pride of place in accounts of America's paranoid past, this portrait of Bacon-as-Shakespeare puts in play the key terms that, I have argued, define a crucial tension within Donnelly's oeuvre and even within populism itself: namely, between reason and rhetoric, transparency and duplicity, argument and emotional persuasion.

Though now considered the most far-fetched notion of his career and the pinnacle of delusion, Donnelly's Bacon-not-Shakespeare theory won him his greatest renown prior to the release of 1890's *Caesar's Column*. *The Great Cryptogram*, which laid out Donnelly's argument in depth, followed his 1887 essay in the *North American Review* on "The Shakespeare Myth." By April of 1888, Donnelly was lecturing on the true authorship of Shakespeare's plays at Westminster Hall to an audience that included Oscar Wilde. The *Cryptogram* itself, however, was ultimately a financial failure, leading to bitter disputes with the publisher, whom Donnelly had assured the cipher would be communicated clearly enough for a popular audience to appreciate.[38] Nonetheless, the spectacle of a largely self-educated Minnesotan debunking England's most beloved literary figure held enough interest that Donnelly long remained in demand as a lecturer in the United States and abroad.[39]

Donnelly's conviction that Bacon was the true author of Shakespeare's oeuvre rested on the idea that the play's stinging political criticism would not have been tolerated if they were known to have come from Bacon:

"The poor player," Will Shakspere, might have written such plays solely for the pence and shillings there were in them, for he had nothing to do with politics.... [B]ut if Francis Bacon...the lawyer, politician, member of Parliament...had acknowledged the authorship of the Plays, the inference would have been irresistible...that these horrible burlesques and travesties of royalty were written with malice and settled intent to...justify the aristocracy in revolution.   (*GC*, 257)

For Donnelly, the act of authorship by one engaged in politics was a risky under-taking. Donnelly himself published his incendiary populist-call-to-arms, *Caesar's Column*, and the later *Doctor Huguet*, pseudonymously, pursuing once again the promise of the print public sphere: a commitment to abstract reason and a realm of letters where ideas can encounter each other free of their authors' embodied particularities.[40] Imagining Bacon to share a similar concern, Donnelly writes sympathetically of the scientist–politician's subterfuge: "The man who sets forth his thoughts in his own name knows that the public will constantly strive to connect his utterances with his personal character; to trace home his opinions to his personal history and circumstances" (*GC*, 252).

It may seem strange to locate Donnelly's investment in the Bacon–Shakespeare theory as a precursor to *Doctor Huguet*. But the work is in many ways the novel's direct antecedent. Donnelly, musing on the brazenness of "Shakspere's" violation of class boundaries, drew a surprising comparison:

The distinction, in the England of 1596, between the yeoman and the gentleman, was almost as wide as the difference to-day in America between the white man and the black man;...[this] will give us some conception of the nature of this attempt made by William Shakspere in 1596.   (*GC*, 55)

Donnelly acknowledged the existence of an actual William Shakspere of Stratford, but saw this man's claims to the authorship of the plays as an instance of brazen class passing. The lowly Shakspere merely capitalized on Bacon's chosen pseudonym. Donnelly appears to denigrate this form of deceptive artifice by comparing it to an act of racial passing, even as he strives to justify Bacon's deceit, and by extension other forms of necessary pretense, in disguising his true authorship of the plays.

And of course a similar tension is visible in Donnelly's own work. While I suggested that Donnelly's pseudonymous authorship was a strategy for separating the logic of his arguments from any personal allegiances or animosities from his life as a politician, *anonymous* authorship would accomplish the same goal without the more extravagant pretense of a false identity.[41] Donnelly's preferred pen name, "Edmund Boisgilbert, M.D.," laid claim to a Huguenot lineage of noble French intellectuals. Exiles from persecution, Huguenot émigrés were often seen to have offered their adoptive countries a distilled dose of European enlightenment knowledge in the form of intellectual elites and trade professionals.[42]

"Doctor Huguet" is thus a complex figure: the fictional counterpart to a fictional author, whose European background sets him apart from the regional strife he observes like a latter-day Alexis de Tocqueville. So, too, the masklike visage of

"William Shakspere" that begins Donnelly's *Cryptogram* illustrates a strange creature: a man of reason and of cunning duplicity, a founding father of empiricism and scientific reason, and a playwright adept at intricate figurative imagery and obscure intertextual citations.[43] The image announces a desire for the political to be a space of transparency, sincerity, and reason, even as the complex layers of trickery, evasion, and misdirection attest to the limits of that ideal. Donnelly imagined that Bacon's texts, simultaneously masking and encoding hints of his true identity, called out for a reader able to unpack the nested secrecy and coded revelation of a "man who under a mask could put forth the Plays to the world; and who, inside the Plays, could, in turn, conceal a cipher" (*GC*, 473).

With Donnelly's earlier meditation on political pretense in mind, it becomes clear that, in *Doctor Huguet*, references to the prior work serve to raise the possibility of *necessary* deceit even as the novel cries out against the hypocrite's duplicity. An early scene mixing flirtation and philosophy directly references this earlier work. In an awkward bit of cross-promotion for *The Great Cryptogram* (and his planned future volume that would reveal Bacon as the author of Ben Jonson's works as well), Donnelly depicts Huguet marveling at Mary's erudition while the two trade favorite quotations from Renaissance thinkers. Huguet is a great fan of Jonson, and Mary wins Huguet's heart by musing that Jonson's works have such poetry they "sound as if they had been written by the Pen of Shakespeare" and "have all the depth and profoundness...of Bacon's compositions" (*D*, 24). Huguet responds with admiration that he "had not supposed...that there was any resemblance between Ben Jonson's prose and Lord Bacon's writings" (*D*, 25), to which Mary offers this particular example from Jonson: "Language most shows a man. *Speak that I may see thee*. It springs out of the most retired and inward parts of us, and is the image of the mind. No glass renders a man's form or likeness so true as his speech" (*D*, 25). Huguet and Mary's courtship itself supports the notion that language reveals the soul, as their emerging love unfolds through bouts of literary analysis and linguistic delectation.

However, after Huguet is turned black, his philosophy is tested and his persuasive powers are so weakened he is forced to realize he may not be able to "convince my friends that I was indeed Doctor Huguet" (*D*, 95). Huguet is predictably jailed when, in the unwashed form of Sam Johnsing, he repeatedly approaches his acquaintances and proclaims himself to be the esteemed doctor. These experiences lead him to a grim conclusion: "It had been taught me that the *mind* is the man; but now I perceived that the *body* is the man" (*D*, 100). In the cruelest irony, Huguet is unable to convince Mary of his corporeal switch, even after he reminds her of their shared fondness for the phrase "Language most shows a man," a phrase Donnelly locates as central to "Bacon's" philosophy: "Alas! I speak as Doctor Huguet, and you cannot see me in this mean habillment" (*D*, 135). Broken by his inability to prove his identity, Huguet juxtaposes citations from Shakespeare's *The Taming of the Shrew* and Jonson's *Sejanus His Fall* to vent his anguish: "My philosophy was all gone. Honor did *not* peer through the meanest habit. The mind did *not* make the body rich. All that was fiction, not fact. I thought of Mary's favorite quotation: 'Tis place, not blood, discerns the noble from the base.' And it seemed to be that Ben Jonson had come nearer to the truth than Shakespeare" (*D*, 155).

Reviewers of the novel scoffed at Donnelly's incorporation of his Baconian theories into *Doctor Huguet* and at his ostentatious and seemingly superfluous citations of Renaissance literature.[44] However, the references are a rather nuanced if unusual piece of intertextual reference. Unjust conditions might demand courageous sincerity: surely, there is something admirable in Donnelly's call for southern politicians to bravely endorse a radical commitment to racial equality. But politics might also require rhetorical forms, canny performances, and representational labor. The point is not that Donnelly was wrong to condemn his protagonist's artifice, but that the apparent clarity of that condemnation papers over a longstanding nervousness about if or when deceit—or even simply measured rhetoric—is justified. Even more importantly, the denunciation of Huguet's hypocrisy is premised on a faith that direct argument works because both black and white laborers share the same "interests." Rhetorical deceit obscures these interests; sincere speech reveals them. Oddly enough, it appears to have been the thought of William Shakspere's supposed act of class "passing" that raised, for Donnelly, a thought in opposition to this rigid commitment to transparency: a holder of unpopular beliefs—especially by one disenfranchised by existing power hierarchies— might not have the luxury of open speech. Is artifice under threat of persecution "hypocrisy"?

These competing conceptions of the legitimacy of pretense intersect with Donnelly's understanding of racial difference in complicated ways. In *The Great Cryptogram*, Donnelly implicitly endorses racist hierarchies in his heated account of the similarities between "Shakspere's" gambit and "the mulatto who would try to pass himself off as a white man, and would support his claim by lies and forgeries" (*C*, 55). By the end of the same decade, however, Donnelly reworked the idea of a racial mask to indict the injustice of those hierarchies themselves. After Huguet's transformation, a mulatto servant, Abigail, is alone among the doctor's former acquaintances who believes his story, precisely because racist laws have made her constantly aware of her body as an obstacle to social equality: "I had touched upon the secret passion of her life. Hers, too, was the proud mind in the proscribed body" (*D*, 131). In his earlier view, there is something disturbing to Donnelly about disguising one's "true" class position, racial identity, or character behind a "false" exterior. In his later view, it is society's own prejudices that have turned the accident of racial embodiment into a tragedy, rendering the outward fact of race more consequential than one's inner being.

Du Bois's Structural Hypocrites

In a speech given at the height of his popularity as a black schoolteacher and community leader (that is, still occupying Sam Johnsing's black body), Doctor Huguet urges his audience to abandon the practice of voting as a bloc for the

Republican candidate: "Let the black men break ranks!...Let them divide politically on other lines than those of color. Great economic questions are arising which have nothing to do with the old struggles" (D, 289). Huguet's political sermon continues: "The black man's interests are the same as [the whites of the South]. He needs prosperity, growth, opportunity, happiness. So do they. He wants to see the robbers struck down. So do they. He desires all that civilization can give him—all that belongs to him. So do they" (D, 289). Once this common political ground is acknowledged, Huguet fantasizes that the white southern population will succumb to a peculiar compulsion: not the enforcement of Reconstruction policies by a victorious federal government but rather, "their own interest will compel him to defend [the black man's] rights" (D, 289). This declaration underscores that the black community must be "true to themselves" (D, 218). Once material interests are aligned, sincerity and political rationality go hand in hand.

In Donnelly's account, existing political institutions sustain debilitating, outmoded affiliations. "Hypocrisy" might be a resource, then, since the hatred of the hypocrite could help dissolve partisan attachments as a first step toward new alliances. However, in moments such as those above, *Doctor Huguet* flirts with the seductive appeal of transparent material interest as a putatively self-evident foundation for this longed-for political unity. But by staging this fantasy of political transparency in the context of post-Reconstruction racial politics and efforts to imagine a black–white class alliance, Donnelly also offers significant, and productive, obstacles to an easy fantasy of interests and sincerity. Economic interest served a rhetorical purpose by helping to figure a utopian horizon beyond the political stalemates of Civil War-era prejudice, but Donnelly's complicated allegorical narrative reveals (perhaps in spite of itself) that the nature of these "interests" was a subject of active negotiation. And while courageous political speech was to be prized, Donnelly offers oblique acknowledgement of the public sphere's hostility to black speech of any sort.

To underscore this point, it's helpful to consider one particular example of populist economic reason, namely, the subtreasury plan, and the problems this rational, relatively plausible economic solution posed to the keenest observer of post-Reconstruction politics, W.E.B. Du Bois. Du Bois offers a powerful take on the ways "interests" might organize political alliance, but also the ways "interest" itself might be a rhetorical ploy. First outlined in the pages of *The National Economist* by the prominent National Farmers Alliance member Charles Macune in 1889 and later incorporated into the populist party platform in 1892, the subtreasury plan inspired the historian Lawrence Goodwyn to end his historical overview of populism by declaring it "democratic...[and] breathtakingly radical," celebrating its capacity to address "a problem that has largely defeated twentieth-century reformers, namely the maldistribution of income within American society."[45] The idea was relatively simple: Rather than falling prey to market fluctuation in harvested goods and rapacious lenders, farmers would be allowed to store their yield in federally owned warehouses, allowing them to ride out periods of depressed prices. More important, a farmer could obtain a loan issued in greenbacks valued at eighty percent of the crop's value. The plan was both defensive and proactive, protecting farmers from the whims of the market and limiting their vulnerability to predatory loans and mortgages during temporary periods of scarcity while freeing up currency for long-term investment and improvement. The plan also provided a relatively clear rallying point for Alliance and People's Party organizing committees, as it "defined the doctrine of fiat money in clear terms of self-interest that had unmistakable appeal to farmers desperately overburdened with debt."[46]

Yet, as Norman Pollack notes, the subtreasury policy could look more like "interest-group politics rather than class-conscious protest" as it "did not provide the economic or ideological basis for generalizing to the larger social welfare."[47] The subtreasury plan was as unappealing to southern black people as it was attractive to southern plantation owners, whose virtually unspoilable cotton crop was well-suited to waiting out the market: "Needless to say, the Negro in the South might as well have cultivated tundra in the Arctic Circle insofar as the subtreasury plan reflected his welfare"—or, we might say, his "economic interests."[48] The question of the subtreasury plan's "interest" for southern black people was clearly on Du Bois's mind when, eight years after the publication of Donnelly's *Doctor Huguet*, he wrote his novel of farm life in the Reconstruction south, *The Silver Fleece*. Arnold Rampersad describes Du Bois's novel as an "epic of cotton," sketching scenes ranging from its harvesting by black laborers, to white landowners struggling against the might of Northern capital, to the Washington power brokering that exerts a powerful influence on the seemingly distant plantation.[49]

Du Bois's view of agrarian economics from the perspective of the oppressed black worker emphasizes that southern land owners were far from developing a biracial "class consciousness." Early in the novel, one scheming Northerner lectures his associate on an inability to dominate the market in agricultural goods: "Last year when you curtailed cotton acreage and warehoused a big chunk of the crop you gave the mill men the scare of their lives," but "you failed...because you couldn't get the banks and big merchants behind you" (Q, 113). Later in the novel, when the plantation owners have transitioned this proto-subtreasury plan into a large-scale financial manipulation, Du Bois relays with irony a newspaper story covering the stratagem: " 'League Beats Trust.'... 'Farmers of South Smash Effort to Bear Market...Send Cotton to Twelve Cents...Common People Triumph'" (Q, 233).

From Du Bois's skeptical viewpoint, a league of white farmers cornering the cotton market hardly deserved lionization as populist heroes, and declaring such a maneuver a people's victory was scarcely sound economic thinking. Du Bois depicts one character in the novel scoffing openly upon reading the above headline and its celebration of an agrarian monopoly as a "common" victory: "Do fools like the American people deserve salvation?...A Man is induced to bite off his own nose and then to sing a paean of victory. It's nauseating—senseless" (Q, 233). Du Bois evokes a queasy disgust with people's capacity to nourish self-defeating loyalties. In a theme familiar to citizens of the twenty-first century, Du Bois was especially wary of faux populisms, or the capacity for corporate, monopolistic wealth to borrow the legitimizing trappings of folk culture.

Du Bois's cynicism toward the subtreasury plan (well after the effective demise of the People's Party) does not mean, however, that he was entirely unconvinced economic interest could serve as the basis for a black–white alliance. *The Silver Fleece* depicts an impoverished white woman musing on the possibility of a black–white alliance: " 'Durned if I don't think these white slaves and black slaves had ought ter git together,' she declared" (Q, 395). A white landowner reflecting with great trepidation on this same possibility, confesses "Of course ... they'll eventually get together; their interests are identical. I'll admit it's our game to delay this as long as possible' " (Q, 397). The primary problem *The Silver Fleece* tackles, however, is revealing how these "interests" are not perfectly transparent or immune to exploitation. In constant danger of being manipulated by the power games of white politicians, Du Bois's protagonist, Bles Alwyn, is talked into becoming a spokesperson for the Republican Party, which is eager to maintain the emotional, "bloody shirt" loyalties of the African American citizenry without actually under-taking any efforts to alleviate their plight. The party leaders seek to gain Alwyn's support, declaring him "just the man to take the stump during September and October and convince the colored people of their real interests" (Q, 271). Of course, for a Republican leadership willing to concede to southern demands and delay extending full political rights to the black population, "real interests" is a perverse euphemism for nostalgia and unthinking party loyalty. According to Rampersad, Republicans' hypocritical invocation of shared interests for the sake of holding power leads Bles to recognize the fundamental "disgrace of public life."[50] As with Donnelly, then, Du Bois evinces both optimism and suspicion toward rational-interest-based political affiliation. Black and white laborers clearly would benefit from economic policies protecting them from exploitation, but it was manifestly false to claim that both groups' interests in all things were identical and self-evident. Claims to the contrary revealed the corrupting power of party politics.

While *The Silver Fleece* works through this ambivalent attraction to economic interest, in *The Souls of Black Folk*, Du Bois thematizes these issues more dramati-cally as a kind of political hypocrisy, most likely unaware that Donnelly had performed a similar rhetorical move in nearly identical terms twelve years earlier. In *Souls*, Du Bois conceptualizes hypocrisy as a "problem of the color line" as a way of describing how complicated consistency and transparency—being "true to oneself"—are within the Veil of Color that splits the racialized subject. Du Bois thus reworks the notion of hypocrisy, going so far as to partially redeem it:

From the double life every American Negro must live, as a Negro and as an American ... [t]he worlds within and without the Veil of Color are changing, and changing rapidly, but not at the same rate, not in the same way; and this must produce a peculiar wrenching of the soul, a peculiar sense of doubt and bewilder-ment. Such a double life, with double thoughts, double duties, and double social classes, must give rise to double words and double ideals, and tempt the mind to pretence or revolt, to hypocrisy or radicalism.[51]

Du Bois recasts hypocrisy as related to radicalism; both are more a result of a violent "wrenching," a painful emotional split borne of intense pain, than a sinister, reasoned calculation of interest masquerading behind false principles or an abandonment of lofty reason to unsublimated passions. The radical is sincere but destructive in his inflexibility. The hypocrite adapts and accommodates to current conditions but can only do so through pretense. Du Bois repeats his pairing of hypocrisy and radicalism throughout the passage, associating anarchy with a worldview overly focused on abstract ideals and the hypocrite as unable to think beyond immediate sensual gratification:

> Thus we have two great and hardly reconcilable streams of thought and ethical strivings; the danger of the one lies in anarchy, that of the other in hypocrisy. The one type of Negro stands almost ready to curse God and die, and the other is too often found a traitor to right and a coward before force; the one is wedded to ideals remote...the other forgets that life is more than meat and the body more than raiment.[52]

Du Bois's conception of hypocrisy as epiphenomenal to the painful racial double consciousness produced by Jim Crow policies turns the hypocrite into an object of sympathy. The black political subject is rent in two by the incapacity to resolve material interest and higher standards in the tainted political atmosphere of the late nineteenth and early twentieth centuries. The hypocrite thus becomes less of a political anomaly or a unique personal failing and more of a structural position.[53]

The Transubstantiation of a Poor White

I have shown how, by the end of the nineteenth century, Du Bois had begun to think about political ethics through the lens of hypocrisy. "Hypocrisy" was both useful and insufficient as a form of condemnation because it identified a split between inner life and social masquerade, but could only moralize that disparity as an individual weakness. This dramatization of "hypocrisy" urged those interested in the plight of African Americans to understand the unique social pressures that made consistency impossible. Peter Coviello has noted that "one of the operative premises of *Souls* [is] that the human is activated by an incalculable array of imperatives, motives, and crossed relations."[54] This fundamental sense of relation leads Du Bois to identify the hypocrite as a troubling political type, but makes it much harder to fantasize (as, I have argued, Donnelly sometimes does) that "rational interests" offered a ready way out of the morass of social antagonism.

Souls thus offers a brief but intense meditation on the politics of hypocrisy. But Du Bois's most troubling and sustained investigation of the hypocrite would not come until 1935's *Black Reconstruction*, as he grappled retrospectively with the consequences for black Americans of *white* hypocrisy during the years 1860 to 1880. To pursue "hypocrisy" as a problem with white and black inflections might seem to risk drawing a false moral equivalency. Even so, in that book's longest chapter,

Du Bois directs intense attention to one hypocrite in particular: Abraham Lincoln's successor, President Andrew Johnson. In "The Transubstantiation of a Poor White," Du Bois describes the process by which Johnson ultimately betrayed his own aversion to oligarchy and caste, driven to wild inconstancy in part by an instinctive deference to southern gentility, but above all by an intense race prejudice. Much as Donnelly turned to supernatural allegory to dramatize the consequences of hypocrisy, Du Bois figures Johnson's duplicity as a form of "transubstantiation," imagining his betrayal of black Americans as an uncanny change in shape or form.

To help understand the import of this idiosyncratic phrasing it's useful to review Du Bois's case against Johnson. In Du Bois's account, Johnson was, to his credit, a democrat at heart; he was a "fanatical hater of aristocracy."[55] He goes on to cite a Johnson biographer to highlight the President's "courage to go up against caste, . . . to stand for the under-dog, whether Catholic, Hebrew, foreigner, mechanic, or child" (*BR*, 199). However, as Du Bois states bluntly, "to all this there is one great qualification. Andrew Johnson could not include Negroes in any conceivable democracy" (*BR*, 199). Du Bois never uses the term hypocrisy to describe Johnson's failings, yet he consistently emphasizes the ways Johnson's racial animosity led him to contradict his own stated principles:

> For the Negro, Andrew Johnson did less than nothing . . . once he realized that the chief beneficiary of labor and economic reform in the South would be freedmen . . . He even . . . change[d] plans which he had thought out and announced before he faced the Negro problem. . . . He had advocated . . . penalties on wealth gained through slavery. When he realized that Negroes would be [the] beneficiaries . . . he said not another word. He was a thick-and-thin advocate of universal suffrage in the hands of the laborer and common man, until he realized that some people actually thought that Negroes were men.   (*BR*, 230)

Like Donnelly's protagonist, Johnson is not a hypocrite because he praises virtue but indulges in vice, but because he abandons a full commitment to a sacred political principle.

In part, Du Bois follows Carl Schurz's account of Johnson's hypocrisy, seeing a vulnerability to flattery as its root—an unacknowledged deference to the caste system Johnson otherwise opposed. *Black Reconstruction* cites Schurz at length: "Mr. Johnson, the plebeian who before the war had been treated with undisguised contempt by the slave-holding aristocracy, could not withstand the subtle flattery of the same aristocracy when they . . . cajol[ed] his vanity" (*BR*, 210). Like Donnelly, Schurz finds that flattery is the royal road to hypocrisy: by inflating Johnson's ego, former slaveholders tempted Johnson to enjoy the benefits of a social hierarchy he opposed on principle. Du Bois goes on to expand on Schurz's point to explain that "sincerity" for Johnson was less an unqualified virtue and more a privilege of wealth and status:

> In fact, personally, Johnson liked the slave-holders. He admired their manners; he enjoyed their carriage and clothes. They were quite naturally his ideal of what a gentleman should be. He could not help being tremendously flattered

when they noticed him and actually sued for his favor. As compared with Northerners, he found them free, natural and expansive, rather than cold, formal and hypocritical.   (*BR*, 210)

Du Bois does not stress the irony, though it is clear enough: Johnson's perception that upper class social graces signaled an absence of Notherner's "hypocritical" formality encouraged Johnson in his own duplicity, creating the context in which he could blithely oppose the very reforms he had earlier advocated.

But why does Du Bois call Johnson's hypocritical about-face a "transubstantiation"? In part, this unusual phrasing is consistent with Du Bois's tendency to mix the sacred and the secular, as for instance in *Souls of Black Folk* where "soul" takes on spiritual and positivistic connotations. But the term is still puzzling. Transubstantiation refers to the Catholic belief that the Eucharist—bread and wine—is transmuted into the body of Christ during Mass. It's hard to imagine that Du Bois means to suggest that Johnson was similarly spiritualized or rendered sacred by his acts of deceit and betrayal. To the contrary, for Du Bois, Johnson's racial hypocrisy made the president something of a rube, an easy mark for the "slaveocracy's" long con: using racism to consolidate white southern power. Rather, the corporeal inflection of "transubstantiation" underscores that a substantive, material transformation has taken place. Even as he cites with apparent admiration Schurz's account of Johnson's susceptibility to flattery, the repeated use of the terms "transformation" and "transubstantiation" pushes back against the psychological reading, hinting at a process by which Johnson came to give shape to an inconsistent set of beliefs that defined this juncture in the history of Reconstruction politics, and not only Johnson's personal failings.

Indeed, despite Schurz's focus on Johnson's shameful aristocratic proclivities it was crucial that Johnson not be seen as a psychological anomaly. Instead, for Du Bois, Johnson "embodies" a split. He gives form to a set of tensions that were endemic to Reconstruction era politics:

The transubstantiation of Andrew Johnson was complete. He had begun as the champion of the poor laborer....He had demanded the punishment of those southerners who by slavery and war had made such an economic program impossible. Suddenly thrust into the Presidency, he had retreated from this attitude....Because he could not conceive of Negroes as men, he refused to advocate universal democracy....This change did not come by deliberate thought or conscious desire to hurt—it was rather the tragedy of American prejudice made flesh.   (*BR*, 266)

As in Donnelly's worldview, to hold office is always to flirt with hypocrisy, since institutional politics demands that unpopular beliefs be disguised. But the language of a tension or contradiction made flesh is closely coupled with Du Bois's insistence that Johnson's hypocrisy was not deliberate or conscious. Earlier Du Bois writes that "It was the drear destiny of the Poor White South that, deserting its economic class and itself, it became the instrument by which democracy in the nation was done to death, race provincialism deified, and the world delivered to plutocracy.

The man who led the way with unconscious paradox and contradiction was Andrew Johnson" (*BR*, 198). In Mandeville's aforementioned scale, unconscious hypocrisy is the least vile sort, underscoring the impression that Du Bois means to mitigate the nature of Johnson's crimes. By stressing the unconsciousness of Johnson's inconsistency, and figuring it as a kind of embodiment, transubstantiation, or contradiction "made flesh," Du Bois also heightens the importance of Johnson's hypocrisy by making it a material symptom of a deep historical problem.

Du Bois returns again and again to this point throughout the chapter. Echoing *Souls'* account of black Americans caught between "two great and hardly reconcilable streams of thought," the section's opening summary describes Johnson as "set between a democracy which included poor whites and black men, and an autocracy that included Big Business and slave barons" and thus "torn between impossible allegiances" (*BR*, 195). Du Bois clearly does not *equate* the gravity of hypocrisy as a form of double consciousness and hypocrisy as racist betrayal. For *Souls'* hypocrites and radicals Du Bois invites compassion; for Johnson he invites anger, disdain, and disgust. Yet the two accounts share a concern with what I have called structural hypocrisy. In Du Bois's schematization, an allegiance between poor whites and slave barons was "impossible," even though this is precisely the alliance that Johnson helped bring into being. Meanwhile, an alliance between poor white people and poor black people—an alliance that in Du Bois's eyes was very much logically possible—was rendered nearly inconceivable in actual fact by the force of racism: [T]here should have been...a union between the champions of universal suffrage and the rights of the freedmen, together with the leaders of labor, the small landholders of the West, and logically, the poor whites of the South.... This union of democratic forces never took place (*BR*, 197). Johnson's hatred of the southern oligarchy and sympathy with labor positioned him as a powerful icon for the possibility of an alliance that "should have been"; his racism and susceptibility to flattery made him instead an agent of grotesque, hypocritical alliances. What could have become "a real party of economic reform" became instead "a reaction of small property-holders against corporations; of a petty bourgeoisie against a new economic monarchy" (*BR*, 197). In Du Bois's account, the tragic transubstantiation of Reconstruction politics was complete.

Johnson set out to oppose the southern aristocracy but "became a puppet, played upon by mighty fingers and selfish, subtle minds; groping, self-made, unlettered and alone; drunk, not so much with liquor, as with the heady wine of sudden and accidental success" (*BR*, 264). Johnson changes forms, but in something of the reverse of Huguet's transmutation. When, in Donnelly's novel, Doctor Huguet is accused by his southern neighbors of being a "Republican in disguise" they mean to accuse him of supporting African Americans' rights to political power, all the while masquerading as a "respectable" southern gentleman (that is, one committed to white supremacy). Because Huguet fails to affirm a belief in black political equality, he becomes a version of what he was accused of being: a radical Republican trapped behind a mask of his own making. In Du Bois's account,

Johnson, too, might be said to be a "Republican in disguise," but in a very different sense. For Du Bois, Johnson came to embody the worst features of the mask of moderate Republicanism itself. Still acting the part of the Negro's savior, but deeply afraid of black political power, Johnson oversaw the dismantling of any possibility for substantive economic reform, and sounded the death knell for dreams of a black–white labor alliance. In the closing paragraph of the chapter, Du Bois writes that, "in some respects, Andrew Johnson is the most pitiful figure of American history."

Conclusion: Monsters of Hypocrisy

Hannah Arendt, musing on the unexpected centrality of hypocrisy to revolutionary thought, writes, "It must seem strange that hypocrisy—one of the minor vices, we are inclined to think—should have been hated more than all the other vices taken together.... Is hypocrisy then such a monster?"[56] If Du Bois's rent subjects and—even more so—Donnelly's body-swapping hypocrite appear as grotesque or even monstrous political subjects, I have tried to show how that monstrosity stems less from moral corruption and more from the inescapable complexity of political representation. By the 1880s, the hypocrite had emerged as the Gilded Age's "suspicious object" par excellence, a figure whose brazen venality made any degree of apathy, anger, or disgust seem justified. Taking a long view of Reconstruction and its wake, Donnelly's and Du Bois's black and white hypocrites trouble the clarity of such emotional judgments. Taken together, their works push readers to seek a response to hypocrisy beyond suspicious, outraged demands for transparency and consistency.

In this, these "monsters" dramatize literature's power to, in Nancy Bentley's terms, "break up and reconfigure approved allotments of speech and appearance" by disturbing "well-ordered distributions of subjectivity and metamorphos[ing] strange new speaking bodies."[57] For Bentley, in other words, literature's counter-factual subjects reveal its power to engage with the aesthetic and emotional terrain of democratic politics. But it's a sign of the intensity of our mistrust of masks that, when the hypocrite is rendered as a fantastic creature of metempsychosis or transubstantiation, these strange bodies can equally provoke a debilitating disgust with the aesthetics of politics.

This is the crucial tension that shapes Donnelly's and Du Bois's hypocrites. Both authors harbor deep and justifiable distrust of manipulative political rhetoric; they reveal the ways political hypocrites foster coalitions that reinforce white supremacist and capitalist power and inhibit genuinely progressive cross-racial alliances. But they also suggest that the hypocrite's internal contradictions may not be internal at all. They may be a symptom of a political context that lacks language and institutional forms for aligning a diverse range of "interests" that are potentially compatible but not therefore identical. It is in this context that even Johnson is "pitiful," a sad relic of a wider failure to find common ground. Suspicion and hatred of the hypocrite are understandable, even commendable, but the predominance of these affective responses also impedes a structural interpretation of hypocrisy.[58]

Tempering our aversion to the hypocrite may also be a necessary step toward distinguishing between genuine betrayals, like Andrew Johnson's, and more mundane political disappointments. Bruno Latour describes political language as "always disappointing," claiming, "the ordinary, banal, daily, limp, tautological character of this form of discourse...shocks the brilliant, the upright, the fast, the organized, the lively, the informed, the great, the decided."[59]

However, to fail to see the circuitous, inefficient, and even contradictory forms of political representation as an inescapable part of social life is to risk "no longer see[ing] the point of political talk," which "seems superfluous, redundant, parasitic, compared to the 'reality' of 'social relations' and of 'groups' which appear 'veiled', 'betrayed' or 'concealed.'"[60] At times, Donnelly and Du Bois cast the hypocrite as an impurity in urgent need of expulsion. At other times they suggest that the more difficult task is to condemn the effects of hypocrisy without rejecting politics altogether.

Cynicism

{ 5 }

Cynical Reason in the Cranky Age

This is supposed by many to be the Gilded Age, but we rather incline to the opinion that it is the cranky age.... One of the experts who was called upon as a witness in the Guiteau trial, declares that one person out of every five is insane.

—*DAILY GLOBE*, 1881[1]

This book began by taking up Mark Twain's first novel, a text thought to so perfectly capture the dishonesty and venality of American politics in the latter decades of the nineteenth century that its title became the period's preferred designation: *The Gilded Age*. In my reading, the novel—co-authored with Charles Dudley Warner—struggled to supply a concrete account of the causes and consequences of corruption, focusing too quickly on the public's emotionality and gullibility.[2] But framing the argument this way misses another perspective from which the novel addresses questions of political emotion. Although Twain and Warner appear deeply suspicious of the public's affects, *The Gilded Age* powerfully evoked a set of *feelings about* and *emotional orientations toward* democracy's degradation. These include the novel's overtly polemical outbursts of moral outrage, its efforts to model styles of calm-headed critique, and its underlying tone of apathetic resignation. Some early critics worried that "the thoughtful reader will rise from the perusal of 'The Gilded Age' in a mood rather depressed than exhilarated," but others found bracing this "satire of the bitterest kind" and its "bitter exposures of American folly."[3]

Despite Twain's anti-sentimental thesis, I have argued that *The Gilded Age* (and the later fiction it inspired) help us understand the ways politics is *always* emotional. Focusing on the novel's tone underscores this point. Sometimes politics' emotionality is dramatic, as when a public figure stokes the passions of the masses. At other times, its affective dimension is less theatrical, as in citizens' everyday efforts to manage the strain of participating in—or simply paying attention to—the political process. This chapter continues the latter investigation, into how Gilded Age literature conceptualized quotidian political moods and feelings. To do so, I turn to a Twain novel, 1891's *The American Claimant*, published nearly twenty years after his first, to examine it in a historical moment when *The Gilded Age* was still seen as a resource for understanding the emotional contours of the political present.

The American Claimant is very much a "Gilded Age novel." It can be thought of as such both because it belongs to the moment given shape by Twain and Warner's titular fiction, and because the phrase "The Gilded Age" foregrounds questions of affect and agency, whether or not we remember the antecedent. Twenty-first-century readers who think of our own moment as a "second gilded age" well know that the benefit and the drawback of this periodization is its bundling together a critique and a temperament. Using the expression "The Gilded Age" announces that we see something rotten behind a deceptive façade; the phrase's affective power derives, in part, from protecting us against that shiny falsehood by announcing us as "in the know." One speaks of "the gilded age"—or "the second gilded"—with a bitter laugh, a weary sigh, or a knowing sneer.[4]

This chapter explores this critical-affective dynamic under the heading of "cynicism," which Peter Sloterdijk famously characterizes as pervasive, defensive, and melancholy bitterness that, nonetheless, does not challenge the status quo. In his account, cynicism is a posture by which "enlightened people see to it that they are not taken for suckers."[5] After tracing the ways *The Gilded Age* models a related form of defensive disillusionment, I argue that *The American Claimant* seeks to pull back from a pervasive form of cynical critique—intensified, as I will show, in late-nineteenth-century legal discourse—that was self-consciously modeled on Twain's own work. *The Gilded Age* has been called "one of [Twain's] most deeply cynical works,"[6] an epithet that appears well earned by a novel more bitterly pessimistic about democracy than nearly every American political satire that has followed in its wake—an impressive feat, as the Washington novel is consistently a "cynical" genre.[7] As recently as 2010, Christopher Hitchens lamented the late-nineteenth-century version of the Washington novel's continued influence: "We still await the novelist who can address the matter of the last, best hope of earth and treat it without frivolity, without cynicism, and without embarrassment."[8]

The "cynicism" of the Gilded Age novel and its progenitors is, in Hitchens's account, an offshoot of the authors' pessimistic perspectives. We await the novelist unfettered by this ailment. But is "cynicism" properly seen as merely an outlook, tone, or view? After all, an alternative interpretation of *The Gilded Age* and related political novels suggests that such works are not themselves "cynical" but rather offer penetrating depictions of the cyni*cism* endemic to the political system, especially in the corrupt postbellum era to which the novel lent its title. It's not the political observers who are cynical; it's the politicians. We learn in one overview of Twain's work, for example, that "*The Gilded Age*...gave its name to the mood of materialistic excess and cynical political corruption that started with the Grant administration in 1869 and prevailed into the 1870s and beyond."[9]

These two inflections of the novel's cynicism hinge on an ambiguity within the vernacular understanding of "cynicism" itself. On the one hand, "cynicism" is an attitude that differs from its near synonym "apathy" both in its affective intensity (more bitter than listless) and by specifying the source of the cynic's hopelessness in a disillusioned awareness that all human behavior, but politics especially, is motivated by unscrupulous self-interest.[10] On the other hand, cynicism can also describe a mode of action, especially the craft of governance, which operates on cynical principles: a brazen, "Machiavellian" pursuit of any means necessary to achieve self-interested ends.[11] We can see an awkward juxtaposition of these dual meanings in a recent screed against the cycle of cynicism in the United States that began in the 1860s and 70s: "The rich became richer and more cynical in their manipulations of government and power. The poor became poorer and more cynical in their disillusionment and helplessness."[12] The first and second instances of the word share a certain emotional resonance, and they both imply sour disenchantment, but the quasi-homonym links divergent degrees of agency between the rich (who have a brutally rational strategy) and the poor (who have a debilitating, negative feeling).[13]

In the pages to come I will argue that Twain helps us see how quite a lot of diverse and contradictory diagnoses of democracy's ills are elided in the apparent affective uniformity of "cynicism." Cynicism alternately looks like a form of reason and emotion, a tactic and a hermeneutic, a mode of intense engagement and weary withdrawal, and a style of both passivity and aggression. This final chapter, together with the first, serves as a two-part exploration of cynicism as an unstable but crucial tonal feature of political literature after the Civil War; as a major thematic in the work of Mark Twain; and as a persistent, powerful, and problematic part of our critical vocabulary. Given this project's ambition to chart the ways in which Gilded Age political literature grappled with the allure and the threat of emotion in politics, it is perhaps inevitable that Twain's oeuvre would bookend this study, since both the targets of his critique and the tenor of his satirical voice are so fundamental to our understanding of this period and its literature. In the decades following *The Gilded Age*'s publication, late-nineteenth-century readers—anticipating Hitchens's critique—already had started to see "The Washington Novel" as a settled genre, defined not only by its DC setting and anti-corruption stance, but also by its distorting and self-defeating negativity, the blame for which could be laid squarely on Twain's shoulders.[14] As the period itself came to be known as "The Gilded Age," a set of assumptions about the nature of postbellum corruption, and popular feelings toward it, revealed the definitive imprint of Twain's political imagination.

This chapter, however, is not only about Twain's novels but also the ongoing dialogue between his work and the legal discourses of emotional insanity. Specifically, I show how the 1881 trial of Charles Guiteau, the assassin of President James Garfield, gave Twain and other commentators a troubling opportunity to examine the violence of cynical reason itself. To that end, I explore the surprising centrality of *The Gilded Age* to the Guiteau trial, as revealed in the trial's transcript and contemporaneous newspaper reports. I then conclude by arguing that *The American Claimant* can be read as a response to the earlier work's cameo appearance in Guiteau's trial. *The American Claimant* is, in my account, a deeply cynical novel by almost any definition but one that also embraces an emphatically unrealistic hope-against-the-evidence as an imperfect but provocative response to cynicism's allure. Reading Twain in light of the Guiteau trial, I argue Twain ultimately suggests that, when politics becomes nothing but rational calculation and an aggressive, paralyzing cynicism is cast as the only rational posture toward a corrupt democracy, then optimism for democracy must be imagined as insane.

An Appointment with Disappointment

On July 2, 1881, a frustrated office seeker named Charles J. Guiteau approached President James Garfield in a Washington, DC, train station and shot Garfield in the back, remaining calm in his insane conviction that God had demanded this act to secure the future of the Republican Party and, by extension, America itself. Guiteau was promptly apprehended, and the trial that followed incited yet another furious debate over the "insanity defense," as a stunned nation contemplated that the confessed murderer of its chief executive might evade legal responsibility by reason of an unsound mind. In trying to comprehend the nature of Guiteau's professed insanity, contemporaneous and subsequent observers frequently have made a somewhat surprising comparison, invoking the fictional character "Colonel" Beriah Sellers, the exuberant, eccentric, and possibly crazy inventor and schemer from Twain and Warner's 1873 satire of Washington corruption, *The Gilded Age*.[15]

Indeed, in the immediate aftermath of the murder, Guiteau's former business associate Simon D. Phelps testified in his deposition to the district attorney's office that, prior to the crime, Phelps had "always looked upon [Guiteau] as a sort of Col. Sellers. Enthusiastic, opinionated, and constantly conceiving new schemes."[16] A witness for the prosecution, Phelps went on to cite in court the catch phrase from *The Gilded Age*'s long-running stage adaptation in an effort to disprove Guiteau's insanity, describing Guiteau's money-making plans as not crazy but merely "of the Colonel Sellers stripe, 'millions in it.'"[17] In his widely reported testimony, Phelps cast Colonel Sellers's, and thus Guiteau's, exaggerated faith in his own entrepreneurial prowess and political prospects as an immoral but essentially rational form of egotism, greed, and ambition.[18]

As I demonstrated in the first chapter, throughout the 1870s Twain had articulated a scathing critique of American political emotion by declaring war on the emergent legal capacity to mount an insanity defense—a symptom, in Twain's reckoning, of an overly sentimental public and legal system. Twain's strict insistence on rational norms of individual responsibility, as well as his rejection of the criminal's "emotional insanity" and the public's misplaced sympathy, thus offered a powerful rhetorical precedent for the prosecution's argument in the Guiteau trial. That is, if the invocation of Sellers was in fact well conceived, reminding the jury of Colonel Sellers may have served as a metonym for Twain's wider anti-insanity oeuvre. In light of Twain's rejection of protagonist Laura Hawkins's insanity defense in *The Gilded Age*, any references made to the novel during the Guiteau trial could seem designed to aid the prosecutorial rebuttal of the assassin's pleas for leniency (despite the complicated reminder of Laura's feigned insanity by reference to Sellers's seemingly more authentic variety).

But if this logic was already complex and fraught with opportunities for misunderstanding, it was doubly so given the widespread popularity of Sellers and Twain's positive depiction of him. In the novel, Colonel Sellers's extravagant profit schemes embodied what Twain critically described as America's "all-pervading speculativeness," but Twain also insisted that speculativeness was "a trait which it is of course better for a people to have and sometimes suffer from than to be without."[19] And while there may have been a benefit for the prosecution in invoking *The Gilded Age*'s rationalist denial of all forms of "emotional insanity," Sellers would still seem to be a particularly poor reference. Twain's bumbling "colonel" is a lovable but compulsively speculative businessman, inventor, Hawkins family friend, and Laura's self-appointed political mentor. He never commits an act of violence and is never charged with any crime. In fact, Colonel Sellers was one of Twain's most beloved and recognized figures prior to Tom Sawyer and Huckleberry Finn.[20] Why invoke a comparison to Sellers when arguing for the conviction and speedy execution of a presidential assassin?

Even as Laura's insanity occupies much of *The Gilded Age*, and even as that plot foregrounds a concern—central to the Guiteau case—with the validity of the insanity defense, there was, in fact, good reason to refocus a jury's attention on Colonel Sellers. As the Guiteau trial got underway, a longstanding discourse about the madness of American politics intensified and coalesced around a form of insanity that Sellers quite precisely embodied: that of the political aspirant. It is difficult to know if the witness Phelps was the first to draw the connection, but in the following decades the comparison had enough staying power that, by 1891, the Georgetown University professor Irving Rosse casually could invoke "Guiteau" and "Sellers" as paired representatives of a uniquely Washingtonian neurosis resulting from disappointed political ambitions: "One will not find relatively in any other city than Washington more persons of broken fortune, dead hopes, and bankrupt nervous systems...men of the Guiteau stamp and Col. Sellers conformation."[21] Men whose mental illness conformed to this pattern suffered from the disconnect between, on the one hand, the apparent possibility of profiting directly or indirectly from the postbellum federal government's expanding bureaucracy and coffers and, on the other, the limits imposed on newcomers' ambitions by nepotism, partisan networks of "influence," and crony capitalism.

In *The Gilded Age*, Charles Dudley Warner foregrounds this brand of madness when the hardworking engineer Philip Sterling encounters the capital for the first time:

> [Philip] was not familiar with Washington, and it was difficult to adjust his feelings and perceptions to its peculiarities....It seemed to him a feverish, unhealthy atmosphere in which lunacy would be easily developed. He fancied that everybody attached to himself an exaggerated importance, from the fact of being at the national capital, the center of political influence, the fountain of patronage, preferment, jobs and opportunities.   (G, 312)

Warner describes the psychological effects of proximity to power as widespread, with everyone in Washington driven mad by the desire for influence and just-out-of-reach routes of access to government. This feverish ambition produces "lunacy" on a mass scale, with the city's entire population imagining itself as enlarged and empowered by contact with the numinous political center.

Although Sterling recoils from insane hallucinations of stately splendor, the novel reveals that Sellers is perfectly in his element:

> The Colonel enjoyed this bustle and confusion amazingly; he thrived in the air of indefinite expectation. All his own schemes took larger shape and more misty and majestic proportions; and in this congenial air, the Colonel seemed even to himself to expand into something large and mysterious. If he respected himself before, he almost worshipped Beriah Sellers now, as a superior being. (*G*, 279)

Insanity is endemic to Washington, DC, and no one is more susceptible to the city's overheated desires than Sellers. Later, when he is called on to substantiate some basic facts of Laura's testimony during her trial, he launches into a wandering monologue in which he name-drops his imaginary connections with governors and senators, appearing nearly deranged with the "grandeur of his position" as witness (*G*, 398). While the authors depict Laura's insanity as a ruse to be rejected, it seems Sellers is actually quite nuts.

But if Sellers shows distinct signs of madness, there is little indication that Twain means for us to regard this lunacy as sinister. While the "air" in Washington was better described as malarial than congenial (according to Irving Rosse, cited above), a late-nineteenth-century audience might have enjoyed the counterintuitive notion that Sellers "thrived" in a political atmosphere widely understood to be deadly and inimical to sanity. His hyperbolic fantasy of the political as a realm of almost mystical possibility would have provided an amusing, even admirable, antithesis to the going cynical take on politics as merely another business venture.[22] By the beginning of the next decade, however, this lighthearted depiction would ultimately take on a disturbing new air. When Guiteau murdered the president less than ten years after *The Gilded Age*'s publication, at a time when the novel's theatrical run continued to draw crowds, Sellers's insane grandiosity seemed decidedly less amusing. Guiteau notoriously imagined he had helped to elect Garfield and was entitled to the Parisian ambassadorship in recompense. In the months leading up to the assassination, Guiteau was a familiar figure in Washington, constantly seeking recognition and favors from party leaders. When he came to feel that Garfield had betrayed the Stalwart faction of the Republican Party, Guiteau launched his assassination plot for what he saw as the good of the country: "This is not murder. It is a political necessity. It will make my friend Arthur President, and save the Republic."[23] In this delusional mindset, Guiteau resembles Sellers, likewise blind to his real capabilities and prospects.

While Sellers is often depicted as lovable, it's easy enough to see how Guiteau's murderous delusions could take the shine off Sellers's cheerful enthusiasm. However, a new problem quickly emerges. If *The Gilded Age* suggests that life in the capital produces "lunacy," and if Sellers offers a satiric portrait of the craziest forms such madness might take, and if Guiteau exceeds this fictional portrait in his real-life insanity, then the Sellers–Guiteau comparison would seem perfectly suited to the *defense*'s case that Guiteau is insane and therefore not legally accountable.

As already indicated, however, when Sellers figures into the trial, it is ostensibly to buttress the *prosecution*'s case for Guiteau's conviction. Sellers does not appear as a symbol of insanity but of eminent rationality, egotism, and ambition—evidence against the defendant's insanity plea. Charles Rosenberg, the foremost historian of the case, notes without comment the prosecution's counterintuitive use of the famously delusional Sellers to prove the defendant's sanity: "Phelps cautioned...he had never thought of [Guiteau] as insane, simply consumed with egotism, ambition, and unadulterated selfishness. 'I have always looked upon him as a sort of Col. Sellers.'"[24] Yet when Phelps speaks so casually of Guiteau's "extraordinary shrewdness and judgment of the Colonel Sellers stripe," he ignores the persistence with which Twain emphasized Sellers as likeable in part for his complete absence of shrewdness and judgment (R, 1055). Indeed, for a novel in which insanity is rampant (two of the primary protagonists are questionably crazy), Twain is quite consistent in maintaining a scheme in which Sellers mirrors Laura Hawkins's madness. Laura is rational; her feigned insanity only attests to her cunning. Sellers is, at best, borderline crazy; his madness manifests as a total lack of guile.

To an audience of the time familiar with Twain's best-selling work, then, the invocation of Sellers would not have communicated Guiteau's sanity as clearly as Phelps might have intended. Perhaps a result of the imprecision of Phelps's reference, the trial's transcript records a revealing inquiry upon cross-examination, when the defense asks Phelps to expand on his literary comparison:

> Q. Please explain yourself a little more fully; perhaps the jury do not know Colonel Sellers as well as you do.—A. Colonel Sellers is the type of the character who has measureless egotism, constantly getting up schemes which are to make him and his friends great fortunes, great names, a general good-natured fellow, willing to let all his friends in—differing from this man, however, who has instead of genial good nature, the most unbounded selfish disposition that I ever met with.   (R, 1056)

Phelps awkwardly invokes both Sellers's egotism and generosity but then, hoping to help convict Guiteau, quickly specifies that, in that latter respect, Guiteau was emphatically unlike Sellers. Guiteau himself was unimpressed by this confusing comparison and, following a characteristically irreverent outburst from the prisoner, the defense challenged Phelps to expand further on the analogy, sensing a productive ambiguity:

> THE PRISONER. That is the best you can do, is it?
>
> THE WITNESS. That is the best I can do.
>
> THE PRISONER. That indicated your brain.
>
> Q [The Defense]. Now, the Colonel Sellers character which you have depicted is recognized as a sort of good natured foolish man, is it not?
>
> A [The Witness]. No, sir; anything but a fool.   (R, 1056)

As the defense's questions to Phelps suggest, Sellers was not an easy point of comparison; rather, he was part of a particularly complicated effort by the prosecution to rewrite Guiteau's life as a history of rationally self-interested behavior.

The rationality of Guiteau's apparent madness was of central concern to the case, a point of contention that required probing the fine line between ordinary political and economic ambitions and delusional egotism. The "alienist" and government expert Allan Hamilton claimed that Guiteau's schemes were, in fact, eminently reasonable and often quite successful: "Guiteau's projects were, as a rule, substantial, and were at some time realized. The Inter-Ocean [publishing] scheme was a pronounced success...and even his last and most fatal 'delusion' was verified, for he did 'unite the Republican party,' and his act has thoroughly changed the features of American politics."[25] In this account, while Garfield's murder was the grotesquely immoral outcome of Guiteau's deluded appraisal of his own political prospects, it was nonetheless the result of calculated, rational choices made with a view to Guiteau's benefit. Guiteau's own brother testified that "he was responsible for his act, which I called moral responsibility, because I believed that some time in his past life he made a choice to follow the path of evil rather than good" (*R*, 491). Recasting Sellers from a lovable lunatic or "good natured foolish man" to a sinister schemer functioned, however imperfectly, as shorthand for the logic by which Guiteau's seemingly insane actions were to be understood as the result of reasoned premeditation.[26] The prosecution repeatedly warned the jury (and, by extension, the public following the trial) that by entertaining the credibility of Guiteau's insanity plea, the people were playing into the hands of a shrewd political aspirant and businessman who thrived on public attention and was always ready to turn notoriety into profit—just like Sellers.

The prosecution thus made a risky gamble. Invoking Sellers threatened to remind the jury of a model for Guiteau's behavior who was genuinely crazy and lovable to boot. But the memory of Sellers's ambitions also functioned to caution the jury that they'd seen this type before: Guiteau was yet another "crazy" schemer, one who was only insane insofar as his estimation of his own greatness exceeded that of the ordinary office seeker. As my epigraph suggests, nine out of ten Washingtonians were said to share this so-called madness during the "cranky age." What's more, if the prosecution could convincingly repurpose Sellers as a figure of shrewd deceit, he could remind them of a style of "cynical" critique that Twain's first novel modeled. Colonel Sellers might well seem affable and good natured—he might even seem "crazy" in his grandiose dreams—and this might tempt us to extend him our sympathy. But to the sober, dispassionate observer, Sellers's (and thus Guiteau's) madness would be revealed for the ruse it always was. We, with a knowing sneer, see that these men are anything but fools.

Interlude I: Cynical Critique

Sellers's unlikely appearance in the trial as an icon of rational decision-making is striking on its own terms—a moment when reading Twain, and reading him correctly, took on national significance. The case capitalized on the flexibility and authority of a cynical critical tone, which had found a powerful early expression via *The Gilded Age*'s sardonic narrative voice. But one might fairly ask: Who cares if the rejection of Guiteau's insanity plea required a "cynical" form of critique? The logic of the argument against Guiteau was certainly strained—laboring to describe a crazy person as "shrewd"—but the prosecution, jury, and concerned onlookers could be forgiven for aggressively prosecuting a presidential assassin. We can also see, however, that the reaction to the Guiteau trial reinforces Sloterdijk's and other theorists' sense that cynicism as a form of "enlightened" critique carries significant risks.

Specifically for Sloterdijk, cynicism presents a twofold problem. First, as "enlightened false consciousness," cynicism describes an attitude of apathetic knowledge: "it has learned its lessons in enlightenment, but it has not…put them into practice. Well-off and miserable at the same time, this consciousness no longer feels affected by any critique of ideology; its falseness is already reflexively buffered" (5). Sloterdijk's formulation of "cynicism" can appear to offer little that "apathy" wouldn't capture; it is a form of disillusioned knowledge that produces "a detached negativity" (6), which leads to paralysis rather than praxis. For Slavoj Žižek, however, Sloterdijk's formulation is useful because it weans critics of the notion that "ideology" can be understood as something like a bad set of thoughts in our heads, which might be corrected by better, truer knowledge. If, for Sloterdijk, "to act against better knowledge" defines the cynical tenor of our "global situation," for Žižek this underscores the ways ideology is *always* materialized in action.[27] "We must avoid the simple metaphors of demasking" because we are "fetishists in practice," not "belief."[28]

Extrapolating from Sloterdijk and Žižek, then, we might say that "cynicism" is dangerous because it feels like ideology *critique* (a penetrating view of hidden truths and deceptive ideologies) but it is more like *ideology* full stop. As Žižek argues:

> Ideology is not a dreamlike illusion that we build to escape insupportable reality;…it is…an "illusion" which structures our effective, real social relations and thereby masks some insupportable, real, impossible kernel (conceptualized by Ernesto Laclau and Chantal Mouffe as "antagonism": a traumatic social division which cannot be symbolized). The function of ideology is not to offer us a point of escape from our reality but to offer us the social reality itself as an escape from some traumatic, real kernel. (44)

The passing reference to Laclau and Mouffe's notion of "antagonism" provides all the positive content Žižek will give to this "kernel" from which we escape. But it's clear that cynicism is conceived here as emphatically *not* a way of seeing through an illusion to reality. Rather, it is an aggressively realistic attitude that allows social reality itself to be experienced as an escape, which in turn acclimates us to that reality's social divisions: "antagonisms" sustained and exploited by existing political and economic structures of capitalism, imperialism, etc.

This conception of cynical reason as an ideological lure helps us to question the posture of disillusioned reason adopted by Twain's early works, and by the prosecution and public during the Guiteau trial. The trial's onlookers, for example, all knew Guiteau was a symptom of rampant corruption and nepotism. Everyone also knew his insanity was a crafty dodge. But the certainty that these forms of knowledge constituted how things really were was of questionable value in the battle against abuses of political power. The "disappointed office seeker" as a character type dramatized the insane excesses of party politics, offering reformers a final, crucial push to bring about the passage of 1883's Pendleton Act, which established a merit-based system of appointment for positions within the federal bureaucracy.[29] However, for some historians, the cleansing and purifying of the civil service spurred on by Garfield's assassination served to radically *contract* opportunities for political involvement. New restrictions on patronage removed an incentive for political participation, and the rhetoric of civil service reformers' assault on political corruption was easily reworked as a critique of "political parties' continuing exploitation of ignorance and venality among voters."[30] This, in turn, justified increasing restrictions on voter eligibility. Vigorously rejecting the illusion that party politics was a contest of principles and ideals, the cynical public "woke up" to an increasingly regimented bureaucracy and contracted citizen agency.

There is also a second cost of cynicism, which Andreas Huyssen—in his introduction to the English translation of Sloterdijk's work—takes to be, ultimately, the more important point: "Even more objectionable to Sloterdijk is the...problematic reification and depersonalization of the opponent:...enlightenment as a war of consciousness aimed at annihilat[ion]."[31] This structuring aggression undermines the idea that "*voluntary* consensus" is at once the Enlightenment's "methodological core and its moral ideal" (12). Sloterdijk notes that it's easy to laugh at this "sublimely peaceful event, where, under the impact of plausible reasons, old, now untenable positions are given up" (13). However, he also suggests that the "academic idyll" of "free dialogue" may be a necessary "healing fiction" (14). A cynical worldview has given up the fantasy of eager pupils ready to be disabused of their errors, though not in favor of a more measured optimism for rational persuasion. Instead, everywhere the cynic looks he "discovers extrarational mechanisms of opinion: interests, passions, fixations, illusions" (18). The utopia of free dialogue is surmounted, but it is replaced with a form of ever more aggressive critique. This cynical critical consciousness seeks "to operate with precision, to reveal the opponents' intentions" (15). It is an aggressive, surgical unmasking.

Sloterdijk provides multiple names for this forceful and bitter mode of rationality, which he designates "dirty realism," (193) "pugnacious reason" (543), and of course "cynical reason." But he is vague about the costs of this aggressive hermeneutic system, noting only that it "risks alienating the opponent more deeply" (19). Nonetheless, it's clear that, for Sloterdijk, the enlightenment procedure of ferreting out error, lie, and ideology has short-circuited, demanding that others' myriad mystifications be laid bare with such righteous fury that the critic becomes carried away to the point of paranoia. The cynic now sees cunning artifice everywhere. Instead of converting, convincing, or persuading, cynical reason reifies an opponent as a pathological specimen of false consciousness. By the time the Enlightenment goal of freeing oneself from illusion has become a more widespread disillusionment, "reason" has become indistinguishable from passionate hostility.

My goal here in tracing Sloterdijk's account of modern cynicism is not to take up his claim that this worldview characterizes modern consciousness writ large, and even less to endorse or contest his more specific claim that modern cynicism's contours first come fully into view in the culture and politics of Weimar Germany. But I would suggest that the "cynicism" early readers detected in Twain's fiction, and the form Sloterdijk delineates, share much in common—above all, the frantic energy of the novel's relentless unmaskings (of piety, principle, etc.). Further, the self-defeating energies of late Enlightenment's cynical methodology help us to understand the stakes of Twain's indirect involvement in the Guiteau trial. There, as I will show in the coming section, commentary on the trial that adopted a "cynical" tone consistently aligned itself with justice; the cynical observer could see through the law's overly complex and sentimental mechanisms for reduced sentencing to the simple fact of guilt or innocence. However, this disillusioned confidence had a cost. The cynical impatience with others' duped feelings and procedural obfuscation segues effortlessly into a ferocious demand for instantaneous justice.

Judge Lynch

In my first chapter I showed how much of Twain's early work lambasted the claims of "temporary," "emotional," "moral," and "volitional" insanity. In the context of Victoria Woodhull's "free love" movement, emotional insanity offered Twain and Harriet Beecher Stowe a ready rubric for pathologizing counterhegemonic affective publics.[32] As Sloterdijk now helps us see, the cynical posture of revealing the venality and irrationality behind an opponent's ideals pivots almost imperceptibly into an aggressive diagnosis of that opponent's pathology, which had real consequences for those caught in the juridico-medical net of "insanity." Twain's and Stowe's cynicism was directed toward the excesses of reform idealism, which both authors denounced and debunked for their "crack-brained" theories. Their novels loosely used insanity as a way of condescending to and deflating utopian idealism. In this they were not alone: Even Walt Whitman could not resist a wry jab at the free lovers gathered in Vermont in 1858, whom he dismissed as "amiable lunatics."[33]

As a legal problem, however, detractors argued the insanity defense revealed a larger pattern in which misguided humanitarian attempts to sympathize with the mentally ill created an atmosphere of diminished social responsibility. That is to say, this related form of cynical critique was directed less at a specific reform movement's idealistic excesses and more at a wider culture of corruption and the legal system, enabled by gullible masses, that sustained it. The chief expert for the prosecution in Guiteau's trial would offer a concise description of this outlook, warning that "a growing tendency...exist[s] in our day to contract the limits of human responsibility. A whole school has risen up, whose aim ... [is] to reduce all the phenomena of voluntary and mental action to problems within the domain of physical law and natural processes."[34] As early as 1870, Twain had laid the rhetorical groundwork for this line of attack in essays responding to a series of high-profile trials that employed the insanity defense, the details of which he later incorporated into the plot of *The Gilded Age*. This trajectory in Twain's thinking again reveals the familiar "cynical," pessimistic voice that critics have so long celebrated as the source of his most powerful insights. But it also reveals another dark side to the cynical posture of disillusioned clarity: the intimate relation between cynicism as a posture of disenchanted reason and an aggressive, even violent insistence on swift and unfeeling justice as a counterpoint to "sentimental" hesitation.[35]

Evidence of this link was on display in my earlier discussion of Twain and Warner's sudden and unexpected narration of Laura Hawkins's punishment at the hands of a boisterous mob in *The Gilded Age*. But no work reveals the violence of cynical reason more directly than 1870's "Our Precious Lunatic," a short story that responded to the real-life trial of Daniel McFarland for the murder of Albert D. Richardson, his wife's lover. McFarland was acquitted on grounds of insanity. In the fictionalized version, Twain indulges in a violent fantasy in which the overly compassionate jury immediately pays for its misguided sentimentality:

> [T]hree tremendous cheers...told where the sympathies of the court and people were. Then a hundred pursed lips were advanced to kiss the liberated prisoner...but presto! with a maniac's own quickness and...fury the lunatic assassin of Richardson fell upon his friends with teeth and nails...and rent and sundered bodies, till nearly a hundred citizens were reduced to mere quivering heaps of fleshy odds and ends.   (C, 386)

If "mania" denotes a form of hyperesthesia, or abnormal sensitivity, Twain implicitly suggests that the law itself should be more anesthetic, or less sensitive to the excesses of emotion that align the "maniac" with the over-passionate "sympathies of the court and people."[36] In a later letter, Twain sarcastically described the characteristics lawyers seek in a prospective juror: "an intellectual vacuum, attached to a melting heart, and perfectly macaronian bowels of compassion" (C, 549). In "Our Precious Lunatic," these "macaronian bowels" are rent by the hands of the maniac, and citizens—already too corporeal in their excessive bodily responses—are reduced to quivering heaps of flesh. While a plea of emotional insanity helped McFarland escape prosecution, Twain holds the jurors and spectators to stricter account. They are summarily executed on account of their emotional stupor, not forgiven because of it.[37]

In Twain's imagination, strict mechanisms for assessing individual responsibility culminate perversely in swift violence, from the slaughter of the crowd in "Our Precious Lunatic" to Laura Hawkins's death in *The Gilded Age*. So, too, in the Guiteau trial, the desire for a kind of immediate, common- sense justice led quickly to the lynch mob. Public opinion was clear: Guiteau was guilty and should be executed with the greatest possible haste. One editorialist extolled the virtues of "an American judge whose decisions are almost always just, and whose work is always well done. His name is Judge Lynch; and...he has [a job] waiting for him in Washington."[38] Crowds eager to murder the assassin quickly formed, anxious to bypass what was perceived, à la Twain's earliest attacks on the insanity defense, as a legal system oversensitive to the humanity of the defendant and thus capable of complicating a simple case with excessive sympathy and legal loopholes.[39] Twain would later condemn lynching as an "epidemic of bloody insanities," but his own impatience with forms of emotion or irrationality could seem to lead directly to an endorsement of such simple, immediate violence.[40]

Echoing the vitriol of Twain's call for swift justice but promoting the mob from debased sentimental public to righteous avenger, the prosecution in Guiteau's trial went so far as to extol the virtues of mob passion over the hopeless quagmire of the legal process and the weary work of presenting and refuting evidence:

> What is your mob?...I am no mob man but I never yet knew the mob however much to be reprehended that had not behind it the highest forms of human passion and human sentiment. [Guiteau] feared...that mob....It does not dawdle over a case week after week and allow interjections and interruptions....There is nobody there to...enforce constitutional or any other provisions. But this great monster growing out of the better side of humanity, says or would have said: "Here is a crime against God, against nature, and against law, and we will sacrifice this wretch."   (R, 1875)

The prosecution's rhetoric is remarkable for its crafted slipperiness. In one moment, the attorney disclaims allegiance to the unreasoning mob but in the next recasts passionate action as the height of reason.[41] The defense, meanwhile, works quickly to counter this picture of virtuous and reasonable mob action, reminding the jury that, in questioning the reality of Guiteau's madness, the nation must not indulge in its own form of insanity:

> If it is possible by your verdict to arrest this tide of public clamor and revenge, this mob law which my brother Davidge has lauded before you,...wherein without reason or reflection, and simply influenced by desire for vengeance...if I can by my efforts stay that tide until reason returns, I am here to do it, so that we shall never have it said in this country...that here we have done what was done in England when Bellingham was rushed to the scaffold in a week's time.   (R, 2144)

Making a canny if ultimately futile appeal to American pride, Guiteau's lawyer urged the jury to be more calm-headed and restrained than those Brits who clamored for the blood of Prime Minister Spencer Perceval's murderer. But as the appeal to "Judge Lynch" reveals, at least some onlookers appeared to think hasty extrajudicial violence was the most properly American form of justice.

Twain's work helps us see that, in Guiteau's trial, America was faced with two versions of legal reason. One was a vision of reasonable immediacy, which Twain elsewhere referred to as "simple, straight forward justice unencumbered with nonsense."[42] From this perspective, Guiteau was guilty of murder and so should be killed without excessive hand wringing.[43] In this formulation, rationality is represented by the passionate mob, whose unthinking violence aligned it precisely with the crazy murderer himself.[44] The alternative version of reason was the formal logic of the legal process, the role of which was to introduce procedural obstacles to the execution of such hurried, emotional, and potentially violent forms of judgment. But this brand of reason could also appear mad, aligned as it was with the obscurantism of elite bureaucracy, including the insanity defense, that provided routes of escape for nearly any crime.[45] In a dynamic that Twain thus endorsed but also helped to critique, the Guiteau trial offers the quintessential version of what I called in the Introduction a "fit of reason," in which the models of rationality serving as normative goals seem always on the verge of equally emotional forms of madness.[46]

Interlude II: Cynicism or Kynicism?

In *The Gilded Age*, a cynical mode of critique venting an angry suspicion of elite corruption slips readily into a critique of the pathology of democratic sovereignty writ large. Everywhere Twain looked, he discovered fresh evidence of blind popular enthusiasm, as he sought to expose the cynical politicians and plutocrats who used this emotionality as cover. In the trial of Charles Guiteau, however, a similar style of critique that drew explicitly on Twain's work authorizes a relentless attribution of rational motives—indeed, the capacity to "unite the Republican party" and fundamentally remap the "features of American politics"—to a low-level clerk with signs of mental illness. Again, as in much of Twain's work, revealing the cynical reason hiding behind the mask of emotionality leads to demands for immediate, clear-headed "justice." Guiteau's putative rationality was understood to justify his execution by any means necessary.

But is it helpful or fair to see the imbrication of violence and reason I am tracking here as indicative of a problem with "cynicism"? While I have already discussed Sloterdijk's account of the deficiencies of modern cynicism, a range of critics and philosophers beginning with Sloterdijk (and Michel Foucault pursuing an independent but parallel track) has also returned to the classical origins of cynic philosophy. They find in the figure of Diogenes and his progeny an alternate mode of cynicism—often denoted kynicism or capital-C Cynicism—that shares with modem cynicism its penetrating view of sham and pretense, but without the aggression or debilitating pessimism. This truer or more radical cynicism, it is suggested, does not fall prey to apathy. Instead it cultivates postures of carnivalesque humor, Zen forbearance, or performative asceticism, which allow the cynic to act as a disruptive and productive force in the public sphere.

This schematization might seem to offer a way of redeeming Twain's oeuvre from charges that his texts are tainted by cynicism's internal contradictions. We might, for example, describe his works as navigating between cynicism and kynicism—apathetic in their cynical knowledge at one moment, subversively comic and disruptive in another. Yet I join those critics who are more convinced by Sloterdijk's analysis of the shortcomings of modern cynicism than by the ideal kynicism he invokes to take its place. As discussed, Sloterdijk's modern cynic knows very well that selfishness, violence, and exploitation hide behind public virtue, but he continues to tolerate and support the structures that sustain this hypocrisy. Against this, Sloterdijk calls for a cheeky, raucous critique that hearkens back to Diogenes' bawdy and bodily provocations. As one recent interlocutor notes, however, it is difficult to differentiate the provocation offered by Sloterdijk's "Kynic" from a Bakhtinian notion of the carnivalesque. Both concepts threaten to hyperbolize the agency of the rebel critic who can upend staid ideological formations through sheer outrageousness.[47] As another skeptical reader puts it bluntly, "it is hard to believe that laughter of any type is really going to solve the world's problems."[48]

It may be, then, that Sloterdijk's proposal for a reinvigorated kynicism is overly optimistic—or at the very least, imprecise—about the subversive power of satire. But more importantly I would suggest that the move to counter bad, modern, apathetic cynicism with good, classical, carnivalesque kynicism misses something useful in the modern understanding of the term. One of cynicism's virtues as a concept, despite its instability, is precisely its capacity to describe an opposition to hegemonic power while also flagging real constraints on critical agency.[49] Because "cynicism" evokes a mode of intensely engaged ideology critique while also associating that critique with lethargy and indifference, it always draws attention to the affective dimension of critical interpretation.

For some, of course, the bitter intensity of "ideology critique" has suggested that it is past its prime. Bruno Latour, in particular, has declared ideology critique to be "out of steam," and Rita Felski has echoed this concern by drawing attention to the aggression and self-defeating negativity of critique's defining postures of "digging down" and "standing back."[50] These provocations to find other interpretive modalities are timely, but exhaustion and disaffection are not necessarily signs of critique's irrelevance. After all, even indispensable acts of critical exposure might leave one feeling depleted. This, as I discussed in my second chapter, is one of the most disturbing lessons to be gleaned from Henry Adams's *Democracy*: revelations of corruption or injustice are rarely invigorating. At a moment when critics have begun (or begun again) to question the limits of "critique," the intense critical energy *and* simultaneous paralysis indicated by "cynicism" foreground questions of agency that always haunt a hermeneutics of suspicion without—and this is the crucial point—thereby invalidating all forms of critical distrust. This virtue of "cynicism," such as it is, is lost if we abandon vernacular cynicism (what we might call modern or simply plain-old cynicism) to celebrate and recuperate a classical kynicism theorized as a heroic form of satiric resistance.

In other words, rather than simply denounce Twain's status as cynic or affirm his role as kynic, I am suggesting it's more productive to see how Twain complicates the affective self-evidence of cynicism's uniformity as a concept by disarticulating the diverse elements that live uncomfortably side-by-side within modern cynicism. Cynicism is paradoxically defined by the intensity of its own involvement in politics (expressed aversively as bitterness, pessimism, anger, exasperation, etc.), and a deep suspicion of others' public affects. It can suggest heroic acts of penetrating critique, a defeatist and self-pitying apathy, and a ruthlessly aggressive gesture of critical unmasking.

What's more, cynicism as a rationalist temperament is perhaps the clearest reminder that denunciations of others' political emotions usually do more to highlight that all politics is inevitably emotional. That is, understanding the tension between cynicism and optimism in Twain's work requires us to see cynicism, which is often opposed to "sentimental" idealism (as it was for Twain), as a peculiar strain of sentimental politics. Like the sentimentality associated with much antebellum literature, particularly *Uncle Tom's Cabin*, we have seen that cynicism links feeling with justice. Twain's fiction—and his admirers in the Guiteau trial— assert again and again that if members of the public could just get right with their feelings, shake off their propensity toward mawkish sentimentality, and gird themselves for the tough task ahead, justice could be done. Because this link between feeling and justice appears to renounce the seductions of naïve emotion, cynicism looks like sentiment's antonym. But if cynicism is as much a temperament as a critical procedure, and if it identifies that mood as a way of being political by feeling right, then we can see that cynicism substitutes suspicion for sympathy as the sentimental feeling par excellence. And if the fellow-feeling of antebellum sentimentality vents impatience with official politics via fantasies of domestic influence, cynicism's exasperation with the inefficiencies of the law mirrors and intensifies this anti-institutional gesture by way of fantasies of extrajudicial violence.[51]

Twain's work thus reveals how ostensibly rational forms of political discourse constitute their own kind of sentimentality. Resisting the move from denouncing cynicism to celebrating kynicism allows us to see that modern cynicism's structuring tension is a virtue of sorts: If we keep the rationalist aspirations *and* affective cost of cynicism in view, we can see that Twain's often-denounced and sometimes-celebrated "cynicism" captures an anxious, quotidian dimension of political emotion, wherein intense engagement might cure apathy or produce it. If Twain's work "reveals" this dynamic, however, this revelation is generally unwitting. *The Gilded Age* gives few clues that its tone and its critical aspirations could ever be at cross-purposes. In the next section, however, I will argue that Twain's later work shows signs of a more direct and purposeful meditation on the cost of his critical temperaments, as Twain plots "cynicism" on an affective scale that ranges from bitter paralysis to naïve optimism.

Optimism and Insanity: On *The American Claimant*

In 1892, ten years after Guiteau's trial, Twain published *The American Claimant*. In this novel, Twain permanently relocates Sellers to Washington and emphasizes the connection to Guiteau by engaging Sellers in the same manic office seeking that characterized the real-life assassin's time in that city. Early in the novel, Sellers reveals to his friend Washington Hawkins that he moved to the capital to "go Minister to St. James" but sadly arrived "*A day too late*, Washington.... [Y]es, sir, the place had been filled.... I offered to compromise and go to Paris. The President was very sorry and all that, but *that* place, you see, didn't belong to the West, so there I was again."[52] Sellers's aspirations directly recall Guiteau's much-ridiculed claim to the French consulate, as though Twain sought to correct the ambiguity in his earlier portrait of Sellers and to emphasize Sellers's self-serving demands for a share of the spoils. At first glance, the Sellers on display early in *Claimant* looks much more like the character drawn by the prosecution in Guiteau's trial: a figure of calculating, essentially rational egotism who assumes a posture of self-sacrifice and deluded political confidence. This Sellers invites the bemused laughter of an audience familiar with gracious so-called offers to take positions of enormous prestige and compensation, with Washington Hawkins, Laura Hawkins's adoptive brother, serving as the naïve dupe who believes such selfless posturing: "And so, after coming here, against your inclination, to satisfy your sense of patriotic duty and appease a selfish public clamor, you get absolutely nothing for it" (*A*, 32). Read this way, *The American Claimant* appears to ratchet up the cynical intensity and, for many readers, stands as Twain's most vitriolic satire of republicanism, ridiculing a faith in American democracy.[53]

These initial signs suggest that Twain sought to complete the transformation begun in the Guiteau trial, ultimately turning Sellers into a Guiteau-like figure of delusional egotism. But the bulk of the novel works to distance Sellers from suspicions of self-interest. In fact, the novel generally delights in Sellers's generosity and resilient optimism, which persist despite the corruption that this otherwise cynical portrait of democracy exposes. Much of the plot, for example, recounts the exploits of Lord Berkeley, a young British aristocrat drawn to the ideal of equality and a potential distant relative of Sellers. The young man has been reading radical political tracts by Lord Tanzy of Tollmache—roughly, Lord Tanzy of "Crazymaking"—that lead him to shed his rank, adopt the pseudonym Howard Tracy, and disembark for America's egalitarian utopia.[54] Tracy's father, upon hearing his son's plan to go to America, declares: "I believe you are insane, my son," which is to say, "Ab-so-lutely cra-zy—ab-so-lutely!" (*A*, 21–2). The novel derives its bitter humor from how thoroughly America cures Tracy of this madness, forcing him to confront a political system in which "competency was no recommendation; political backing, without competency, was worth six of it" (*A*, 104). Tracy, like Sellers, is an office seeker, but his experiences lead him to the conclusion that "there is an aristocracy of position here, and an aristocracy of prosperity, and apparently there is also an aristocracy of the ins as opposed to the outs, and I am with the outs" (*A*, 130). Tracy's father, horrified by his son's republican fantasy, does not need to wait long for the "cure of [this] insane dream" (*A*, 237).

In *The American Claimant*, then, "insanity" names an overly enthusiastic devotion to American democracy, and regaining one's sanity requires accepting the reality that everyone in America is not "free and equal" (*A*, 129). As such, the novel reproduces in remarkably condensed form a cynical critique of ideology: If only we'd wake up and see clearly, the falsity of precious "ideals" will reveal themselves. In this often-bitter novel, however, Twain narrates Sellers's fantasies with affectionate glee in part because the latter's enthusiasm is immune to such reality. Confronted with his failure to find a place in government, Sellers goes to extraordinary imaginative heights to avoid concluding that money and influence are the only routes to political power. Denied a series of appointments, Sellers fantasizes that he has been granted a position that bypasses party politics entirely, an appointment decreed directly by popular fiat:

> What was due to a man...made permanently and diplomatically sacred, so to speak, by having been connected, temporarily, through solicitation, with every single diplomatic post in the roster of this government...? By the common voice of this community, by acclamation of the people...I was named Perpetual Member of the Diplomatic Body representing the multifarious sovereignties and civilizations of the globe near the republican court of the United States of America. (*A*, 33)

Depicting Sellers as pursuing "every single diplomatic post" was sure to call to the minds of most readers Guiteau's manic office seeking, and Sellers's claim to an eternal, global ambassadorship surely marks him as somewhat insane.[55] Yet Twain's tone is hardly one of moral condemnation. In fact, Twain is far more consistent in portraying Sellers's sincerity and idealism in *The American Claimant* than he was in *The Gilded Age*, maintaining a sense that Sellers is unusually generous and well meaning, and resilient in his willingness to help others without recompense. As Sellers's wife relates: "[H]e's been shamefully treated, many times, by people that had used him for a ladder to climb up by.... Any selfish tramp out of nobody knows where can come and put up a poor mouth and walk right into his heart with his boots on" (*A*, 37). In light of his propensity for self-sacrifice, Sellers starts to look like a genuine, if misguided, office seeker hoping to serve the American people, as his emotional insanity is repeatedly manifested in symptoms of liberality and creativity: "when his sentimentals are up, he's a numskull, and there's no knowing what extravagance he'll contrive" (*A*, 88). Far from the antisentimental assault on the emotional insanity of "naïve optimism" that some read Sellers as designed to evoke, it is when Sellers's "sentimentals" suspend his capacity for rational action that he emerges most strikingly as the novel's hero and emotional center—even as his political schemes remain tainted by reckless ambition and even as they neglect to offer any substantive response to the failures of American democracy.[56]

Assuming Twain was thinking of Guiteau as he returned to Sellers, then the figure of Sellers in *The American Claimant* offers a strange twist on the discourse of insanity that played out in Guiteau's trial. Reversing the prosecution's efforts to paint portraits of Sellers and Guiteau as shrewd political mercenaries, Twain reimagines the delusional patronage seeker as an unexpected figure of optimism.

In the process, Twain was surprisingly true to Guiteau. Guiteau, after all, seems to
have been genuinely insane; there is little evidence that his lunacy was a mask for
calculated rational self-interest, and the only people he ever fully convinced of his
rationality were the twelve jurists who had him hanged.[57] Guiteau consistently
held that his crime was an act of inspired devotion to a higher ideal and spent
much of the trial contradicting his defense attorney's portrait of his madness,
echoing an earlier letter in which he detailed his impending greatness: "If a man
have big ideas he is usually deemed *insane*" (*R*, 686). Civil service reformers were
quick to declare the president's assassination the "logical consequence of a political
system predicated on self-aggrandizement, not principle," yet it was precisely
Guiteau's vocabulary of "principle," "big ideas," and "inspiration" that made him an
object of popular fascination and that marked him most clearly as insane.[58] What's
more, before Guiteau gained the oft-repeated designation of "disappointed office
seeker" in subsequent decades' historical accounts, he was widely considered crazy
precisely because of his immunity to disappointment.[59]

In other words, *The American Claimant*'s real provocation may be its recovery
of this occluded, optimistic aspect of Guiteau's personality, rewriting Sellers more
consistently as a dreamer inspired by bigger ideals. In *Claimant*, Twain's depiction
of Sellers focuses on the difference between delusional schemes undertaken as
expressions of such ideals and the faux insanity of frantic self-aggrandizement.
For example, in a rare instance of entrepreneurial triumph, Sellers invents a game,
Pigs in the Clover, that sparks a nationwide fad:

> The business of the country had now come to a standstill. . . . Everybody, indeed,
> could be seen from morning till midnight, absorbed in one deep project and
> purpose. . . —to pen those pigs, work out that puzzle successfully; that all gayety,
> all cheerfulness had departed from the nation . . . and all faces were drawn, dis-
> tressed, and furrowed with the signs of age and trouble, and marked with the still
> sadder signs of mental decay and incipient madness.   (*A*, 250)

In moments like this one, which recalls the public that formed around Laura
Hawkins's trial, Twain reveals himself to be keenly aware of the operations by which
a kind of incipient madness might constitute an emergent public. This public looks
something like Mark Seltzer's broader notion of the "pathological public sphere,"
the boundaries of which are destabilized by the traumatic scenes (accidents,
crimes, and other atrocities) that serve as the occasion for their formation.[60]
In Twain's version, the total self-absorption and isolation of those engaged in
Sellers's puzzle are paradoxically connected: "all the populations" united in "one
deep project and purpose"—the absurd task of penning those pigs.[61] Twain, however, presents this as a vision of national unity founded on the empty competition
of a parlor game, an insanity-inducing quest for whatever self-aggrandizement
such a petty victory might afford.[62]

Twain emphasizes, moreover, that Sellers is not content with the game's success.
Faced with financial gain so significant it promises to line his friends' pockets as

well as his own, Sellers is disappointed nonetheless by the absence of a higher ideal driving this national unity, complaining: "That's just the way things go. A man invents a thing which could revolutionize the arts...and bless the earth, and who will bother with it or show any interest in it?...But you invent some worthless thing to amuse yourself with, and would throw it away if let alone, and all of a sudden the whole world makes a snatch for it and out crops a fortune" (A, 250). In search of a project with more revolutionary potential, Sellers becomes obsessed with the population of Siberia, where the uniquely virtuous denizens have been "sifted, sifted, sifted, by myriads of trained experts....[W]henever they catch a man, woman, or child that has got any brains or education or character, they ship that person straight to Siberia" (A, 186). This obsession leads Sellers to an ambitious plan: "to buy Siberia and start a Republic" (A, 185). When Sellers describes this republican plot, he glows with the light of inspired insanity: "his breast began to heave and his eye to burn, under the impulse of strong emotion. Then his words began to stream forth, with constantly increasing energy and fire, and he rose to his feet as if to give himself larger freedom" (A, 186–7). By the novel's concluding paragraph, Sellers, engrossed in his utopian project, is far from the self-interested Guiteaulike office seeker he first seemed, expressing instead an unbridled generosity and optimism: "I will send you a greeting...for I will waft a vast sun-spot across the disk like drifting smoke, and you will know it for my love-sign, and will say 'Mulberry Sellers throws us a kiss across the universe'" (A, 273).[63] In seeking to fund his Siberian republic with the proceeds from a weather-altering machine, Sellers undoubtedly looks crazy. Yet his craziness is unexpectedly desirable—the only positive attachment to political ideals that remains possible in an utterly cynical age.[64]

As strange as it may seem to embody optimism in a figure of delusional egotism, this is precisely how Alphonso Lingis begins his recent meditation on hope. For Lingis, "hope" is always "against the evidence," and thus the most hopeful figure is he who, like Guiteau, has no grounds for his optimistic self-evaluation: "I am always struck with those people who have great hopes and who are in fact no better endowed than anyone else—they are not more beautiful or more gifted or more intelligent or more healthy or more strong. So hope doesn't come out of those things."[65] Indeed, recuperating the counterfactual optimism of Sellers's insanity puts Twain in line with a range of recent critics who have responded to aforementioned concerns about the bitterness of critique by seeking new resources for political optimism.

We might say that Twain sees in Sellers something like what Chris Castiglia has called "marvelousness," a capacity to imagine alternative futures, which was rejected in antebellum literature and politics' rush to privatize and institutionalize democracy: "The public orders of the state had no need for the capacity to marvel— to be surprised out of the expected and the already known, to see the unimaginable as if it were real."[66] It's as though marvelousness, due to its expulsion from politics, resurfaces here in its only available idiom: madness. This madness carries with it a positive valence buried beneath the anti-romantic impulse of what Castiglia calls "institutionalism." Even more surprising, this marvelous craziness emerges as a *facet of* institutional life, since Sellers's optimism alternately fixates on and breaks with the institutions of formal politics and governance. It is, of course, far from clear whether Sellers's insane optimism can do the work Twain seems to desire: Sellers's democratic dreams remain cockeyed and unattainable, and his idealism appears as an admixture of egotism and delusion. Even so, Twain's attachment to Sellers ultimately serves to disclose a double bind faced by Americans of the Gilded Age: a moment when an enervating, cynical detachment looked like the only sane response to political corruption, and insane idealism was the only model for political optimism.

Conclusion

Throughout this chapter I have argued that Twain's works offer tonal training in a mode of cynical critique that poses as rational but is distinctively sentimental: His fiction implies a causal link between feelings of shrewd discernment, exasperation, and suspicion and the conditions for legal and political justice. Based on the references to Twain's character Colonel Sellers during the trial of Guiteau, not to mention the continued popularity of "the Gilded Age" as a phrase and cultural reference point, it seems many were listening. Though I have argued that Peter Sloterdijk's relatively recent conceptualization of cynicism as "enlightened false consciousness" helps understand the contours of this cynicism, it's worth noting this reading also continues a much older conversation about the tone of Twain's critical voice. In 1920 Van Wyck Brooks declared, "To those who are interested in American life and letters there has been no question of greater significance . . . than the pessimism of Mark Twain."[67] For Brooks, the negativity of Twain's oeuvre could not possibly stem from political commitments; he asserted we cannot "say that Mark Twain's pessimism was due to anything so external as the hatred of tyranny" (9). Instead, Brooks claimed it was "perfectly plain" that the "far more personal root" was Twain's disappointment in the aftermath of his psychic castration by a prudish wife. Bernard de Voto set the stage for much later Twain criticism by redeeming that pessimism as an insightful, critical cynicism in his famous rebuttal: "Pessimism is only the name that men of weak nerves give to wisdom."[68]

De Voto's claim for Twain's pessimism as a form of knowledge benefits from what Michael Taussig has described as a widespread tendency to correlate "lack of hope with being smart, or lack of hope with profundity."[69] But not all criticism has been so sanguine about the relation between a pessimistic tone and critical wisdom. Without using the term, John Carlos Rowe offers one of the better recent accounts of Twain's cynicism. Rowe challenges "the romantic idealist assumption that rigorous reflection on the process of thought and representation constitutes in itself a critique of social reality."[70] While Rowe never quite links his chapter on

The Gilded Age to the main strain of his book's argument, he implicitly suggests that Twain's novel articulates a particularly apathetic version of what he calls "aesthetic dissent." In Twain's paired historical romances of *The Gilded Age* and *Pudd'nhead Wilson*, Rowe suggests, the speculative economy has so thoroughly enslaved both "freed" African Americans and the white working class that literature can only "wisecrack," a form of social criticism reduced to wry observations about the irredeemable corruption of the age.[71] Unlike Sloterdijk's longed-for radical "cheekiness," the wisecrack is easily ignored.

Rowe's reading is perceptive, although I'd submit that things are both better and worse than he suggests. By engaging with the perceived emotionality of the women's movement, Twain revealed himself to be very aware of other forms of active dissent; indeed, he denigrates them. But the longer history of Twain's work suggests a hesitant effort to examine the affective economy of this apathetic cynicism. If the "wisecrack" signals a satiric mode neutralized by its own apathy, Twain draws attention to the affective dimensions of critique by juxtaposing his trademark cynicism with crazy forms of indefatigable optimism. In other words, Twain actively theorizes and draws attention to how the tone of a critique can both enhance and undercut the substance of its intervention.

In his earlier critiques of late-nineteenth-century democracy, Twain rejected all political emotion as a species of madness, a forfeiture of free will that contributed to the erosion of legal norms of accountability. Even as Twain labeled so much of American democracy insane, he continually revised what this term meant, later using the trope of insanity to imagine an alternative to a strain of reason that, in the Guiteau trial, found its expression in fantasies of mob justice. In the face of this violently rationalist political pessimism, the often cynical Twain reasserted Sellers's eccentric idealism and optimism. Conceptually, this move is surprising, as we have come to understand cynicism and optimism as mutually exclusive terms; as Sloterdijk puts it, "a consciousness diseased with Enlightenment…refuses cheap optimism….In the new cynicism, we see a detached negativity which scarcely allows itself any hope, at most a little irony and self-pity."[72] However, at the center of two of America's supposedly most cynical, most pessimistic political novels, we find Sellers, who remains the same "scheming, generous, good-hearted, moon-shiny, hopeful, no-account failure he always was," a figure of always disappointed but unrelenting optimism.[73]

Twain's investigation of disappointment, cynicism, and optimism was well-timed: Sellers is a frustrated spoilsman, just as Guiteau was famously a "disappointed office seeker," in an era when George Beard, one of the nation's leading psychologists, warned of the damaging effects of political disappointment:

> To-day, just after the inauguration, those whose minds are philosophically bent, may well occupy themselves with making an estimate of the cost in brain and nerve of these months of excitement and disappointment; for it is the very essence of politics to disappoint those who have to do with it, and disappointment, like love, is one of the most expensive of human emotions.[74]

For Beard, the nervous strain of democratic participation made it an undertaking best avoided: "one of my patients informed me, to my alarm, that he was getting interested in politics....I said to him...fold your arms and go to bed."[75] *The Gilded Age* and *The American Claimant* similarly depict political participation as producing a type of madness: a bipolar nervous disposition that oscillates between too much or too little optimism, too much or too little pessimism, or what William James would later refer to as "circular insanity."[76]

Twain's alternately idealistic and cynical texts are afflicted by a version of this insanity, although they do not join Beard in prescribing a defensive apathy and bed rest. Instead, I argue that Twain's greatest contribution to political thought may be his commitment to undergoing the emotional and intellectual labor—even to the edge of madness—required to articulate a penetrating political critique without detaching from the legal and political institutions he criticized.[77] In the process, he expresses an ambivalent or self-contradictory diagnosis of the peculiar insanity of Gilded Age politics, judging it the product of an excess of either emotion or cynical reason. But surely Twain would have known how to escape responsibility for these grave charges: "With these evidences of a wandering mind present to the reader, am I to be debarred from offering the customary plea of Insanity?" (*C*, 355).

Exhaustion

{ Coda }

Election Fatigue
POLITICAL EMOTION IN SPACE AND TIME

In July 2016, six in ten Americans reported being "worn out" by election coverage.[1] But even this widespread "voter fatigue" pales in comparison to the "post-election stress disorder" that set in after Donald Trump's victory.[2] Given the discomfort brought on by intense political seasons, it's amusing—and, perhaps, disheartening—to encounter the hopeful fervor that characterized Walt Whitman's nineteenth-century musings on the presidential calendar. Whitman lobbied repeatedly and unsuccessfully for the term "Presidentiad," a way of measuring national time, to be added to the *Century Dictionary*:

> I have almost been disposed to write to Gilder or one of the fellows myself, cautioning them not to omit my word "Presidentiad." Oh! that is eminently a word to be cherished—adopted. Its allusion, the four years of the Presidency: its origin that of the Olympiad—but as I flatter myself, bravely appropriate, where not another one word, signifying the same thing, exists![3]

Whitman first deployed his coinage in the poem "Year of Meteors," where the term unites an atmospheric event ("YEAR of meteors! brooding year!"), the lead- up to the 1860 election ("I would sing your contest for the 19th Presidentiad"), with the execution of John Brown ("I would sing how an old man, tall, with white hair, mounted the scaffold in Virginia...").[4] While "administration" might serve per-fectly well to denote a four-year presidential term, Whitman's promotion of "Presidentiad" underscores the temporal unit's wider cultural significance.

A "Presidentiad" is thus coterminous with—but not a mere synonym for, as it would need to be given Whitman's suspicion of official politics—a quadrennial period. Peter Coviello reminds us that, for Whitman, "The 'real America' is not to be found in the government...because governments deal only in proclamations and in strictures" rather than the more important fact of "specifically affective attachments" among strangers.[5] "Presidentiad" allows Whitman to explore how national life is synchronized to the rhythms of the natural world and to official calendric time (interrupted by violence and other historical events) while ultimately elevating the figure of the poet, who can elucidate the embodied temporalities of national life. That is, thinking in terms of a "Presidentiad" helps make politics warm and intimate: "Your chants, O year all mottled with evil and good! year of forebodings! year of the youth I love!"[6]

With our own frazzled nerves and Whitman's enthusiasm in mind, I want to use these remaining pages to think about the temporalities of political affect. Doing so provides an occasion to interrogate, and to depart from, what we might call the spatial—or better, "atmospheric"—logic that has been implicit in many of the novels I have studied thus far. According to the Gilded Age novels studied throughout *Not Quite Hope*: Postbellum Washington, DC, was a city populated primarily by "disappointed office seekers" desperate to enter the halls of power; the distant capital's elites cared little for the depression or illness that characterized indigenous life on the nation's southwestern border; and the "backroom" and "lobby" were arenas of venality and avarice. Entering these political and politicized spaces—whether in fact or virtually, through fiction—was always to risk being impacted by their affective atmospheres. Such dramas rely on a fantasy, and sometimes even a presumption, of access: In book after book, with righteous indignation, Gilded Age authors narrate tales of frustrated political ambition, implicitly suggesting Washington *should* be more accommodating to their protagonists' demands. For Adams's *Democracy* to be engaging, one has to identify to some degree with an elite heroine who assumes, as a matter of course, she will be granted an audience with a senator.[7]

If the Gilded Age novel invited readers to see themselves poised on the threshold of senatorial chambers or overhearing the double entendre of the lobby, if it imagined characters peering through binoculars down toward the senate floor, these fantasies belong to a precise historical moment, when the scale of the federal government was large enough to provide potential appointments for myriad "office seekers" but small enough to inspire dreams of unfettered access. But in its allegorical dimension, this fiction also dramatizes "politics" as an activity that has an emotional cost, even for those on its margins. Gilded Age fiction's spatial tease (its promise to smuggle the reader "behind the scenes") is limited in that it links fantasies of agency with physical intimacy with power. But the ready accessibility of the novels' *affective* atmospheres nonetheless speaks to a more general condition of being roused, incensed, and drained by a pervasive backdrop of political aspiration and disappointment.

The concept of literary "tone" has provided one way of thinking about readers' relationship to the Gilded Age novel and how it evokes democracy's emotional ambience. By way of a brief reading of Frances Hodgson Burnett's *Through One Administration* (1881), a novel that links its narrative in surprising ways to the DC calendar, I will end by suggesting that the rhythms of the political public sphere offer another model for conceptualizing how citizens are impacted affectively by involvement in or attention to the political process. That is, I suggest that attending to time, and queer theories of temporality in particular, provides an alternative to the spatial or atmospheric model explored thus far for understanding how we are caught up in and impacted affectively by a zone of political activity to which we have limited access. It is a common lament that, for many, the act of politics today has been reduced to casting a vote for president every four years. That may be true, but my opening glimpse above of a twenty-first-century electorate overtaxed by media saturation and my nineteenth-century archive of intimate political tempo-ralities underscore that citizens can have limited opportunities for political expres-sion and yet feel broadly political nearly all the time.

Through One Presidentiad

Throughout this book, I have argued that understanding the Gilded Age political novel requires suspending a presumption: that proximity to formal politics is in-compatible with affecting fiction. But even given the importance of this basic dynamic—intense emotion versus lifeless formality—to much of American litera-ture, it would be hard to imagine a novel title more perfectly suited to ensure its place in the dustbin of American literary history than Frances Hodgson Burnett's *Through One Administration*. If Whitman's "Presidentiad" is also a "year of the youth I love" and thus a queering of the national frame, Burnett's novel looks emphatically straight and straightlaced.

After all, for much recent queer theory, it is the out-of-step or out-of-sync quality of queerness that once had been denigrated but now is recuperated and celebrated.[8] Against the strictures of official time (figured as "homogeneous empty time," "straight time," or the normative rhythms of "chronobiolitics"[9]), critics have explored asynchronous queer temporalities as "points of resistance to this tempo-ral order."[10] As Thomas Allen warns of an analogous dynamic within Postcolonial and American Studies, however, normative discourses have proved adept at accom-modating diverse temporal registers.[11] Yet I sound this note of caution not to deny a link between queerness, backwardness, and subversion—although aspects of such a warning may be timely.[12] Rather, I want to pursue an opposing question, which Burnett helps articulate: If we should hesitate before *equating* anachronism and arrhythmia with resistance, what forms of political imagination might we discover if we disassociate synchronization from ideological complicity? Despite its seeming devotion to official time, Burnett's focus on an administration's four-year time frame foregrounds the rhythms of electoral politics in order to explore how this temporal scaffold might sustain alternate forms of sociality and intimacy.

Through One Administration tells the story of Bertha Armory, a DC society woman torn between her corrupt husband, Richard; her Indian-killing former flame, Colonel Philip Tredennis; and her sardonic companion, Larry Arbuthnot (who may be either another potential love interest or a fellow traveler at the mar-gins of reproductive heteronormativity). The novel tracks the temporalities of desire in at least two ways: First, it offers an account of the DC social calendar, which organizes the superficial rituals and fake feelings that lubricate the machin-ery of official politics.[13] Second, Burnett presents a quintessential post-Grant-era account of presidential administrations as units of unregulated desire, the effects of which can be observed in a peculiar specimen: "the man of broken career, whose wasted ambitions and frustrated purposes were buried in the monotonous routine of a Government clerkship" (*T*, 67). As I have shown in previous chapters, appointments in an expanding postbellum bureaucracy increasingly served as partisan bargaining chips, turning the ravages of the electoral calendar on political appointees into a remarkably common trope for heartlessly self-interested party elites. This high-stakes power brokering also set the stage for the historical emergence of the "female lobbyist," who was seen to make explicit the eroticism already underlying the mutual backscratching of quid-pro-quo democracy.[14]

Burnett, like all of the period's political novelists I have discussed thus far, turned a taxonomic eye on the glittering hostess, the seductive lobbyist, and the disappointed office seeker, developing a pre-Freudian account of these subjects' political desires. Arbuthnot, for example, acutely registers DC's libidinal frustrations. In an early scene—after noting that someone in the social circle always punctuates his departures by remarking, "What a queer fellow!"—Bertha, Richard, and Philip try to get to the bottom of Arbuthnot's queerness. The passage is worth quoting at length:

> "Well...he is a queer fellow...rambling about with...bonbons in his fastidious overcoat pocket, to be bestowed on children without any particular claim on him. Why does he do it?"
>
> "It doesn't exactly arise from enthusiasm awakened by their infant charms," said Bertha...
>
> " But he must care for them a little," returned Richard.
>
> "The fact is that you don't know what he cares for," said Bertha, "and it is rather one of his fascinations. I suppose that is really what we mean by saying he is a queer fellow."
>
> "At all events," said Richard, amiably, "he is a nice fellow...All I complain of is that he hasn't any object. A man ought to have an object—two or three, if he likes."
>
> "He doesn't like...for he certainly hasn't an object—though...that belongs to his mode of life."
>
> "I should like," said Tredennis, "to know...the mode of life of a man who hasn't an object."
>
> "You will gain a good deal of information on the subject if you remain long in Washington," answered Bertha. "We generally have either too many objects or none at all. If it is not your object to get into the White House, or the Cabinet, or somewhere else, it is probably your fate to be installed in a 'department' and, as you cannot hope to retain your position through any particular circumspectness or fitness for it, you have not any object left you." (*T*, 55)

As a "mode of life" defined vaguely by fastidiousness, a lack of enthusiasm for children, and a dearth of suitable objects, Arbuthnot's "queerness" looks queer, indeed.[15] While "object" initially seems a transparent euphemism for erotic interest, Bertha's commentary suddenly shifts registers, making "object" signify *any* attachment, whether professional or sensual. If this move partially desexualizes Arbuthnot's queerness, it also eroticizes politics as a scene of shifting investments, where one would need to improvise a theory of cathexis and decathexis to describe the anxious, desiring subjects from which "politics" is composed.

To be sure, the novel ostensibly rejects all of this political promiscuity and object-less desire. Bertha, perpetually tempted to leave her husband for one man or another, must constantly be reminded of her children and thereby resutured to motherhood and domesticity.[16] And the novel ultimately makes clear that we are meant to reject superficial banter in favor of Tredennis's seriousness, solidity, and sincerity: "His grave face and large figure were rather out of place among all this airy badinage. His... seriousness and silence was not a Washingtonian quality... Here were people who could treat lightly, not only their subjects, but themselves and each other" (T, 53). Tredennis, in short, "does not exactly belong to the nineteenth century" (T, 339), and Burnett highlights his anachronism to critique the then-current flightiness, queerness, and narcissism of life in the capital:

> "You are not modern," [Bertha] said. "You must learn to adjust yourself rapidly to changes of mental attitude." "No, I am not modern," he returned; "and I am always behindhand. I do not enjoy myself when you tell me it is a fine day, and that it was colder yesterday, and will be warmer to-morrow; and I am at a loss when you analyze Mr. Arbuthnot's struggles with his vanity." (T, 249)

Given queer theory's engagement with marginalized sexuality as a mode of back-wardness, it's valuable to note how this novel instead casts normative masculinity as a "behindhand" relic. Queerness, artificiality, and superficiality, meanwhile, are distinctly—and, in Tredennis's estimation, to their detriment—very much *au courant*.[17]

The opposition of solid sincerity and queer superficiality is not so simple, how-ever, as Burnett's narrator emphasizes in her account of the small talk that so alien-ates Tredennis: "It was nonsense, but it was often sparkling nonsense... and the rooms were rarely ever so gay... as when there was among the guests a sprinkling of men no longer young, who had come there to forget that they were jaded, or secretly anxious, or bitterly disappointed" (T, 94). In a quasi-camp dynamic, extrav-agant displays of manufactured emotion come to look like signs of intense, all-too-real affect.[18] "Sparkling nonsense" might be seen as a necessary, if compromised, alternative to the "monotonous routine" and disappointments of public life. Richard, convinced of Bertha's and Arbuthnot's commitment to fake feeling, is gently corrected by the latter:

> "All that I have to complain of in you two people," said [Richard] gayly... "is that you have no sentiment—none whatever."
>
> "We are full of it," said Arbuthnot, "both of us, but we conceal it, and we feel that it makes us interesting. Nothing is more interesting than repressed emotion. The appearance of sardonic coldness and stoicism which has deceived you is but a hollow mockery; beneath it I secrete a maelstrom of impassioned feeling and a mausoleum of blighted hopes." (T, 52)

The novel insistently links sparkling banter with the ugly feelings of some barely named social traumas.[19] Chief among these are the "disappointments" of bad or absent objects, which never seem fully equivalent to sexual partners or to political goals.

For Burnett, then, Washington's official calendar appears to have synchronized negative feelings—frustration, anger, shame—as well as the labor of their management, but in so doing also produced a sense of the political as a shared affective ambience. The novel is fascinated by the public life of feeling, even if Burnett is often pessimistic about the antidemocratic effects of mass affect. For example, after tracing in great detail the corruption of DC politics, she unexpectedly imagines a reading public likewise caught up in the rhythms of formal democracy—but only to scold these readers for their unseemly interest in political scandal. After a "well-seasoned Washingtonian" makes an insinuating remark about "what goes on in these tip-top parlors around here," the narrator observes:

> He said it with modest pride and exultation, and his companions were delighted. They represented the average American, with all his ingenuous eagerness for the dramatic exposure of crime in his fellow-man. They had existed joyously for years in the belief that Washington was the seat of corruption, bribery, and fraud; that it was populated chiefly with brilliant female lobbyists and depraved officials.... [They] would have felt a keen pang of disappointment if they had been suddenly confronted with the fact that there was actually an element of most unpicturesque honesty in the House and...Senate. They had heard delightful stories of "jobs" and "schemes," and had hoped to hear more. When they had been taken to the visitors gallery, they had exhibited an earnest anxiety to be shown the members connected with the last investigation, and had received with private rapture all anecdotes connected with the ruling political scandal.   (*T*, 382)

Despite Burnett's reprimand, I would submit that, in this novel, a range of affects, from "keen disappointment" to "private rapture," defines an emotional atmosphere with a troubled attachment to institutional politics. If a rhetoric of feeling in the antebellum period has been said to turn depoliticized citizens away from politics and toward their interior lives, emotion—even, or especially, negative emotion—is depicted here as insistently public, tying individuals to forms of social life that are deeply draining but also more expansive than those of the home.[20]

That the negative affects of the political public sphere could anchor a "queer" imagining of social life is less surprising than it might seem at first. Burnett's own "queerness" might best be located in her search for alternatives to heterosexual domesticity and in her apparent sympathy for aspects of Victoria Woodhull's "free love" movement (examined at length in my first chapter), which, in Woodhull's famous 1871 pronouncement, explicitly grounded its radicalism in a new relationship to the temporality of desire: "Yes, I am a Free Lover. I have an inalienable, constitutional and natural right to love whom I may, to love as long or as short a period as I can; to change that love every day if I please."[21] This is not to say, however, that *Through One Administration* simply offers a condensed and displaced autobiography of its author.[22] Rather, in a dynamic akin to Mark Seltzer's notion of a "wounded public," Burnett casts "earnest anxiety" as both a worrying sign of democratic cynicism and an important placeholder for an embodied sociality that exceeds the family form.[23] If, for Woodhull, only the free-form temporality of whim ("to love as long or as short" as she will) takes full advantage of her constitutional rights then Burnett's queer loves and queerer disappointments stay in surprising sync with the rhythms of official time.

One might further object that to describe this sociality as "queer" is a contradiction in terms if, as Michael Warner has argued, queer activism distinguishes itself from "gay and lesbian politics" precisely through its suspicion of the state.[24] But perhaps we need new ways of conceptualizing the ambivalence that marks citizens' everyday relations to the sphere of official democracy. For Warner, writing in the midst of challenges to the military's "don't ask don't tell" policy, nothing more powerfully dramatized the danger of a "turn back to a state-oriented politics" than the spectacle of marchers chanting, "We're here, we're queer, we want to serve our country."[25] Yet it's rare that such a turn to the state so fully parrots institutional patriotism.

Indeed, for good or for ill, politics rarely holds citizens' undivided interest. Lauren Berlant argues, politics is often "overheard" and shaped by practices of diffuse attention and reluctant recommitment that might feel ambivalent, even if they function structurally as a cruelly optimistic affirmation:

> Voting is one thing; collective caring, listening, and scanning the airwaves, are others. All of these modes of orientation and having a feeling about it confirm our attachment to the system and thereby confirm the system and the legitimacy of the affects that make one feel bound to it, even if the manifest content of the binding has the negative force of cynicism or the dark attenuation of political depression.[26]

In Burnett's novel, "disappointment" knits together the thwarted desires of Bertha's salon and the nation at large, a loosely political community of feeling that is irreducible to the domestic. Unlike the biological and theological chronologies that are said to tie Bertha to her husband and children—"That's her woman's way. God made it so" (T, 90)—an "administration" is a manifestly artificial and political temporal unit.[27] Like the diverse forms of fatigue that already defined American politics in the run-up to the 2016 election, Through One Administration depicts citizens moving alongside but not fully in step with administrative time, diagnosing a subject of politics who is not an autonomous individual but is instead inescapably social, always and necessarily permeated by the affective rhythms of the political. In this, the novel offers a surprisingly ambivalent counterpart to Whitman's "Presidentiad." And it speaks to a twenty-first-century moment when "voter fatigue" and related forms of exhaustion diagnose a desire for the political that is intimately attuned, for better or worse, to democracy's official calendars.[28]

Burnett confirms a dynamic I have sought to elucidate throughout *Not Quite Hope*: According to major works of the American literary canon, the political realm will always disappoint. The state's vision of political life will always be artificially contracted and enervated. Politically provoked feelings of cynicism, frustration, and disgust will always require digging deep to uncover a countervailing optimism, and readers will always need to seek the resources to do so outside of the political arena—in literature, perhaps. Charles Olson notes, "Whitman we have called our greatest voice because he gave us hope."[29] Critics have prized literature's evocation of democratic sentiments—hope, sympathy, fellow feeling— for putting the failures of existing political institutions into relief. In short, we celebrate great literature for the opportunity it offers to imagine better democracies. But I have tried to demonstrate that Gilded Age literature—often messier and more easily overlooked than its canonical counterparts—demands our attention, too, precisely because it probes the familiar feelings that define actually existing democracy, not in an idealized state but in the tainted, disappointing, depressing, and exhausting work of quotidian politics.

The Gilded Age novel never redeems its fallen democracy; a heroic nation never arrives to eclipse the corrupt one; the warm bonds of sentiment never revive democracy's dead forms; a political naïf never reminds jaded power brokers of the ideals that once motivated them; the people never take back the reins of power in a groundswell of enthusiasm. At best, these novels' often-cynical tone suggests bitter disillusionment may be the first step toward getting the nation on sounder, more rational footing. I have shown that this rationalist and disenchanted outlook constitutes its own form of aversive attachment. By tracking these novels' shifting tones of madness, disgust, depression, agitation, and suspicion, I have sought to uncover a deeply ambivalent critical optimism, which Gilded Age authors repeatedly cast as an (in Twain's memorable formulation) "ab-so-lutely crazy"—and absolutely necessary—component of everyday political life.

{ ENDNOTES }

Introduction

1. The epigraph can be found in Alexis de Tocqueville, *Democracy in America*, trans. Harvey C. Mansfield and Delba Winthrop (Chicago: University of Chicago Press, 2000), 189.

2. George Miller Beard, *American Nervousness: Its Causes and Consequences* (New York: G.P. Putnam's Sons, 1881), 122.

3. Frances Hodgson Burnett, *Through One Administration* (Boston: J.R. Osgood and Co., 1883), 365.

4. In Tocqueville's and Beard's accounts, "agitation" is less a principled enthusiasm than a pervasive anxiety. Even in the derogatory sense, however, agitation may describe a necessary condition. After all, "agitation" is also "to keep a political or other issue constantly under discussion, so as to arouse public concern and bring about action" ("agitation, n." *OED Online*. Oxford University Press. http://www.oed.com/view/Entry/4011, accessed December 2015).

5. Work that focuses on this period in literary history—just after the heyday of the romance and just before the dominance of realism, regionalism, and naturalism—remains surprisingly rare. I share with James B. Salazar a desire to attend to "the many diverse and hybrid literary forms obscured by the critical and historical emphasis on realism in the late nineteenth century" (*Bodies of Reform: The Rhetoric of Character in Gilded Age America* [New York: New York University Press, 2010], 31). My focus on hybrid genres is taken up most directly in Chapter 4. Like Peter Coviello, although in a different register, I'm intrigued by nineteenth-century visions of social life shaped by an impending sexological modernity yet enough in advance of that future to picture forms of intimacy not captured by later taxonomies. See *Tomorrow's Parties: Sex and the Untimely in Nineteenth-Century America* (New York: New York University Press, 2013). This aspect of my project is explored most directly in my first chapter, on "free love." I also echo Jane Thrailkill's interest in overturning the idea that late nineteenth-century literature was "immune to affective concerns" (*Affecting Fictions: Mind, Body, and Emotion in American Literary Realism* [Cambridge: Harvard University Press, 2007], 185). My work differs from hers by focusing on texts that directly explore the tensions between reason and emotion in specifically political contexts, asserting neither the autonomy of affect nor the autonomy of artistic expression.

6. Mark Wahlgren Summers, *The Era of Good Stealings* (New York: Oxford University Press, 1993).

7. For early versions of this debate, see Ann Douglas, *The Feminization of American Culture* (New York: Avon, 1977) and Jane Tompkins, *Sensational Designs: The Cultural Work of American Fiction, 1790–1860* (New York: Oxford University Press, 1985). On the depoliticizing effects of sentimentality's representation of structural problems through personal stories, see Lauren Berlant, *The Female Complaint* (Durham: Duke University Press, 2008), 41.

8. On the powerful erotics and troubling erasures of Whitman's "poetics of embodiment," see Karen Sanchez-Eppler, *Touching Liberty: Abolition, Feminism, and the Politics of the Body* (Berkeley: University of California Press, 1993), 74–82.

9. For important exceptions, see Justine Murison, *The Politics of Anxiety in Nineteenth-Century American Literature* (New York: Cambridge University Press, 2013); Dana Luciano, *Arranging Grief: Sacred Time and the Body in Nineteenth-Century America* (New York: New York University Press, 2007); and Paul Hurh, *American Terror: The Feeling of Thinking in Edwards, Poe, and Melville* (Stanford: Stanford University Press, 2015). These texts have expanded our understanding of the range of affective idioms through which American literature does its cultural work. They differ from this book, however, in delineating one key feeling (e.g. anxiety, grief, terror) in order to lend it the stability of a named emotion rather than focusing on the instability of affect itself. These negative affects can also have surprising affinities with sympathy. Luciano's *Arranging Grief*, for example, which explores in such rich detail the diverse temporalities and affective experiences associated with mourning, primarily sees grief as a framework for organizing "affective nationalism" and "feeling-in-common" (218). That is to say, grief joins sympathy as a binding, unifying feeling.

10. Sympathy is by far the most studied structure of feeling in pre-1900 American literature. A partial bibliography would include Gordon Hutner, *Secrets and Sympathy: Forms of Disclosure in Hawthorne's Novels* (Athens: University of Georgia Press, 1988); Kristin Boudreau, *Sympathy in American Literature: American Sentiments from Jefferson to the Jameses* (Gainesville: University Press of Florida, 2002); Glenn Hendler's study of the "logic of sympathy" in *Public Sentiments: Structures of Feeling in Nineteenth-Century American Literature* (Chapel Hill: University of North Carolina Press, 2001); Elizabeth Barnes, *States of Sympathy* (New York: Columbia University Press, 1997); and Julia Stern, *The Plight of Feeling: Sympathy and Dissent in the Early American Novel* (Chicago: University of Chicago Press, 1997).

11. Samantha Smith, "6 Key Takeaways About How Americans View Their Government," Pew Research Center Fact Tank: News in the Numbers (November 23, 2015). http://pewrsr.ch/1lEgKvX.

12. On anxieties about political representation and the fantasy of a seamless transmission of voters' collective will, see F.R. Ankersmit, *Political Representation* (Stanford: Stanford University Press, 2002), 112.

13. The story is, of course, more complex than this. Whitman's *Democratic Vistas* is productively inconsistent on the question of whether the negative emotions he associates with institutional politics are a problem for democracy or instead make up democracy's necessary core.

14. Eric Slauter, "Revolutions in the Meaning and Study of Politics," *American Literary History* 22, no. 2 (Summer 2010): 326.

15. Ibid.

16. Ibid., 338 n. 2.

17. "Correspondence: Novels of Washington Life," *The Literary World: A Monthly Review of Current Literature* (August 25, 1883): 273.

18. Henry James, *Literary Criticism: Essays on Literature, American Writers, English Writers*, ed. Leon Edel and Mark Wilson (New York: Library of America, 1984), 232.

19. For more on the ways authors used the genre of the Washington novel to overcome the challenge of representing an increasingly complex federal bureaucracy, see Amanda

Claybaugh, "Washington Novels and the Machinery of Government," in *The World the Civil War Made*, eds. Gregory P. Downs and Kate Masur (Chapel Hill: University of North Carolina Press, 2015).

20. Burnett, *Through One Administration*, 503.

21. In the most iconic gesture of this ambivalence, which I will discuss in Chapter 5, Mark Twain offers a biting satire of American politics and culture, only to append a preface to the London edition of *The Gilded Age* asserting the importance of the same delusional ambitions he had just lambasted.

22. Nancy Glazener, *Literature in the Making: A History of U.S. Literary Culture in the Long Nineteenth Century* (New York: Oxford University Press, 2015), 59.

23. Ibid., 63.

24. Ibid., 61.

25. Summers, *The Era of Good Stealings*, 84.

26. Gordon Milne, *The American Political Novel* (Norman: University of Oklahoma Press, 1966), 27.

27. In my third chapter, for example, I will show how Helen Hunt Jackson was both drawn toward and on guard against the capacity for "feeling right" to represent a first step toward personhood for the members of indigenous tribes.

28. On the "countersentimental," see Lauren Berlant, *The Female Complaint: The Unfinished Business of Sentimentality in American Culture* (Durham: Duke University Press, 2008), 56.

29. Steve Fraser, "The Gilded Age, Past and Present," *Salon.com*, April 28, 2008, https://www.salon.com/2008/04/28/gilded_age/.

30. Tom Lutz, *American Nervousness, 1903: An Anecdotal History* (Ithaca: Cornell University Press, 1991), 154. Michael O'Malley examines a similar, early-twentieth-century dynamic in which an acquisitive instinct was widely regarded as an essential feature of the *fin de siècle* American temperament but also provoked a worry that fixating on "business" might lapse into "busyness": a wasteful, restless, agitation. See "That Busyness That Is Not Business: Nervousness and Character at the Turn of the Last Century," *Social Research: An International Quarterly* 72, no. 2 (Summer 2005): 398.

31. Justine Murison does consider "nervousness" an outgrowth of both political and economic activity: "The market revolution and the ascendancy of Jacksonian democracy during the 1820s and 1830s together fueled the perception that the United States produced uniquely nervous citizens" (*The Politics of Anxiety in Nineteenth-Century American Literature* [New York: Cambridge University Press, 2011], 11). Yet it's clear that, for most of the authors in her study, nervousness was not directly linked to political activity. Indeed, Murison's powerful evocation of the range of the antebellum period's anxiogenic obsessions puts into relief the ways these fears would later coalesce around "politics" in the postbellum era.

32. As Kathryn Jacob notes, Washington, DC, "was an artificial town, created by compromise and plunked down in semi-wilderness. Its sole raison d'être was to serve as the nation's capital" (*King of the Lobby: The Life and Times of Sam Ward, Man-About-Washington in the Gilded Age* [Baltimore: Johns Hopkins University Press, 2010], 9).

33. On a more recent version of the dynamic in which a seemingly salacious interest in the scandals of democracy may also constitute a meaningful, or at least inescapable, mode of relation to the workings of American politics, see Lauren Berlant and Lisa Duggan,

Our Monica, Ourselves: The Clinton Affair and the National Interest (New York: New York University Press, 2001); Eric Lott, "The First Boomer: Bill Clinton, George W., and Fictions of State," *Representations* 84 (2004): 100–22.

34. Here I draw on Lauren Berlant's notion of "aversive identifications" (as, for instance, the uncomfortable empathy that pro-life activists foster with the fetus as an innocent, damaged subject) and Stanley Cavell's "aversive thinking" (an Emersonian mode of critical, productive withdrawal). See Lauren Berlant, "The Subject of True Feeling: Pain, Privacy, and Politics," in *Cultural Pluralism, Identity Politics, and the Law*, eds. Austin Sarat and Thomas Kearns (Ann Arbor: University of Michigan Press, 1998), 55; Stanley Cavell, *Conditions Handsome and Unhandsome: The Constitution of Emersonian Perfectionism* (Chicago: University of Chicago Press, 1990), 33–63. Combined, these concepts suggest something of the peril and promise of an aversive attachment to democratic institutions.

35. Christopher Castiglia likewise focuses "on the state as a series of interconnected institutions" in order "to displace the restrictive focus…on the nation and on nationalism" (Christopher Castiglia, *Interior States: Institutional Consciousness and the Inner Life of Democracy in the Antebellum United States* [Durham: Duke University Press, 2008], 7). The literary works Castiglia studies are interesting cases, as they mostly displace institutions from view by describing citizens' core responsibility as the management of their own feelings.

36. This is not to downplay the vital importance of studies, like Dana Nelson's recent work, that uncover early republican experiments in "non-hierarchical political power generated outside of formal institutions" (*Commons Democracy: Reading the Politics of Participation in the Early United States* [New York: Fordham University Press, 2016], 7). However, the fantasies and anxieties driving several decades of Gilded Age political literature remain invisible if we only attend to the power of extra-institutional politics.

37. Many of McCann's and Szalay's interlocutors have heard them, understandably, to make an error that is the reverse of the one they decry. Eric Lott, for example, calls their position one of "political complacency dressed up as tough-minded realism" ("Chants Demagogic," *The Yale Journal of Criticism* 18 no. 2 [2005], 472).

38. McCann and Szalay sacrifice some of the nuance present in their wider body of work for the sake of polemical thrust. McCann's earlier monograph makes clear that political institutions (in this case, the executive branch) can be objects of fantasy, misrecognition, creativity, and both productive and debilitating attachments. See Sean McCann, *A Pinnacle of Feeling: American Literature and Presidential Government* (Princeton: Princeton University Press, 2008).

39. Brooks D. Simpson, *The Political Education of Henry Adams* (Columbia, SC: University of South Carolina Press, 1996), 105.

40. Ron Powers, *Mark Twain: A Life* (New York: Free Press, 2005), 394; Albert Bigelow Paine, *Mark Twain, A Biography: The Personal and Literary Life of Samuel Langhorne Clemens*, vol. 3 (New York: Harper & Bros., 1912), 1147.

41. Jacques Rancière, *Disagreement: Politics and Philosophy* (Minneapolis: University of Minnesota Press, 1999), 29–30.

42. Ibid., 28.

43. Ibid.

44. In the context of US literary studies, "dissensus" may evoke Sacvan Bercovitch's anxious meditation on the fragmented field of Americanist criticism in the mid to late 1980s. See Sacvan Bercovitch, "The Problem of Ideology in American Literary History,"

Critical Inquiry 12, no. 4 (Summer 1986): 631–53. Don Pease has argued that Bercovitch threatens to cast dissensus as a deterioration of some flawed but useful agreement. Pease's approach accords more or less with Rancière's understanding of disagreement as the necessary condition for politics. See Donald E. Pease, *Revisionary Interventions into the Americanist Canon* (Durham: Duke University Press, 1994), 20–9.

45. Lisi Schoenbach, *Pragmatic Modernism* (New York: Oxford University Press, 2014), 68.

46. Ibid.

47. Lauren Berlant and Dana Luciano, "Conversation: Lauren Berlant with Dana Luciano," *Social Text Online* (January 13, 2013), https://socialtextjournal.org/periscope_article/conversation-lauren-berlant-with-dana-luciano/.

48. Fredric Jameson, "Magical Narratives: Romance as Genre," *New Literary History* 7, no. 1 (1975), 135.

49. Ibid., 153.

50. Slavoj Žižek has used the term "post-political" to describe "the reduction of politics proper to the rational administration of conflicting interests" ("Against the Populist Temptation," *Critical Inquiry* 32 [2006], 555).

51. This is why I do not see my focus on emotion as opposed to works, like Sandra Gustafson's *Imagining Deliberative Democracy in the Early American Republic* (Chicago: University of Chicago Press, 2011), that stress the importance of rational-critical debate. Gilded Age literature forces us to contend with affect as a feature of deliberation not its opposite. The yearning for cool reason as a respite from hot tempers can have democratic and antidemocratic effects.

52. Rancière, *Dis-Agreement*, 55.

53. For the best overview of this philosophical tradition, see the introductory essay in Melissa Gregg and Gregory J. Seigworth, eds., *The Affect Theory Reader* (Durham: Duke University Press, 2010).

54. Michael Hardt, in an admirable act of concision, summarizes the turn to affect in this way: "One way of understanding this complex set of propositions, then, is simply to say that the perspective of the affects requires us constantly to pose as a problem the relation between actions and passions, between reason and the emotions" ("Foreword: What Are Affects Good For," in *The Affective Turn: Theorizing The Social*, ed. Patricia Ticineto Clough [Durham: Duke University Press, 2007], x).

55. On the affective body politic, see especially John Protevi, *Political Affect: Connecting the Social and the Somatic* (Minneapolis: University of Minnesota Press, 2009).

56. Brian Massumi's work best demonstrates the tension between the utopian and dystopian strains of affect theory. For much of his work, affect appears almost inherently radical because it "escapes confinement" in any "particular body whose vitality, or potential for interaction, it is" (*Parables for the Virtual: Movement, Affect, Sensation* [Durham: Duke University Press, 2002], 35, 40–2). Yet his most prominent example of the workings of affect is Ronald Reagan's affective manipulation of the electorate.

57. Raymond Williams, *Marxism and Literature* (New York: Oxford University Press, 1977).

58. See, for example, Frantz Fanon, *Black Skin White Masks* (New York: Grove Press, 1967); José Esteban Muñoz, "Feeling Down, Feeling Brown: Latina Affect, the Performativity of Race, and the Depressive Position," *Signs* 31, No. 3 (Spring 2006): 675–88; David L. Eng

and Shinhee Han, "A Dialogue on Racial Melancholia" in *Loss: The Politics of Mourning*, eds. David L. Eng and David Kazanjian (Berkeley: University of California Press, 2003).

59. Ann Cvetkovich, "Everyday Feeling and its Genres," in *Political Emotions*, eds. Janet Staiger, Ann Cvetkovich, and Ann Reynolds (New York: Routledge, 2010), 6.

60. Ngai studies those "minor affects that are far less intentional or object-directed, and thus more likely to produce political and aesthetic ambiguities, than the passions in the philosophical canon" (*Ugly Feelings* [Cambridge: Harvard University Press, 2005], 20). On the novel and more traditional emotions, see Philip Fisher, *The Vehement Passions* (Princeton: Princeton University Press, 2003).

61. Fredric Jameson, *The Antinomies of Realism* (London: Verso, 2013), 34.

62. Castiglia, *Interior States*, 86.

63. Ibid., 84.

64. I build here and throughout on Lauren Berlant's work, which makes clear that the *structure* of an optimistic relation to an object can feel or be experienced in all sorts of ways. See *Cruel Optimism* (Durham: Duke University Press, 2011), 2.

65. Leys claims that "the whole point of the turn to affect" is to "shift attention away from considerations of meaning or 'ideology' ... to the subject's subpersonal material-affective responses." This "produces as one of its consequences a relative indifference to the role of ideas and beliefs in politics, culture, and art" ("The Turn to Affect: A Critique," *Critical Inquiry* 37, no. 3 [Spring 2011]: 450–1). While Leys exposes serious gaps in Brian Massumi's work, in particular, I am not persuaded that it accounts for the affective turn *tout court*. The study of "affect" in the humanities has strong genealogical ties to queer theory, from which it borrows an interest in forms of experience that are imperfectly captured by scientific taxonomies or vernacular designations. To put it much too simply, this can be good (there may be ways of living or loving that exceed narrow definitions) or bad (a disparity between experience and normative vocabularies of visibility and legitimation), but these are clearly concerns that bear on "ideas and beliefs." Thinking about affect neither guarantees nor excludes taking on questions of ideology.

66. The tension between affect and bureaucracy is a theme throughout this book, but it is most fully on display in Chapter 2 (on Henry Adams's ambivalent endorsement of civil service reform) and in Chapter 3 (on Helen Hunt Jackson's engagement with the Department of the Interior's management of the so-called "Indian problem").

67. See, for example, Michael Snediker, *Queer Optimism: Lyric Personhood and Other Felicitous Persuasions* (Minneapolis: University of Minnesota Press, 2009).

68. See especially José Esteban Muñoz, *Cruising Utopia: The Then and There of Queer Futurity* (New York: New York University Press, 2009).

69. Wendy Brown, "Resisting Left Melancholy," *Boundary 2* 26, no. 3 (1999): 19–27.

70. Amanda Anderson, "Postwar Aesthetics: The Case of Trilling and Adorno," *Critical Inquiry* 40, no. 4 (2014): 418–38.

71. Eve Kosofsky Sedgwick, *Touching Feeling: Affect, Pedagogy, Performativity* (Durham: Duke University Press, 2003). On critical optimism as an alternative to critique's negative affects, see Christopher Castiglia, "Critiquiness," *English Language Notes* 51, no. 2 (Fall/Winter 2013): 79–85.

72. Ellis Hanson, "The Future's Eve: Reparative Reading after Sedgwick," *South Atlantic Quarterly* 110, no. 1 (2011): 101–19.

73. Bruno Latour, "Why Has Critique Run out of Steam? From Matters of Fact to Matters of Concern," *Critical Inquiry* 30 (Winter 2004): 225–48. Rita Felski has recently tracked

critique's dominant "style, attitude, and tone" across four decades of literary and cultural studies. See "Digging Down and Standing Back," *English Language Notes* 51, no. 2 (Fall/Winter 2013): 7–23.

74. Stephen Best and Sharon Marcus, "Surface Reading: An Introduction," *Representations* 108, no. 1 (2008): 1–21.

75. For an argument that disappointment and hope, critique and idealism, must be viewed as deeply entwined, see Christopher Castiglia's essay "Twists and Turns," in *Turns of Event: Nineteenth-Century American Literary Studies in Motion*, ed. Hester Blum (University of Pennsylvania Press, 2016) and his book *The Practices of Hope: Literary Criticism in Disenchanted Times* (New York: New York University Press, 2017). I argue that Gilded Age political literature is a particularly important and challenging archive through which to test this claim, precisely because it contains so little that resembles what Castiglia, citing Michael Taussig, calls "demystification and re-enchantment." The world of Gilded Age politics looks small, sordid, and perpetually demystified. It is all the more important, then, to see what critical practices of hope can be excavated from contexts that appear resistant to such a project.

76. The nested references here are to Castiglia, "Critiquiness" and Berlant, *Cruel Optimism*.

77. Jacob, *King of the Lobby*, 129. As Richard Hofstadter notes, "One of the ironic problems confronting reformers around the turn of the century was that the very activities they pursued in attempting to defend...individualistic values...brought them closer to the techniques of the organization they feared" (*The Age of Reform: From Bryan to F. D. R.* [New York: Vintage Books, 1960], 7).

78. Jacob, *King of the Lobby*, 72.

79. Jacob notes, "There were nearly fifteen million more people in the United States in 1876 than in 1861...[T]hese changes spelled skyrocketing demands for the post offices, law enforcement, courts, internal improvements, and revenue, land, customs and pension agents that citizens looked to the federal government to provide" (Ibid., 69, 72).

80. Andrew W. Robertson, *The Language of Democracy: Political Rhetoric in the United States and Britain, 1790–1900* (Charlottesville: University of Virginia Press, 2005), 159.

81. Ibid., 163.

82. Historians have noted the appeal of this reform program with some surprise: "No major historical event of the late 1860s or the 1870s could be said to cry out that the republic was endangered by the patronage system" (Bernard S. Silberman, *Cages of Reason: The Rise of the Rational State in France, Japan, the United States, and Great Britain* [Chicago: University of Chicago Press, 1993], 252).

83. Hofstadter, *The Age of Reform*, 135.

84. Ari Arthur Hoogenboom, *Outlawing the Spoils: A History of the Civil Service Reform Movement, 1865–1883* (Westport, CT: Greenwood Press, 1982), 30.

85. For an overview of postbellum antisentimentalism, see June Howard, "What Is Sentimentality?" *American Literary History* 11, no. 1 (1999): 63–81.

86. See especially Teresa Brennan, *The Transmission of Affect* (Ithaca: Cornell University Press, 2004); Brian Massumi, *Parables for the Virtual: Movement, Affect, Sensation* (Durham: Duke University Press, 2002); Rei Terada, *Feeling in Theory: Emotion After the Death of the Subject* (Cambridge: Harvard University Press, 2003); Adela Pinch, *Strange Fits of Passion: Epistemologies of Emotion, Hume to Austen* (Stanford: Stanford University Press, 1996).

87. Susan Wells, *Sweet Reason: Rhetoric and the Discourses of Modernity* (Chicago: University of Chicago Press, 1996), 151.

88. On "tone" as a text's "global or organizing affect," see Ngai, *Ugly Feelings*, 28.

89. For a critique of any so-called politics founded on an intuition about justice, see Raymond Geuss, *Philosophy and Real Politics* (Princeton: Princeton University Press, 2008), 97.

90. This formulation is from Ann Cvetkovich's caution against a view of realism as the opposite of sentimentality or melodrama. See Staiger et al., *Political Emotions*, 7–8.

91. Again, Susan Wells's work is apposite in the ways it reads discursive forms that announce their transparent rationality as instances and expressions of the instability of language and desire. See *Sweet Reason*, 50–1.

92. "The Old and New Cynics," *The Eclectic Magazine of Foreign Literature* (March 1884): 408–10.

Chapter 1

1. Mark Twain and Charles Dudley Warner, *The Gilded Age: A Tale of Today* (New York: Penguin Books, 2001), 185. All references to this text are hereafter cited parenthetically by page number and abbreviated *G*.

2. On the novel's co-authorship and its chapter breakdown, see Louis Budd's introduction in *G*, xi–xii.

3. Harriet Beecher Stowe, *My Wife and I: Or, Harry Henderson's History* (New York: Fords, Howard & Hulbert, 1871), 431. All references to this text are hereafter cited parenthetically by page number and abbreviated *M*. In effect, love arrives to correct what Edmund Burke decried as the "abuse of reason," the fantasy that a fallen humanity can conform to rational theories. On Burkean conservatism's skeptical critique of reformist theory, see Jerry Z. Muller's introduction to his *Conservatism: An Anthology of Social and Political Thought from David Hume to the Present* (Princeton: Princeton University Press, 1997).

4. For an account of emotional insanity contemporary with *The Gilded Age*, see David Dudley Field, *Emotional Insanity* (New York: Russell Brothers, 1873). For Field, the key question in insanity cases was whether the defendant had the capacity to resist whatever emotional impulse produced their criminal action.

5. On *My Wife and I* as a critique of the commodification of women in marriage see Astrid Recker, "To Market! Consuming Women in Harriet Beecher Stowe's *My Wife and I* and *We and Our Neighbors*," in *Beyond Uncle Tom's Cabin*, eds. Sylvia Mayer and Monika Mueller (Madison: Fairleigh Dickinson University Press, 2011), 209–35.

6. On the history of free love and other forms of sex radicalism see Joanne E. Passet, *Sex Radicals and the Quest for Women's Equality* (Chicago: University of Illinois Press, 2003); John C. Spurlock, *Free Love: Marriage and Middle-Class Radicalism in America, 1825–1860* (New York: New York University Press, 1990).

7. On the ways Whitman's "Calamus" poetry sought to "release sex into every register of sociability, to saturate the social field with the adhesive vibrancy of desire," see Peter Coviello, *Tomorrow's Parties: Sex and the Untimely in Nineteenth-Century America* (New York: New York University Press, 2013), 50. We might say it is this saturation against which *The Gilded Age* and *My Wife and I* position their visions of social life. These novels implicitly suggest the erotic was *already* released into social life—not by poets but by capitalist appetites, political ambition, and the public's promiscuous desires.

8. For a dialogue about the need for a "properly political" concept of love, see Michael Hardt, "For Love or Money," *Cultural Anthropology* 26, no. 4 (2011): 676–82; Lauren Berlant, "A Properly Political Concept of Love: Three Approaches in Ten Pages," *Cultural Anthropology* 26, no. 4 (2011): 683–91.

9. Michael Hardt and Antonio Negri, *Commonwealth* (Cambridge: Harvard University Press, 2009), 181.

10. Alain Badiou with Nicolas Truong, *In Praise of Love*, Peter Bush, trans. (London: Serpent's Tail, 2012), 2.

11. Ibid., 79.

12. Berlant takes up questions of love's power and pitfalls throughout *The Female Complaint* (Durham: Duke University Press, 2008) and *Cruel Optimism* (Durham: Duke University Press, 2011). See also "Love, a Queer Feeling," in *Homosexuality and Psychoanalysis*, eds. Tim Dean and Christopher Lane (Chicago: University of Chicago Press, 2001), 432–51, and *Desire/Love* (Brooklyn, NY: Punctum Books, 2012).

13. For Berlant, this is a dynamic of "cruel optimism" that keeps nearly everyone, but especially women, attached to the social forms that sustain that vulnerability.

14. Posing the question this way allows crazy love to join the more overtly "negative" feelings studied in this book, like cynicism and disgust, as a deeply ambivalent mode of relation to democratic institutions and the forms of social life they stabilize. Conversely, in Chapter 2 I will explore disgust in political contexts as a feeling defined by its violent recoil from degraded institutions but also as a form of repulsion that energizes a strange desire for the political.

15. On the limited liability of corporations, see Alan Trachtenberg, *The Incorporation of America: Culture and Society in the Gilded Age* (New York: Hill and Wang, 1982), 84–5.

16. Isaac Ray, *A Treatise on the Medical Jurisprudence of Insanity* (Cambridge, MA: Belknap Press of Harvard University Press, 1962).

17. Ray published his second edition in 1843, with further editions appearing throughout the century. On the McNaughton test, see Thomas Maeder, *Crime and Madness: The Origins and Evolution of the Insanity Defense* (New York: Harper & Row, 1985). Daniel McNaughton mistakenly killed British Prime Minister Robert Peel's secretary in an attempt on the prime minister's life. The McNaughton test was made law in the United States via *Commonwealth v. Rogers* in 1844. See also Da Zheng, "Twain's and Warner's The Gilded Age: The Economy of Insanity," *College Language Association Journal* 39 (1995): 71–93.

18. Cited in Maeder, *Crime and Madness*, 50.

19. Louis E. Reik, "The Doe–Ray Correspondence: A Pioneer Collaboration in the Jurisprudence of Mental Disease," *Yale Law Journal* 63 (1953): 183–96.

20. Maeder, *Crime and Madness*, 46.

21. On Wharton and the conflict among medical experts, see Janet A. Tighe, "Francis Wharton and the Nineteenth-Century Insanity Defense: The Origins of a Reform Tradition," *The American Journal of Legal History* 27, no. 3 (July 1983): 243.

22. Mark Twain, *Collected Tales, Sketches, Speeches & Essays* (New York: The Library of America, 1992), 354. All references to this text are hereafter cited parenthetically by page number and abbreviated *C*.

23. An 1843 poem in London's *Times* responding to the McNaughton case sums up these anxieties for an English audience: "Why say ye that but three authorities reign/ Crown, Commons, and Lords?—You omit the insane. / They're a privileged class whom no

statute controls / And their murderous charter exists in their souls." Cited in Maeder, *Crime and Madness*, 30.

24. Cited in Albert Bigelow Paine, *Mark Twain: A Biography* (New York: Harper and Brothers, 1912), 474.

25. Critics have long noted how Twain's works expose the obstacles, from the momentous to the absurd, that modernity created for notions of individual responsibility: uncertain racial identity, cross dressing, corporate agency, Siamese twins, and technology and mechanization, among others. See especially Nan Goodman, *Shifting the Blame: Literature, Law, and the Theory of Accidents in Nineteenth Century America* (Princeton: Princeton University Press, 1999); Susan Gillman, *Dark Twins: Imposture and Identity in Mark Twain's America* (Chicago: University of Chicago Press, 1989). By contrast, I am arguing that the discourse of insanity helps us see how Twain's own insistence on individual responsibility was the problem, as this rationalist discourse led to an indiscriminate critique of all political emotion.

26. For a reading of this scene in the context of tort law, see Stacey Margolis, *The Public Life of Privacy in Nineteenth-Century American Literature* (Durham: Duke University Press, 2005), 90. See also Goodman, *Shifting the Blame*, 65. Twain lost his brother in just such an explosion and was hardly sanguine about the psychological effects of the experience. See Ron Powers, *Mark Twain: A Life* (New York: Free Press, 2005), 86–7.

27. As Ray bluntly states, "The hereditary character of insanity has long since passed into the category of established things" (Ray, *A Treatise on the Medical Jurisprudence of Insanity*, 172.)

28. For an overview of Child's involvement in the case, see Carolyn L. Karcher, *The First Woman in the Republic: A Cultural Biography of Lydia Maria Child* (Durham: Duke University Press), 328–9.

29. Andrea L. Hibbard and John T. Parry, "Law, Seduction, and the Sentimental Heroine: The Case of Amelia Norman," *American Literature* 78.2 (June 2006): 325–55.

30. Lydia Maria Child, *A Lydia Maria Child Reader*, ed. Carolyn L. Karcher (Durham: Duke University Press, 1997), 373.

31. On Twain's Nook Farm friends and colleagues, and their critique of sensationalism and sentimentalism, see Bryant Morey French, *Mark Twain and The Gilded Age* (Dallas: Southern Methodist University Press, 1965), 25–59.

32. Susan Harris discusses this statement and Twain's contradictory portrait of Laura in "Four Ways to Inscribe a Mackerel: Mark Twain and Laura Hawkins," *Studies in the Novel* 21 (1989): 151. Harris focuses on Twain's oversimplification of fiction written by women, which he simultaneously parodies and mimics.

33. For a resonant discussion of the potentially inverse relationship between moral virtue and publicity (in the context of the rise of named authorship and the importance of literary reputation), see Susan M. Ryan, *The Moral Economies of American Authorship: Reputation, Scandal, and the Nineteenth-Century Literary Marketplace* (New York: Oxford University Press, 2016).

34. On the mid-nineteenth-century emergence of free love advocates, see Nancy F. Cott, *Public Vows: A History of Marriage and the Nation* (Cambridge, MA: Harvard University Press, 2000), 68.

35. Barbara Goldsmith, *Other Powers: The Age of Suffrage, Spiritualism, and the Scandalous Victoria Woodhull* (New York: A.A. Knopf, 1998). Future citations will be given

parenthetically in the text and abbreviated *O*. This definition of Woodhull as a kind of "queen" helpfully invokes the accounts of women's precarious acts of political agency analyzed by Lauren Berlant in *The Queen of America Goes to Washington City: Essays on Sex and Citizenship* (Durham: Duke University Press, 1997). Woodhull is a quintessential "Diva Citizen": one who "stages a dramatic coup in the public sphere in which she does not have privilege" and engages in acts of "risky dramatic persuasion" (223).

36. See Carole Haber, *The Trials of Laura Fair: Sex, Murder, and Insanity in the Victorian West* (Chapel Hill: The University of North Carolina Press, 2015).

37. One way to track what's odd about Twain's critique would be to say it combines what Richard Hofstadter calls the "populist" and "progressive" reform dispositions. The former was rowdy, "rancorous," and agrarian, with populists protesting "economic deprivations"; the latter, or the "mugwump type," were urban, educated men who were victims of "an upheaval in status," seeking not to organize the masses but to form a "responsible elite." See *The Age of Reform* (New York: Vintage, 1955), 163.

38. On the rise of "the lobbyist," see Joel H. Silbey, *The American Political Nation, 1838–1893* (Stanford: Stanford University Press, 1991), 193. I examine the figure of the "female lobbyist" at greater length in the following chapter.

39. "fascinate, v." *OED Online.* Oxford University Press. http://www.oed.com/view/Entry/68362, accessed December 2015.

40. Laura's "fascination" is the dark mirror of earlier nineteenth-century notions of "female influence": the natural emission of moral goodness by which female power could seep indirectly into the public sphere. For an account of female benevolence emphasizing the real labor of "influence," see Lori D. Ginzberg, *Women and the Work of Benevolence: Morality, Politics, and Class in the Nineteenth-century United States* (New Haven: Yale University Press, 1990).

41. For a concise account of how Woodhull's rise led Stowe to scale back her support of radical reformers, see Margaret Wyman, "Harriet Beecher Stowe's Topical Novel on Woman Suffrage," *The New England Quarterly* 25, no. 3 (1952): 386.

42. Though the comparison would surely have horrified all parties, Stowe's *My Wife and I* could be put in dialogue with the "Free Love" novels surveyed by Holly Jackson in "The Marriage Trap in the Free-Love Novel and Queer Critique," *American Literature* 87, no. 4 (December 2015): 681–708. Jackson shows that while many free lovers desired to escape from marriage, others questioned if or how marriage could accommodate more flexible forms of kinship. Stowe, too, could be said to refuse "to relinquish marriage" even as she often seems "hungry for alternatives" (702). Tess Chakkalakal underscores the intimacy between Stowe and free love advocates by highlighting her antagonism toward them. She argues that Stowe's exploration of freedom within marriage in *The Minister's Wooing* is a rebuke to radicals who could only imagine noncoercive love outside of it. See " 'Whimsical Contrasts': Love and Marriage in 'The Minister's Wooing' and 'Our Nig,' " *The New England Quarterly* 84, no. 1 (March 2011): 159–71.

43. Jon Mee, *Romanticism, Enthusiasm, and Regulation: Poetics and the Policing of Culture in the Romantic Period* (New York: Oxford University Press), 2005.

44. Fears of love's effects on unbalanced minds were justified according to medical experts. Testimony in the Laura Fair case warned, "that when [women] are in love, and at the same time of nervous hysterical disposition, they are capable of doing anything." Cited in Haber, *The Trials of Laura Fair,* 101.

45. Christopher Castiglia, *Interior States: Institutional Consciousness and the Inner Life of Democracy in the Antebellum United States* (Durham: Duke University Press, 2008), 2.

46. Ibid., 74.

47. On the importance of print culture to late-nineteenth-century sex radicalism, in general, and the history of Woodhull's *Weekly*, in particular, see the fourth chapter, "The Power of Print," in Passet, *Sex Radicals*, 39–63.

48. Elsewhere Stowe shows herself keenly aware that madness was a ready rhetorical tool to discredit reformers: "a woman belonging to the upper classes, who undertakes to get wealth by honest exertion and independent industry, loses caste, and is condemned by a thousand voices as an oddity and a deranged person" (*M*, 74–5).

49. Justine Murison, *The Politics of Anxiety in Nineteenth-Century American Literature* (New York: Cambridge University Press, 2011), 110; John Mac Kilgore, *Mania for Freedom: American Literatures of Enthusiasm from the Revolution to the Civil War* (Chapel Hill: University of North Carolina Press, 2016), 5. Murison and Kilgore also see Stowe as probing the limits of enthusiasm, especially when embodied by the eponymous black prophet and revolutionary in *Dred: A Tale of the Great Dismal Swamp* (1856).

50. This parallels Gillian Brown's account of the problematic politics of sentimental possession in relation to slaves and servants. For Brown, "these conjunctions of market value and color underscore the identity of black people with commodities that Stowe retains even as her ethic of sentimental possession offers a way of transforming commodities into citizens" (*Domestic Individualism: Imagining Self in Nineteenth-Century America* [Berkeley: University of California Press, 1990], 59–60).

51. "home-wrecker, n." *OED Online*. Oxford University Press. http://www.oed.com/view/Entry/248675, accessed December 2015.

52. Lori Merish, *Sentimental Materialism* (Durham: Duke University Press, 2000), 152, 161.

53. What we might call Stowe's "Robinsonade" imagines domestic goods freed into circulation by unseen and unspecified familial crises, transformed effortlessly into the backdrop for wholesome domesticity. For Karl Marx, the Robinsonade described a philosophical genre for imagining the origins of society—"history's point of departure"—in the isolated individual. Stowe's updated Crusoe fantasy does the likes of Smith and Ricardo one better by positing unclaimed, free-floating manufactured commodities as the pre-existing point of departure for the matrimonial phase of "Harry Henderson's History." See Karl Marx, *Grundrisse* (New York: Penguin Books, 1973), 83.

54. The notion of marriage as a national "institution"—that is, more than a private contract—was still relatively new at the time of Stowe's writing. Nancy Cott sees the consensus about the importance of marriage as a stable social form solidifying from the late 1860s through the subsequent two decades, such that by 1888 the US Supreme Court Justice Stephen Field could insist that marriage was "an institution, the maintenance of which *in its purity* the public is deeply interested." Cited in *Public Vows*, 102–3.

55. "SLC to OLC, 3 Oct. 1872, London, England (UCCL 00817)." In *Mark Twain Project Online*. Berkeley: University of California Press. 2007; http://www.marktwainproject.org/xtf/view?docId=letters/UCCL00817.xml;style=letter;brand=mtp, accessed 20 January, 2009.

56. For Foucault, the history of madness is "primarily concerned with scandal." See Michel Foucault, *Madness and Civilization: A History of Insanity in the Age of Reason* (New York: Vintage Books, 1988), 66. Showing remarkable sensitivity toward the function of scandal to neutralize radical political thinking, Elizabeth Cady Stanton argued that the public needed to foster a certain taste for the scandalous: "To those who take a surface view

of the scandal, it is possibly prurient, disgusting, nauseating.... This, to my mind, is an evidence, not of a depraved popular taste, but of a vital interest in the social problems that puzzle and perplex the best of us" (*O*, 404).

57. On the kissing of Graham, the real-life counterpart to Braham, see French, "Mark Twain, Laura D. Fair, and the New York Criminal Courts," *American Quarterly* 16, no. 4 (Winter 1964): 561.

58. On free love as free lust, see Cott, *Public Vows*, 68.

59. Gustave Le Bon, *The Crowd: A Study of the Popular Mind* (New York: The Macmillan Co., 1897), 12.

60. William McDougall, *The Group Mind* (London: Cambridge University Press, 1920), 45.

61. Le Bon, 116.

62. William Mazzarella, "The Myth of the Multitude, or, Who's Afraid of the Crowd?," *Critical Inquiry* 36, no. 4 (Summer 2010): 707.

63. Ibid., 721.

64. Ibid., 716.

65. Haber, *Trials of Laura Fair*, 112.

66. Mari Jo Buhle and Paul Buhle, eds., *The Concise History of Woman Suffrage* (Urbana: University of Illinois Press, 2005), 284.

67. The quote is drawn from a website that offers a partial archive of *Woodhull and Claflin's Weekly*: http://www.victoria-woodhull.com/wc112599.htm

Chapter 2

1. Gustafson argues that calling a novel focused on the capital's "social and governing elites" *Democracy* is a "deliberate irony" that "points to the gap between the abstract ideal of 'democracy'... and the actual circumstances of democracy's implementation" ("Democratic Fictions," in *A Companion to American Fiction 1780–1865*, ed. Shirley Samuels [Malden, MA: Blackwell Publishing, 2004], 33).

2. Stanley Cavell, *The Senses of Walden* (Chicago: The University of Chicago Press, 1992), 9.

3. Nathaniel Hawthorne, *The House of the Seven Gables* (New York: Penguin, 1986), 315.

4. Ibid., 179.

5. Edmund Burke, *The Portable Edmund Burke*, ed. Isaac Kramnick (New York: Penguin Books), 34.

6. E.H. Chapin, *The Philosophy of Reform: A Lecture Delivered Before the Berean Institute* (New York: C.L. Stickney, 1843), 17.

7. Michael Davitt Bell, *The Development of American Romance* (Chicago: The University of Chicago Press, 1981), 196. For an account that troubles claims about the radicalism of the romance by casting the genre as a phobic response to the vicissitudes of property in a capitalist economy, see Walter Benn Michaels, "Romance and Real Estate," in *The American Renaissance Reconsidered*, eds. Walter Benn Michaels and Donald E. Pease (Baltimore: Johns Hopkins University Press, 1985), 164.

8. Christopher Hitchens, "In Search of the Washington Novel: A Colorful Genre Awaits Its Masterpiece," *City Journal* 20, no. 4 (Autumn 2010), www.city-journal.org/2010/20_4_ urb-the-washington-novel.html.

9. This state of affairs may explain the new interest in post-critical practices of "repair" even as anti-institutional romanticism remains highly lauded. In other words,

"conservatism's" failure to stake its legitimacy on an ethics of institutional responsibility makes "repair" available for other political ends. There are of course other ways to contextualize the turn to post-critique: Eve Sedgwick argued that the naked violence of modern power demands rethinking the now superfluous gesture of "unmasking." And Robyn Wiegman questions "the attraction, in a time of declining…support for the…humanities, of a critical practice that…nurture[s] its objects of study." See Eve Kosofsky Sedgwick, "Paranoid Reading and Reparative Reading, or You're So Paranoid, You Probably Think This Essay is About You," in *Touching Feeling: Affect, Pedagogy, Performativity* (Durham: Duke University Press, 2003), 123–51; Robyn Wiegman, "The Times We're in: Queer Feminist Criticism and the Reparative 'turn,'" *Feminist Theory* 15, no. 1 (April 1, 2014): 4–25.

10. David Brooks, "The Republicans' Incompetence Caucus," The *New York Times*, October 13, 2015, http://www.nytimes.com/2015/10/13/opinion/the-republicans-incompetence-caucus.html.

11. Ibid.

12. Cited in Arthur Schlesinger, "On Henry Adams and Democracy," *New York Review of Books*, March 27, 2003.

13. Russell Kirk, *The Conservative Mind From Burke to Eliot* (Washington DC: Regnery Publishing Inc., 2001), 357.

14. Michael Brendan Dougherty, "Henry Adams and the Gift of Pessimism," *The Week*, April 13, 2014, http://theweek.com/articles/444563/henry-adams-gift-pessimism.

15. For a concise account of conservatism's suspicion of efforts to reform institutions see Jerry Z. Muller, "What is Conservative Social and Political Thought?" in *Conservatism: An Anthology of Social and Political Thought from David Hume to the Present*, ed. J.Z. Muller (Princeton: Princeton University Press, 1997).

16. There isn't space to fully pursue the profound but complex resonance between the novel and twenty-first-century politics, but a condensed schematization could go like this: In the late nineteenth century, a widespread disgust with politics fueled fantasies of elite, technocratic administration. In the twenty-first century, Donald Trump's promises to "drain the swamp" fed off a similar disgust with corruption, helping to position him as an authoritarian strongman who could cut through the morass. These are two different styles of post-political fantasy but they are both fueled by repulsion and are both broadly extra- or anti-democratic.

17. For Richard Hofstadter, the "mugwump type" denotes a waning aristocracy of eastern elites casting a suspicious eye at both the laboring classes and the industrialist nouveau riche. See *The Age of Reform* (New York: Vintage, 1955), 163.

18. A range of recent work has explored the vicissitudes of disgust as a problem for classical aesthetics, a troubling emotion for democratic theory, and both a challenge and resource for modern art. Martha Nussbaum argues that disgust's "cognitive content"—its refusal of contamination—is too readily put to racist, misogynist, anti-Semitic, and homophobic ends. William Miller considers when and how disgust, as a feeling that will inevitably occur in political contexts, may reinforce meaningful judgments about social life. That this is more of an ethical and aesthetic question than a legal one puts Miller's account in line with Winfried Menninghaus's philosophical genealogy of disgust, which focuses on aesthetic theory, and Sianne Ngai's recent work on "ugly feelings," which emphasizes the ways artists provoke disgust to refuse indifference or weak toleration. See Martha Nussbaum,

Hiding from Humanity: Disgust, Shame, and the Law (Princeton: Princeton University Press, 2004); William Ian Miller, *The Anatomy of Disgust* (Cambridge: Harvard University Press, 1997); Winfried Menninghaus, *Disgust: Theory and History of a Strong Sensation*, trans. Howard Eiland and Joel Golb (Albany, NY: State University of New York Press, 2003); Sianne Ngai, *Ugly Feelings* (Cambridge: Harvard University Press, 2005).

19. On William Cobbett's anti-revolutionary rhetoric of repulsion see Jason Frank, "Democracy and Disgust," *J19* 5, no. 2 (Fall 2017): 396–403. Frank's essay came out after I wrote this chapter, but it helps highlight important continuities and shifts in disgust as an eighteenth- and nineteenth-century political emotion. For Cobbett in 1790, the very concept of democracy—its disorganization of hierarchies and boundaries—is disgusting. Frank outlines the importance of contending with such antidemocratic deployments of affect. For Henry Adams in 1880, "democracy" is still an abstract principle but it is also the name for the all-too-concrete institutions of Gilded Age governance. In this context, as I show, disgust is at the center of a complex negotiation of affective positions between apathy and desire, withdrawal and engagement.

20. Henry Adams, *Democracy: An American Novel* (New York: Penguin Books, 2008), 3. All references to this text are hereafter cited parenthetically by page number and abbreviated *D*.

21. From one angle Madeleine's journey to Washington looks like an instance of what Lauren Berlant has called an act of Diva Citizenship, in which "a person stages a dramatic coup in a public sphere in which she does not have privilege." On the other hand, Madeleine emphasizes that she is not mobilizing her gendered particularity but rather abandoning it, and she already has a significant degree of social and financial power to leverage. See Lauren Berlant, *The Queen of America Goes to Washington City* (Durham: Duke University Press, 1997), 223.

22. Berlant has argued that "the desire to become national seems to call for a *release* from sensuality—this is the cost, indeed the promise, of citizenship." See *Queen of America*, 239. For another, extended account of this loss of particularity as a condition for access to the public sphere, see, Seyla Benhabib, *Democracy and Difference: Contesting the Boundaries of the Political* (Princeton: Princeton University Press, 1996).

23. Clinton Rossiter, ed., *The Federalist Papers* (New York: Penguin Putnam, 1999), 217.

24. Brooks D. Simpson, *The Political Education of Henry Adams* (Columbia: University of South Carolina Press, 1995), 108.

25. On the ways "allegorical thinking helps to provide ways of explaining the relation between individuals' lives, the life of the collectivity, and the story of the nation form itself" see Berlant, *Queen of America*, 48.

26. Menninghaus, *Disgust: Theory and History of a Strong Sensation*, 22.

27. Ibid.

28. For an account of this scene as expressing Adams's ambivalence about American's slavish devotion to foreign culture, see Charles Vandersee, "The Pursuit of Culture in Adams' *Democracy*," *American Quarterly* 19 (1967): 239–48. For a general account of America's anxieties about the lack of culture, refinement and taste in the young nation's capital city, see Carl Abbott, *Political Terrain: Washington, D.C., from Tidewater Town to Global Metropolis* (Chapel Hill: University of North Carolina Press, 2005).

29. Art exhibitions at the Philadelphia Centennial Exhibition of 1876 and Oscar Wilde's 1882 visit to the United States bookend the writing and publication of Adams's *Democracy*

as two significant markers of the height of aestheticism in America. In historian Mary Blanchard's telling, relays between the private interior and the public life of politics reached an all-time low during the Gilded Age. See Mary Warner Blanchard, *Oscar Wilde's America: Counterculture in the Gilded Age* (New Haven: Yale University Press, 1998), 86.

30. Blanchard, 120.

31. For a relevant discussion of the widespread use of anesthetic narcotics in the late nineteenth century, see T.J. Jackson Lears, *No Place of Grace: Antimodernism and the Transformation of American Culture, 1880–1920* (New York: Pantheon Books, 1981), 11.

32. Domesticity thus becomes paradoxically outward looking: "domesticity must be spatially and conceptually mobile to travel to the nation's far-flung frontiers." Amy Kaplan, *The Anarchy of Empire in the Making of U.S. Culture* (Cambridge, MA: Harvard University Press, 2002), 34.

33. For a description of the decorating style of Adams and his wife, Clover, see Ernest Samuels, *Henry Adams, the Middle Years* (Cambridge, MA: Belknap Press, 1958), 127.

34. Cited in Blanchard, *Oscar Wilde's America*, 85.

35. Or we might say that Madeleine wants the solidity of objects to compensate for a lack of political stability. For an analysis of another literary scene in which material objects appear to fill a disturbing absence at the heart of American democracy, see especially the first chapter of Bill Brown, *A Sense of Things: The Object Matter of American Literature* (Chicago: University of Chicago Press, 2003).

36. Christopher P. Wilson, "Secrets of the Master's Deed Box: Narrative and Class," in *A Companion to American Fiction 1865–1914*, eds. Robert Paul Lamb and G.R. Thompson (John Wiley & Sons, 2008), 347.

37. Matthew Taylor discusses *The Education* as a "remarkably uninhabited autobiography" in *Universes Without Us: Posthuman Cosmologies in American Literature* (Minneapolis: University of Minnesota Press, 2013), 57–83.

38. Martha Banta, "Being a 'Begonia' in a Man's World," *New Essays on the Education of Henry Adams*, ed. John Carlos Rowe (Cambridge: Cambridge University Press, 1996): 49–86.

39. John Carlos Rowe, "Introduction," *New Essays on the Education of Henry Adams*, 16.

40. Cindy Weinstein, "From True Woman to New Woman to Virgin," in *Henry Adams and the Need to Know*, eds. William Merrill Decker and Earl N. Harbert (Boston: Massachusetts Historical Society, 2005), 301.

41. For a short history of the lobbyist's rise see Conor McGrath and Phil Harris, "The Creation of the U.S. Lobbying Industry," in *The Routledge Handbook of Political Management*, ed. Dennis W. Johnson (New York: Routledge, 2009).

42. "lobbyist, n.". *OED Online*. March 2016. Oxford University Press. http://www.oed.com/view/Entry/109499?redirectedFrom=lobbyist, accessed March 2016.

43. Kathryn A. Jacob, *King of the Lobby: The Life and Times of Sam Ward, Man-About-Washington in the Gilded Age* (Baltimore: Johns Hopkins University Press, 2010).

44. *The National Police Gazette* 350 (June 7, 1884), 6.

45. Joyce W. Warren, *Fanny Fern: An Independent Woman* (New Brunswick, NJ: Rutgers University Press, 1992), 3.

46. Catherine Allgor, *Parlor Politics: In Which the Ladies of Washington Help Build a City and a Government* (Charlottesville: University Press of Virginia, 2000).

47. See, for example, "Women at the Capital," *Every Saturday: A Journal of Choice Reading* (August 12, 1871): 167.

48. This notion of the "mysteries of the lobby" recalls "mysteries of the city" novels such as George Lippard's 1845 *The Quaker City*, which anticipates *Democracy* in its desire to conceptualize the state of political power spatially, constructing a gothic mansion in which secret rites conducted in hidden chambers figuratively evoke the inaccessibility of elite power. George Lippard, *The Quaker City; or, The Monks of Monk Hall: a Romance of Philadelphia Life, Mystery, and Crime* (Amherst: University of Massachusetts Press, 1995).

49. On the rhetoric of sexual indiscretions policing gendered access to Reconstruction politics, see Rebecca Edwards, *Angels in the Machinery: Gender in American Party Politics from the Civil War to the Progressive Era* (New York: Oxford University Press, 1997), 23.

50. Sianne Ngai, *Ugly Feelings* (Cambridge: Harvard University Press, 2005), 28.

51. Lauren Berlant defines the juxtapolitical as a zone "proximate to, without being compromised by, the instrumentalities of power that govern social life" in *Cruel Optimism* (Durham: Duke University Press, 2011), 224. In Madeleine's case, however, the juxtapolitical space of the parlor fails to maintain its critical distance from compromised and compromising political institutions.

52. Teresa Brennan, *The Transmission of Affect* (Ithaca: Cornell University Press, 2004), 1.

53. Ibid., 6.

54. William Ian Miller, *The Anatomy of Disgust* (Cambridge: Harvard University Press, 1997).

55. "Correspondence: Novels of Washington Life," *The Literary World: a Monthly Review of Current Literature* (August 25, 1883): 273.

56. Henry James, *Literary Criticism: Essays on Literature, American Writers, English Writers*, eds. Leon Edel and Mark Wilson (New York: Library of America, 1984), 232.

57. Ngai, *Ugly Feelings*, 22.

58. Ibid., 120.

59. Ibid., 170.

60. "Several Recent Novels," *Christian Union* 21, no. 17 (April 28, 1880): 398.

61. Warren Susman, *Culture as History* (New York: Pantheon Books, 1984), xxiii.

62. Emily S. Rosenberg, *Spreading the American Dream: American Economic and Cultural Expansion, 1890–1945* (New York: Hill and Wang, 1982), 42.

63. Ari Arthur Hoogenboom, *Outlawing the Spoils: A History of the Civil Service Reform Movement, 1865–1883* (Westport, CT: Greenwood Press, 1982).

64. Simpson, *The Political Education of Henry Adams*, 63.

65. Henry Adams, "Civil Service Reform," *The North American Review* 109, no. 225 (October 1869): 4.

66. Ibid., 32.

67. In this book's final chapter I will examine the case of Garfield's assassin, Charles Guiteau, who came to embody in the popular imagination the literally insane excesses of the frustrated office seeker.

68. In a letter to his brother Charles, Henry Adams declared, "I have learned to think [Alexis] de Tocqueville my model, and I study his life and works as the Gospel of my private religion" (Henry Adams and J.C. Levenson, *The Letters of Henry Adams*, vol. 1, 6th ed. [Cambridge, MA: Belknap Press of Harvard University Press, 1982], 350).

69. Noah K. Davis, "The Moral Aspects of Vivisection," *The North American Review* 140, no. 340 (March, 1885): 210.

70. Susan L. Mizruchi, *The Science of Sacrifice: American Literature and Modern Social Theory* (Princeton: Princeton University Press, 1998), 11.

71. Henry Adams, *The Education of Henry Adams* (New York: Penguin Books, 1995), 43.

72. In *The Education,* this process is narrated in terms of the effects of the political sphere on private friendships, a theme to which I will return in the conclusion of this essay.

73. See for example Maurice Blanchot, *Friendship* (Stanford: Stanford University Press, 1997); Jacques Derrida, "Politics of Friendship," *American Imago* 50 (1993): 353–91; Michel Foucault, *Ethics: Subjectivity and Truth* (New York: New Press, 1997); Leela Gandhi, *Affective Communities: Anticolonial Thought, Fin-De-Siècle Radicalism, and the Politics of Friendship* (Durham: Duke University Press, 2006).

74. Charles M. Oliver, *Critical Companion to Walt Whitman: A Literary Reference to His Life and Work* (New York: Facts on File, Inc.), 386.

75. Helen Vendler, *Invisible Listeners: Lyric Intimacy in Herbert, Whitman, and Ashbery* (Princeton: Princeton University Press, 2009), 56.

76. Peter Goodrich, "The New Casuistry," *Critical Inquiry* 33 (2007): 676.

77. Ibid., 5.

78. Derrida, "Politics of Friendship," 380.

79. Immanuel Kant, *The Metaphysics of Morals,* trans. Mary Gregor (London: Cambridge University Press, 1991), 262.

80. Fenves, "Politics of Friendship," 142.

81. Walt Whitman, *Leaves of Grass: The Original 1855 Edition* (New York: Dover Publications, Inc., 2007), 49.

82. Miller, *Anatomy of Disgust,* 199–200.

83. Nussbaum, *Hiding from Humanity,* 117.

84. Miller, *Anatomy of Disgust,* 204.

85. Sigmund Freud, *Three Essays on the Theory of Sexuality* (New York: Basic Books, 1975), 18. Miller expands on this connection explaining, "disgust must always repel in some sense or it is not disgust. Repulsion, however, might bring in its train affects that work to move one closer again to what one just backed away from" (*Anatomy of Disgust,* 111).

86. Nussbaum, *Hiding from Humanity,* 121.

87. Ngai, *Ugly Feelings,* 336.

88. Ibid., 343.

89. Nussbaum argues, "anger at U.S. politicians tends in the direction of protest and constructive engagement. Disgust at U.S. politicians leads to escape and disengagement" (*Hiding from Humanity,* 106).

90. The original: "And if we cannot end now our differences, at least we can help make the world safe for diversity. For, in the final analysis, our most basic common link is that we all inhabit this small planet. We all breathe the same air" (John F. Kennedy, "Commencement Address at American University, Washington D.C., June 10, 1963," http://www.jfklibrary. org/Research/Research-Aids/JFK-Speeches/American-University_19630610.aspx).

Chapter 3

1. Helen Hunt Jackson, *The Indian Reform Letters of Helen Hunt Jackson, 1879–1885,* ed. Valerie Sherer Mathes (Norman: University of Oklahoma Press, 1998), 22. All references to this text are hereafter cited parenthetically by page number and abbreviated *L.* Jackson's evocation of the story's power echoes a contemporaneous review, which also stressed the tale's ability to affect even normally unfeeling readers: "The pathetic story of the doe's flight

for life and her heartless butchery ought to touch the heart of the most hardened hunter" ("Miscellaneous Books," *The American Bookseller* [July 15, 1878], 71).

2. Charles Dudley Warner, *In the Wilderness* (Boston: Houghton, Mifflin, 1878), 80.

3. Though the aforementioned review touted the tale's "pathetic" quality, the journal's editors also made clear that they regarded the collection as light reading, calling it a book that "every one should take on his vacation" ("Miscellaneous Books," 71).

4. For a concise history of Jackson's linking of her novel to Stowe's work, as well as early critical re-echoes of the comparison, see Susan Gillman, "Whose Protest Novel? *Ramona*, the *Uncle Tom's Cabin* of the Indian," in *The Oxford Handbook of Nineteenth-Century American Literature*, ed. Russ Castronovo (New York: Oxford University Press, 2012), 382.

5. Most criticism on the operation of sympathy in Stowe's novel seeks to complicate this commonsense account. Elizabeth Barnes, for example, argues that in Stowe's work "sympathy is made contingent upon similarity," and thus "Stowe must first elide the personal differences that constitute individuality" (*States of Sympathy: Seduction and Democracy in the American Novel* [New York: Columbia University Press, 1997], 92). Gillian Brown claims that the novel "underscore[s] the identity of blacks with commodities that Stowe retains even as her ethic of sentimental possession offers a way of transforming commodities into citizens" (*Domestic Individualism: Imagining Self in Nineteenth-Century America* [Berkeley: University of California Press, 1992], 59).

6. See especially the first chapter, "Poor Eliza," in Lauren Berlant, *The Female Complaint: The Unfinished Business of Sentimentality in American Culture* (Durham: Duke University Press, 2008).

7. For a summary of the "debate between a dismissal of the sentimental move outside or beyond the boundaries of a gendered or radicalized body…and, alternately, a celebration of the emancipatory strategies" of sentimentality, see Shirley Samuels, ed., *The Culture of Sentiment: Race, Gender, and Sentimentality in the Nineteenth-Century* (New York: Oxford University Press, 1992), 5.

8. See especially Carl Gutiérrez-Jones, *Rethinking the Borderlands: Between Chicano Culture and Legal Discourse* (Berkeley: University of California Press, 1995), and John M. Gonzalez, "The Warp of Whiteness: Domesticity and Empire in Helen Hunt Jackson's Ramona," *American Literary History* 16, no. 3 (2004): 437–65. For the novel's afterlife as a marketing tool, see Dydia DeLyser, *Ramona Memories: Tourism and the Shaping of Southern California* (Minneapolis: University of Minnesota Press, 2005).

9. In Berlant's account, "countersentimental texts withdraw from the contract that presumes consent with the conventionally desired outcomes of identification and compassion" (*The Female Complaint*, 56). Arguing that comparisons between *Ramona* and *Uncle Tom's Cabin* often obscure an alternate, "countersentimental" component to Jackson's political project is not to deny, however, that the comparison is potentially productive. Susan Gillman has argued that, for the Cuban author and activist José Martí, the Stowe–Jackson connection reflects "the intertwined hemispheric histories, aboriginal, slave, European, of the New World" ("Whose Protest Novel?," 386).

10. I am indebted throughout to the discussion of sovereignty in Lauren Berlant, "Slow Death (Sovereignty, Obesity, Lateral Agency)," *Critical Inquiry* 33 (2007): 754–80. Thinking about "slow death" understood as "the physical wearing out of a population…that is very nearly a defining condition of their experience" forces a consideration of the agency or sovereignty of less monumentalized "activity oriented toward the reproduction of ordinary

life" (758–9). This is the distinctly un-hyperbolic temporality of "sovereignty" that I hope to gesture toward here in the phrase "barely living."

11. Eva Ziarek, "Bare Life on Strike," *South Atlantic Quarterly* 107, no. 1 (2008): 89. Ziarek explores bare life as a potentially "contested terrain in which new forms of domination, dependence, and emancipatory struggles can emerge" (98). In this essay, as in Ziarek's work, this means finding ways to locate the potential for meaningful critique in the absence of fully realized political agency.

12. Alexander Weheliye claims that "bare life and biopolitics discourse" aspires "to transcend racialization via recourse to absolute biological matter" (*Habeas Viscus: Racializing Assemblages, Biopolitics, and Black Feminist Theories of the Human* [Durham: Duke University Press, 2014], 4). I suggest, however, that tracking the links in Jackson's text between animal and Indian makes very clear how the bare life on display reflects, to borrow Weheliye's formulation, "a set of socio political processes that discipline humanity into full humans, not-quite-humans, and nonhumans" (ibid.), processes that rely fundamentally on racializing taxonomies. This is not to say, however, that Jackson's strategy is without risk, as I explore throughout this chapter.

13. For an overview of the shifting status of tribal sovereignty, see David E. Wilkins and K. Tsianina Lomawaima, *Uneven Ground: American Indian Sovereignty and Federal Law* (Tulsa: University of Oklahoma Press, 2002). It should be noted that examining the instabilities of legal definitions of tribal sovereignty is not to doubt the ample evidence that indigenous tribes constituted self-governing collectivities and that the US government repeatedly treated them as such. On this point see David E. Wilkins, *American Indian Sovereignty and the U.S. Supreme Court: The Making of Justice* (Austin: University of Texas Press, 1997), 20. On the General Allotment Act and the rise of a bureaucratic apparatus for managing indigenous peoples and lands, see Vine Deloria Jr. and Clifford M. Lytle, *The Nations Within: The Past and Future of American Indian Sovereignty* (Austin: University of Texas Press, 1984), 5.

14. Kevin Bruyneel reclaims the uncertain status of Native Americans as a space of critique in *The Third Space of Sovereignty: The Postcolonial Politics of U.S.–Indigenous Relations* (Minneapolis: University of Minnesota Press, 2007). I suggest that Jackson's text likewise pursues the productive possibilities latent in hybrid forms of Indian agency.

15. For classic accounts of the biochemical basis of depression see Peter D. Kramer, *Listening to Prozac: The Landmark Book About Antidepressants and the Remaking of the Self* (New York: Penguin Books, 1997) and Peter D. Kramer, *Against Depression* (New York: Penguin Books, 2006).

16. Andrew Solomon has written that "depression is a disease of loneliness.... [I]t imposes a dread isolation" in *The Noonday Demon: An Atlas Of Depression* (New York: Scribner Classics, 2001), 214.

17. My interest in depression as exhausted sovereignty draws on Alain Ehrenberg, *Weariness of the Self: Diagnosing the History of Depression in the Contemporary Age* (Montreal, QC: McGill-Queen's University Press, 2010). Though I de-emphasize the focus on lost or internalized objects that characterize accounts of melancholia, I have also benefitted from Kelly Oliver's account of the "affects of oppression" in *Colonization of Psychic Space: A Psychoanalytic Social Theory of Oppression* (Minneapolis and London: University of Minnesota Press, 2004). Similarly, I take inspiration from Christopher Castiglia's discussion of how "Melancholy...preserves the power of social imagining itself"

in *Interior States: Institutional Consciousness and the Inner Life of Democracy in the Antebellum United States* (Durham: Duke University Press, 2008), 18.

18. Sara Ahmed, *The Promise of Happiness* (Durham: Duke University Press, 2010), 125.

19. For a concise overview of the "era of assimilation" see the introduction to Beth H. Piatote, *Domestic Subjects: Gender, Citizenship, and Law in Native American Literature* (New Haven: Yale University Press, 2013). Piatote's study focuses on the first of what she identifies as "the two most dominant policies of the era: the forced removal of indigenous children from their families to attend government-funded boarding and day schools and the allotment of reservation land in severalty" (5). I am focusing here primarily on the latter set of policies.

20. Mark S. Weiner, *Americans Without Law: The Racial Boundaries of Citizenship* (New York and London: New York University Press, 2006), 25.

21. Schurz expressed confidence that when Indians "hold their lands by the same title by which white men hold theirs…they will, as a matter of course, have the same standing in the courts, and the same legal protection of their property." Cited in Valerie Sherer Mathes, "Helen Hunt Jackson and the Campaign for Ponca Restitution, 1880–1881," *South Dakota History* 17 (Spring 1987): 33. As Mathes shows, Jackson repeatedly questioned how Schurz could both oppose Indians' legal rights and presume that those rights would follow "as a matter of course" from allotment.

22. Colleen Glenney Boggs, *Animalia Americana* (New York: Columbia University Press, 2013), 38.

23. On the idea that "identification with pain, a universal true feeling, then leads to structural social change," see Lauren Berlant, "The Subject of True Feeling: Pain, Privacy, and Politics," in *Cultural Pluralism, Identity Politics, and the Law*, ed. Austin Sarat and Thomas Kearns (Ann Arbor: University of Michigan Press, 1998), 53.

24. Helen Hunt Jackson, *Ramona* (New York: Avon Books, 1970), 142. All references to this text are hereafter cited parenthetically by page number and abbreviated *R*.

25. Berlant notes that "historically, the execution of the project of universalizing society through identification with paradigms of pain and love has required much lying about and mis-recognition of how to think about relative privilege within the sentimental field of the universal human" ("Poor Eliza," *American Literature* 70, no. 3 [September 1998]: 643). In *Ramona*, Felipe's sympathy for his mother (the very agent of irrational and unjust law) rather than for Ramona (the victim of the Señora's hasty judgment) dramatizes a similar point about sentimentality's failure to adjudicate relative suffering.

26. For an overview of the history of the Ponca case, see Valerie Sherer Mathes and Richard Lowitt, *The Standing Bear Controversy: Prelude to Indian Reform* (Urbana: University of Illinois Press, 2003).

27. For a discussion of Schurz's faith in civil service reform as an improvement in "efficiency and economy" see Martin J. Schiesl, *The Politics of Efficiency: Municipal Administration and Reform in America, 1800–1920* (Berkeley: University of California Press, 1980), 43.

28. Helen Hunt Jackson, *A Century of Dishonor: A Sketch of the United States Government's Dealings with Some of the Indian Tribes* (New York: Harper and Bros., 1881), 212.

29. See James T. King, "A Better Way: General George Crook and the Ponca Indians," *Nebraska History* 50 (1969): 239–56. Like Tibbles and other prominent voices in the reform movement including Piute author Sarah Winnemucca, Jackson believed that the military often embodied the order, discipline, and honor to which the civilian bureaucracy only paid

lip service. Tibbles and Winnemucca explicitly argued for Indian affairs to be removed from Department of the Interior oversight and transferred to military jurisdiction. See Sarah Winnemucca Hopkins, *Life Among the Piutes* (Reno, NV: University of Nevada Press, 1994), 178.

30. *Century of Dishonor*, 215.

31. Loring Benson Priest, *Uncle Sam's Stepchildren: The Reformation of United States Indian Policy, 1865–1887* (New York: Octagon Books, 1969), 79. Francis Paul Prucha agrees that "Schurz was a severely practical and unsentimental man" (*The Great Father: The United States Government and the American Indians* [Lincoln: University of Nebraska Press, 1986], 185).

32. Allan Nevins, "Helen Hunt Jackson, Sentimentalist vs. Realist," *The American Scholar* 10, no. 3 (Summer 1941): 284.

33. Thomas Henry Tibbles, *The Ponca Chiefs: An Account of the Trial of Standing Bear* (Lincoln: University of Nebraska Press, 1972), 47. All references to this text are hereafter cited parenthetically by page number and abbreviated *P*.

34. John Gonzalez, for example, writes that the Señora's persuasive power is a model for Jackson's own "art of indirect influence" ("The Warp of Whiteness," 444).

35. On the antebellum "cult of the vanishing American," in which the disappearance of indigenous people was presented as a fait accompli, see especially the second chapter in Lora Romero, *Home Fronts: Domesticity and Its Critics in the Antebellum United States* (Durham: Duke University Press, 1997).

36. Thomas Henry Tibbles, *Hidden Power. A Secret History of the Indian Ring, Its Operations, Intrigues, and Machinations. Revealing the Manner in Which It Controls Three Important Departments of the United States Government. A Defense of the U. S. Army, and a Solution of the Indian Problem* (New York: G. W. Carleton and Co., 1881), 246.

37. See Mark Rifkin, "Indigenizing Agamben: Rethinking Sovereignty in Light of the 'Peculiar' Status of Native Peoples," *Cultural Critique* 73 (2009): 88–124. Rifkin writes, "Typifying 'the relations of the Indians to the United States' as 'peculiar' and 'anomalous'... indexes the failure of U.S. discourses to encompass them while speaking as if they were incorporated via their incommensurability" (89).

38. On the production of "bare life [as] the originary activity of sovereignty" see *Homo Sacer: Sovereign Power and Bare Life* (Stanford, CA: Stanford University Press, 1998), 83.

39. Ibid., 124.

40. Stephen Dando-Collins, *Standing Bear Is a Person: The True Story of a Native American's Quest for Justice* (Cambridge, MA: Da Capo Press, 2004); Joe Starita, *"I Am a Man": Chief Standing Bear's Journey for Justice* (New York: St. Martin's Press, 2008).

41. For a resonant discussion of the ways the term "person" can imply "an entity on the verge of entering a political community" or a subject that is already "inside of a political community," see Monique Allewaert, *Ariel's Ecology: Plantations, Personhood, and Colonialism in the American Tropics* (Minneapolis: University of Minnesota Press, 2013), 10.

42. Here I echo Saidiya Hartman's account of "burdened individuality," a term that "attempts to convey the antagonistic production of the liberal individual, rights bearer, and raced subject as equal yet inferior, independent yet servile, freed yet bound by duty, reckless yet responsible, blithe yet brokenhearted" (*Scenes of Subjection: Terror, Slavery, and Self-Making in Nineteenth-Century America* [New York: Oxford University Press, 1997], 121).

43. Ehrenberg, *Weariness of Self*, 9.

44. Sianne Ngai, *Ugly Feelings* (Cambridge: Harvard University Press, 2005), 2.

45. *Rethinking the Borderlands*, 64.

46. Gutiérrez-Jones worries, for example, that Alessandro's "growing anger over the discrimination his community confronts leads him not to overt political acts of reprisal and protest but to increasingly severe mental lapses" (*Rethinking the Borderlands*, 64).

47. In thinking about the violence of Ramona's optimism, I am informed by Lee Edelman's refutation of the compulsory affirmation of the status quo that so often masquerades as "hope." See Lee Edelman, *No Future: Queer Theory and the Death Drive* (Durham: Duke University Press, 2004). See also Ahmed, *The Promise of Happiness*.

48. Siobhan Senier, *Voices of American Indian Resistance: Helen Hunt Jackson, Sarah Winnemucca, and Victoria Howard* (Norman, OK: University of Oklahoma Press, 2001), 41.

49. For another critique of the critical tendency to tie *Ramona* directly to the Dawes Act see Senier, *Voices of American Indian Resistance*, 35. I also follow Senier in questioning whether *Ramona* can justly be called "sentimental," though she emphasizes stylistic differences as the somewhat under-theorized crux of Jackson's aesthetics, describing as "rather unsentimental" Jackson's "tamping down of the didactic narrator" (72).

50. I take this phrase from Laura Wexler's account of how peaceful images of domestic scenes reinforced America's imperialist policies at the turn of the century in *Tender Violence: Domestic Visions in an Age of U.S. Imperialism* (Chapel Hill: University of North Carolina Press, 2000).

51. "Subject of True Feeling," 84.

52. Ibid.

53. *Rethinking the Borderlands*, 62.

54. Ehrenberg, *Weariness of Self*, 8.

55. Ibid.

56. Audra Simpson, for example, challenges a politics of "recognition" and "reconciliation" by seeking alternate, antagonistic postures toward the state: "As well as producing affectively structured citizens…the state produces the conditions for what I want to suggest are 'distantiations,' 'disaffiliations' or outright refusals—a willful distancing from state-driven forms of recognition" (Audra Simpson, *Mohawk Interruptus: Political Life Across the Borders of Settler States* [Durham: Duke University Press, 2014], 16).

57. Glen Sean Coulthard, *Red Skin, White Masks: Rejecting the Colonial Politics of Recognition* (Minneapolis: University Of Minnesota Press, 2014). Speaking of contemporary Canadian–Indian relations, Couthard argues that "what implicitly gets interpreted by the state as Indigenous peoples' *ressentiment*—understood as an incapacitating inability or unwillingness to get over the past—is actually an entirely appropriate manifestation of our *resentment*: a politicized expression of Indigenous anger" (109).

58. *In the Wilderness*, 17.

59. The story was reprinted in later years. See, for example, Charles Dudley Warner, "How I Killed a Bear," *Outlook*, June 4, 1898.

60. John C. Havard, "Sentimentalism, Interracial Romance, and Helen Hunt Jackson and Clorinda Matto De Turner's Attacks on Abuses of Native Americans in *Ramona* and *Aves Sin Nido*," *Intertexts* 11 (2007): 109.

61. *Rethinking the Borderlands*, 68; "The Warp of Whiteness," 454. For a similar reading, see Yolanda Venegas, "The Erotics of Racialization: Gender and Sexuality in the Making of California," *Frontiers: A Journal of Women Studies* 25 (2004): Dean's critique of political transparency 74.

62. Havard, "Sentimentalism," 109.

63. Agamben, *Homo Sacer*, 131. See also the discussion of "Melancholy Migrants," in Ahmed, *Happiness*, 121.

64. Ramona's traumatized half-life might be usefully contrasted with those necrophilic and somnambulistic fantasies of transcending politics that Russ Castronovo tracks in *Necro Citizenship* (Durham: Duke University Press, 2001).

65. Ann Cvetkovich, *Depression: A Public Feeling* (Durham: Duke University Press, 2012), 12.

Chapter 4

1. Thomas Frank, *What's the Matter with Kansas? How Conservatives Won the Heart of America* (New York: Metropolitan Books, 2004), 114.

2. Walter Benn Michaels, *The Trouble with Diversity: How We Learned to Love Identity and Ignore Inequality* (New York: Macmillan, 2007).

3. Robert H. Craig claims that, "like so many well-meaning radicals before and since, Debs tried to subsume the race question in the class struggle, and in the process he moderated his radicalism and failed to come to terms with the unique quality of the African-American experience" (*Religion and Radical Politics: An Alternative Christian Tradition in the United States* [Philadelphia: Temple University Press, 1995], 91–2). For an opposing position that offers a concise summary of this critique, see William P. Jones, "Something to Offer," *Jacobin*, August 11, 2015, https://www.jacobinmag.com/2015/08/debs-socialism-race-du-bois-socialist-party-black-liberation/. Sanders—an avowed Debs admirer—seemed to some detractors to replay the story of populism's inevitable failure to acknowledge the specific pressures shaping black life.

4. Judith N. Shklar, *Ordinary Vices* (Cambridge: Harvard University Press, 1984), 75. David Runciman makes a similar point about hypocrisy's outsized affective impact: "however much one might recognise its essential triviality as a vice, it is impossible to avoid its potential significance as a motor of political conflict, given its capacity to provoke people beyond measure" (*Political Hypocrisy: The Mask of Power, from Hobbes to Orwell and Beyond* [Princeton: Princeton University Press, 2010], 18).

5. Sara Ahmed, *The Promise of Happiness* (Durham: Duke University Press, 2010), 46–9.

6. Walt Whitman, *Democratic Vistas* [1871]. Edited by Ed Folsom (Iowa City: University of Iowa Press, 2010), 11.

7. Ibid.

8. Here I emphasize Donnelly's achievements, though he is most often remembered for his failures. He is the discredited proponent of the Atlantis myth and a defeated populist vice-presidential candidate. Known to admiring contemporaries as the "Sage of Nininger," after the Minnesota town he founded, and the "Prophet of Protest" for his provocative, dystopic imagination, Donnelly has more recently been recrowned the "Prince of Cranks." For a more recent use of this epithet, albeit with a degree of admiration for Donnelly's eccentricity, see J.M. Tyree, "Ignatius Donnelly, Prince of Cranks," *The Believer* 3 (2005).

9. Here I follow a number of critics who have looked to Du Bois especially for a way of understanding the aesthetics of politics and politics of aesthetics. See especially Nancy Bentley, "Warped Conjunctions: Jacques Rancière and African American Twoness," in *American Literature's Aesthetic Dimensions*, ed. Cindy Weinstein and Christopher Looby

(New York: Columbia University Press, 2012.) I engage with Bentley's account in the conclusion of this essay. See also Ross Posnock, "The Distinction of Du Bois: Aesthetics, Pragmatism, Politics," *American Literary History* 7, no. 3 (Autumn 1995): 500–24.

10. Bruno Latour, "What If We Talked Politics a Little?" *Contemporary Political Theory* 2 (2003): 151.

11. On the cynic's view of institutions as themselves "hypocritical, soulless, or otherwise devoid of the beliefs that once animated them," see David Mazella, *The Making of Modern Cynicism* (Charlottesville: University of Virginia Press, 2007), 5.

12. That some of Kenneth Warren's recent work has been regarded as controversial attests to how fraught the race/class debate remains. Warren describes his aim as "mundane" precisely because it is so charged: "Crafting a political left that does not merely reflect existing racial divisions starts with the relatively mundane proposition that it is possible to make a persuasive appeal to the given interests of working and unemployed women and men, regardless of race, in support of a program for economic justice" (" 'As White as Anybody': Race and the Politics of Counting as Black," *New Literary History* 31, no. 4 [2000]: 725).

13. For a political cartoon depicting Donnelly as the father of the People's Party, see Martin Ridge, *Ignatius Donnelly: The Portrait of a Politician* (St. Paul: Minnesota Historical Society Press, 1991), 277.

14. The novel repulsed many white critics—one denounced its "revolting" plot—though it appeared to strike a chord with some black readers. See John S. Patterson, "Alliance and Antipathy: Ignatius Donnelly's Ambivalent Vision in *Doctor Huguet*," *American Quarterly* 22 (1970): 835. A minor *succès de scandale*, *Doctor Huguet* nonetheless fell far short of the reported one thousand copies per day that Donnelly's publisher claimed for *Caesar's Column*, though the author proudly boasted that this later novel was in its fifth edition by 1899. See Ridge, *Ignatius Donnelly: The Portrait of a Politician*, 90, 267.

15. See Patterson, "Alliance and Antipathy." For a summary of other, largely negative responses to the novel, see John R. Bovee, "Doctor Huguet: Donnelly on Being Black," *Minnesota History* (1969): 288.

16. Ignatius Donnelly, *Doctor Huguet: A Novel* (Chicago: F.J. Schulte & Co., 1891), 36. All references to this text are hereafter cited parenthetically by page number and abbreviated *D.*

17. Runciman, *Political Hypocrisy*, 24.

18. For a resonant expression of frustration with the idea that "logic is going to stop people being racist" see the interview with Ernesto Laclau in Mary Zournazi, *Hope: New Philosophies for Change* (New York: Routledge, 2003), 144.

19. "hypocrisy, n." *OED Online*. Oxford University Press. http://www.oed.com/view/Entry/90491?redirectedFrom=hypocrisy, accessed June 2016.

20. Runciman, *Political Hypocrisy*, 58. Emphasis added.

21. Donnelly's importance for the history of populism is often obscured by the movement's co-optation by Democratic presidential candidate William Jennings Bryan's "shadow movement" populism. For Lawrence Goodwyn, this term describes the political maneuvering of a range of politicians who supported isolated elements of the populist platform for immediate political gain. See Lawrence Goodwyn, *The Populist Moment: A Short History of the Agrarian Revolt in America* (New York: Oxford University Press, 1978), 311.

22. Huguet hews closely to Donnelly's beliefs. Donnelly had long been an outspoken advocate for the rights of African Americans, and as a radical Republican he argued

especially for the establishment of a national bureau of education to ensure opportunities regardless of race. St. Paul's Democratic-leaning *Pioneer* sought to discredit Donnelly with white voters, denouncing "Donnelly's Nigger Bureau [and] Nigger Schools." Cited in Ridge, *Ignatius Donnelly*, 104.

23. Nancy Fraser, "Rethinking the Public Sphere: A Contribution to the Critique of Actually Existing Democracy," *Social Text* 25–6 (1990): 117. Italics added.

24. See Patterson, "Alliance and Antipathy."

25. See Looby's introduction to Robert Montgomery Bird, *Sheppard Lee* (New York: New York Review Books, 2008), xvii.

26. *Sheppard Lee*, 140.

27. Edgar Allan Poe, "Robert M. Bird" in *Essays and Reviews* (New York: The Library of America, 1984).

28. That is to say that, for Donnelly, an inquiry into the evolutionary biology of race provides insights into why skin tones differ, but humanity's common ancestry and the more recent evolutionary forces of environment invalidate race's exaggerated social importance.

29. For a fruitful discussion of another text, George Schuyler's *Black No More* (1931), that uses a racial transformation to think about the history and future of black political movements, see Kenneth Warren, *What Was African American Literature?* (Cambridge: Harvard University Press, 2011).

30. Jacques Rancière, *Disagreement: Politics and Philosophy* (University of Minnesota Press, 1999), 30.

31. Jodi Dean, *Publicity's Secret: How Technoculture Capitalizes on Democracy* (Ithaca: Cornell University Press, 2002), 32.

32. Ibid., 46.

33. Dean's critique of political transparency mirrors Eve Sedgwick's critique of "paranoid reading" and the hermeneutics of suspicion, in which the frantic desire to unmask and deconstruct hinders a politics of construction and repair. See Eve Kosofsky Sedgwick, *Touching Feeling: Affect, Pedagogy, Performativity* (Durham: Duke University Press, 2003).

34. Hannah Arendt, *On Revolution* (New York: Penguin, 1990), 98.

35. Shklar, *Ordinary Vices*, 77.

36. Ignatius Donnelly, *The Great Cryptogram: Francis Bacon's Cipher in the So-Called Shakespeare Plays* (London: S. Low, Marston, Searle & Rivington, 1888), 64. All references to this text are hereafter cited parenthetically by page number and abbreviated *GC*.

37. Norman Pollack, one of Donnelly's more sympathetic readers, notes with regret that his Bacon-not-Shakespeare theory "may have suggested to contemporaries an erratic quality which harmed his later credibility" (*The Just Polity: Populism, Law, and Human Welfare* [Urbana: University of Illinois Press, 1987], 229). Donnelly's eccentric theories earn him pride of place in Charles P. Pierce's history of American culture's rampant anti-intellectualism, *Idiot America: How Stupidity Became a Virtue in the Land of the Free* (New York: Anchor Books, 2009). On Donnelly's conspiratorial fantasies see Alex J. Beringer, "'Some Unsuspected Author': Ignatius Donnelly and the Conspiracy Novel," *Arizona Quarterly: A Journal of American Literature, Culture, and Theory* 68, no. 4 (2012): 35–60.

38. The *Cryptogram*'s American publisher, R.S. Peale, admonished Donnelly for misrepresenting the code's promised clarity: "Before I took your book, I questioned you on the one point which the sale of the book would depend. That point was, as to the INTRICACY of the cipher. You stated that it would be so plain and simple that a CHILD would understand it." Cited in Ridge, *Ignatius Donnelly*, 243.

39. For a reading that takes seriously the debates over the authorship of Shakespeare's plays and the models of public reading they reveal, see Nancy Glazener's work "Lost Episodes in Public Literary Culture" in her *Literature in the Making* (New York: Oxford University Press, 2016), 119–60.

40. Michael Warner writes, "virtue comes to be defined by the negation of other traits of personhood, in particular as rational and disinterested concern for the public good" (*The Letters of the Republic: Publication and the Public Sphere in Eighteenth-Century America* [Cambridge: Harvard University Press, 1990], 6).

41. On the history of anonymous and pseudonymous authorship see Robert J. Griffin, "Anonymity and Authorship," *New Literary History* 30, no. 4 (1999): 877–95; Carmela Ciuraru, *Nom de Plume: A (Secret) History of Pseudonyms* (New York: Harper Perennial, 2012).

42. On the "Huguenot diaspora" to colonial America, see especially the first chapter in Paula Wheeler Carlo, *Huguenot Refugees in Colonial New York: Becoming American in the Hudson Valley* (Brighton: Sussex Academic Press, 2014).

43. As David Runciman notes, hypocrisy "has always had some connection with the business of hiding behind a mask" (*Political Hypocrisy*, 31). The image thus raises the awkward possibility that Bacon—who Lorraine Daston has called the "patron saint of objectivity"—was also a master of two-faced deceit. See Daston, "Baconian Facts, Academic Civility, and the Prehistory of Objectivity," in *Rethinking Objectivity*, ed. Allan Megill (Durham: Duke University Press, 1994), 37.

44. See for example the review in *The Critic: A Weekly Review of Literature and the Arts* (October 03, 1891), 165.

45. Goodwyn, *The Populist Moment*, 302.

46. Ibid., 92.

47. Pollack, *The Just Polity*, 221.

48. Pollack is blunt: "The subtreasury plan was not radical. It was thoroughly capitalistic... one searches in vain here for a program of land reform" (ibid., 222).

49. W.E.B. Du Bois, *The Quest of the Silver Fleece* (Boston: Northeastern University Press, 1989), 6. All references to this text are hereafter cited parenthetically by page number and abbreviated Q.

50. Arnold Rampersad, *The Art and Imagination of W.E.B. Du Bois* (Cambridge: Harvard University Press, 1976), 117.

51. W.E.B. Du Bois, *The Souls of Black Folk* (New York: Penguin Books, 1989), 165.

52. Ibid.

53. Albert Hirschman's *The Passions and the Interests* described how a subtle shift in political and moral philosophy saw "interest" emerge in the seventeenth and eighteenth centuries as a form of rational ambition and how this in turn helped legitimize a capitalist order by imagining "money making as a calm passion" (*The Passions and the Interests: Political Arguments for Capitalism Before Its Triumph* [Princeton: Princeton University Press, 1977], 63). Here Du Bois joined other anxious observers of Gilded Age politics for whom the acquisitive instinct was, on the contrary, capable of driving men to a craven betrayal of their own principles.

54. Peter Coviello, "Intimacy and Affliction: DuBois, Race, and Psychoanalysis," *MLQ: Modern Language Quarterly* 64, no. 1 (March 2003): 27.

55. W.E.B. Du Bois, *Black Reconstruction in America: An Essay Toward a History of the Part Which Black Folk Played in the Attempt to Reconstruct Democracy in America, 1860–1880*

(New York: Oxford University Press, 2014), 199. All references to this text are hereafter cited parenthetically by page number and abbreviated *BR*.

56. Arendt, *On Revolution*, 101.

57. Nancy Bentley, "Warped Conjunctions," 304.

58. For a resonant discussion of "compassion" for Du Bois as a critical recognition of a social relatedness distinct from liberal conceptions of sympathy, see Jonathan Flatley, *Affective Mapping: Melancholia and the Politics of Modernism* (Cambridge: Harvard University Press, 2008), 116.

59. Latour, "What if we Talked Politics a Little?" 145.

60. Ibid., 148.

Chapter 5

1. Cited in Scott Sandage, "The Gilded Age," in *A Companion to American Cultural History*, ed. Karen Halttunen (Malden, MA: Blackwell Publishing, 2008), 139.

2. In the first chapter I argued that Twain occludes important differences between apparently like forms of mass enthusiasm, grouping them all under the heading "emotional insanity."

3. Cited in Bryant Morey French, *Mark Twain and The Gilded Age* (Dallas: Southern Methodist University Press, 1965), 21, 24. As I have shown in the intervening chapters, the novel's multifaceted affective-critical tone set a crucial precedent for later political fiction. Henry Adams tackled disgust's complex relation to political investment; Helen Hunt Jackson used depression as an index of indigenous suffering and worried about the misdirection and depletion of reform sentiment; Ignatius Donnelly and W.E.B. Du Bois oscillated between suspicion and pity toward the figure of the hypocrite and the hypocrisy that defined the craft of postbellum practical politics, especially at the fraught intersection of race and class.

4. The "sneer" is central to modern, vernacular definitions (emerging in the 1860s and 1870s) of the cynic: "One who shows a disposition to disbelieve in the sincerity or goodness of human motives and actions, and is wont to express this by sneers and sarcasms; a sneering fault-finder" ("cynic, adj. and n.". *OED Online*. Oxford University Press. http://www.oed.com/view/Entry/46638?redirectedFrom=cynic, accessed January 2015).

5. Peter Sloterdijk, *Critique of Cynical Reason* (Minneapolis: University of Minnesota Press, 1987), 5. All references to this text are hereafter cited parenthetically by page number and abbreviated *CR*.

6. Mary Louise Kete, *Sentimental Collaborations: Mourning and Middle-Class Identity in Nineteenth-Century America* (Durham: Duke University Press, 2000), 185.

7. Writing of the failure of DC satires—from Adams's *Democracy*, discussed at length in the second chapter, to television's "The West Wing"—to match the acerbic intensity of the genre's British counterparts, one commentator recently lumped *The Gilded Age* in with narratives tracking a political naïf struggling to reform a fallen democracy. This is a dominant strain of political satire in America, yet it puts into relief how *different* the genre's progenitor is from its offspring. That is, in Twain and Warner's novel one is hard-pressed to find a sincere reformer (though clueless ingénues abound). See Christopher Lehmann, "Why Americans Can't Write Political Fiction," *The Washington Monthly*, October 1, 2010.

8. Christopher Hitchens, "In Search of the Washington Novel: A colorful genre awaits its masterpiece," *City Journal*, Autumn 2010.

9. https://marktwainhouse.org/about/mark-twain/major-works/.

10. Disillusionment is key to most modern definitions of cynicism. David Mazella speaks of the "modern, disillusioned cynicism that has lost all hope of ameliorating social problems with reasoned political solutions" (*The Making of Modern Cynicism* [Charlottesville: University of Virginia Press, 2007], 20). Louisa Shea calls modern cynicism an attitude of "disillusioned self-interest" and indicates that in current usage the term evokes "an unprincipled person who holds all ideals in contempt" in *The Cynic Enlightenment* (Baltimore: The Johns Hopkins University Press, 2010), xiii, 20.

11. On Machiavelli's place in the history of cynicism, see Sloterdijk, *Critique of Cynical Reason*, 238–9.

12. Wilber W. Caldwell, *Cynicism and the Evolution of the American Dream* (Washington, DC: Potomac Books, Inc., 2011), 92.

13. One of "cynicism's" confusing aspects is thus that, as Mazella notes, it names a "form of political rationality" associated with a ruling class, and an attitude of the "passive, excluded 'public' " (*Making of Modern Cynicism,* 9). Mazella argues persuasively for the importance of taxonomizing the cynical attitude according to its insider and outsider forms. Even Sloterdijk, launching an extended study of the concept, is nearly thrown off course at the get-go by the distinction between elite and popular cynicisms: "that fatally clever smile plays on the lips of those in the know. More precisely, it is the powerful who smile this way, while the kynical plebeians let out a satirical laugh" (*CR*, 4).

14. One reader accused the novel's authors of manufacturing a "conventional type" out of the worst specimens of congressional corruption, and making him "the center of a bad world of their own creation." This reader felt that all later fiction "tend[s] to confirm and perpetuate the erroneous view of Washington life in which they had their origin." See "Correspondence: A Washington Winter," *The Literary World: A Monthly Review of Current Literature (1870–1904)*, September 8, 1883.

15. Guiteau and Sellers have been compared over the decades, though without much attention being given to the logic of the pairing. As I discuss in the coming pages, Sellers and Guiteau were casually assumed to be of the same type, or "conformation"; a psychologist observing the Guiteau trial later described Guiteau as exhibiting "the visionary enthusiasm of…Colonel Sellers"; and the historian Charles Rosenberg begins his twentieth-century analysis of Guiteau's case by remarking that "It was hard to believe that such a trial had ever taken place; certainly it could only have taken place in the America of Jay Gould and Colonel Sellers." Allan McLane Hamilton, "The Case of Guiteau," *The Boston Medical and Surgical Journal* 106 (March 9, 1882): 237; Charles E. Rosenberg, *The Trial of the Assassin Guiteau: Psychiatry and Law in the Gilded Age* (Chicago: University of Chicago Press, 1968), xvi.

16. Cited in Rosenberg, *The Trial of the Assassin Guiteau*, 80.

17. *Report of the Proceedings in the Case of the United States vs. Charles J. Guiteau. Tried in the Supreme Court of the District of Columbia, Holding a Criminal Term, and Beginning November 14, 1881.* 3 vols. (Washington, DC: Government Printing Office, 1882), 1055. All references to this text are hereafter cited parenthetically by page number and abbreviated *R*.

18. For a report of Phelps's testimony see, for example, "More Medical Opinions; New York Doctors Disagree in Guiteau's Case," *The New York Times,* December 14, 1881. In

Chicago, the public could read a summary of Phelps's testimony in the *Inter Ocean*, the newspaper Guiteau famously imagined he might purchase and control, and for which Phelps had been a staff writer. "A Doomed Wretch's Laugh. Like That of the Hyena, a Hollow, Melancholy Mockery of a Laugh," *The Daily Inter Ocean*, December 14, 1881.

19. Irving Rosse, "Washington Malaria and Politics as Genetic Factors in Nervous Disease," *Virginia Medical Monthly* XVIII, no. 7 (October 1891): 531. Mark Twain and Charles Dudley Warner, *The Gilded Age: A Tale of Today* (New York: Penguin Books, 2001), 451. All references to this text are hereafter cited parenthetically by page number and abbreviated *G*.

20. Following Twain's lead, William Dean Howells defended Sellers's irrational ambition as a distinctively American form of tireless optimism, proclaiming him "the American character." Cited in Warner Berthoff, *American Trajectories: Authors and Readings 1790–1970* (University Park, PA: Pennsylvania State University Press, 1994), 33. See also Howells's positive appraisal of Sellers in W.D. Howells, "Mark Twain," *Century Illustrated Magazine* 24 (September 1882): 780–4.

21. Irving Rosse, "Washington Malaria and Politics as Genetic Factors in Nervous Disease," *Virginia Medical Monthly* 18 (October 1891): 531.

22. Even the sensationalistic and flippant journal *Puck* called for self-reflection on the state of American democracy: "We have lowered politics to the level of a disgraceful trade.... Is it unnatural that such system should breed such a man as Guiteau? The wretch is simply the ordinary office-seeker, a trifle exaggerated." "Cartoons and Comments," *Puck* (July 13, 1881): 318.

23. Cited in Rosenberg, *The Trial of the Assassin Guiteau*, 80.

24. Ibid.

25. Allan McLane Hamilton, "The Case of Guiteau," 237.

26. For Derrida, if there is a "law of genre" it is "a principle of contamination, a law of impurity, a parasitical economy" (Jacques Derrida, "The Law of Genre," *Critical Inquiry* 7, no. 1 [Autumn 1980]: 59). In the Guiteau trial, we see a resonant failure of efforts to make Guiteau narrate a coherent life story of rational choice or to obey the generic norms of legal testimony, as the law itself increasingly takes on an insanity of its own.

27. Louisa Shea notes that Foucault's take on classical cynicism also stresses its status as an embodied form of critique, a commitment "to living differently as the basis for thinking differently." Cynicism therefore "topples ... the idea, long associated with the Enlightenment, that better knowledge will dispel foolish behavior" (*The Cynic Enlightenment* [Baltimore: The Johns Hopkins University Press, 2010], 187).

28. Slavoj Žižek, *The Sublime Object of Ideology* (London and New York: Verso, 1989), 28.

29. Glenn C. Altschuler and Stuart M. Blumin, *Rude Republic: Americans and Their Politics in the Nineteenth Century* (Princeton: Princeton University Press, 2001), 252.

30. Altschuler and Blumin, 257.

31. Andreas Huyssen, "Foreword" in *CR*, xii.

32. Zizi Papacharissi defines "affective publics" as "networked publics that are mobilized and connected, identified, and potentially disconnected through expressions of sentiment" ("Affective Publics and Structures of Storytelling: Sentiment, Events and Mediality" *Information, Communication & Society* 19:3 [2016]: 311). While the term has seemed especially useful for describing twenty-first-century social media, it also offers a useful rubric for the circulation of sentiment in the nineteenth-century print public sphere.

33. David S. Reynolds, *Walt Whitman's America: A Cultural Biography* (New York: Vintage Books, 1996), 223.

34. John Gray, "The Guiteau Trial," *The American Journal of Insanity* 38 (1882): 304.

35. For an account of how lynching and other forms of mob justice were seen as a rejection of middle-class "sentimental" conceptions of justice, see Michael James Pfeifer, *Rough Justice: Lynching and American Society, 1874–1947* (Urbana and Chicago: University of Illinois Press, 2004), 14. Apologists for one lynching memorably and redundantly exalted that "sentimental sentimentality [was] rebuked" (102).

36. The association of mania with increased sensitivity was complicated by the fact that this same hyperesthesia could paradoxically induce numbness, what Foucault calls "an insensibility taut with interior vibration" (Michel Foucualt, *Madness and Civilization* [New York: Vintage Books, 1988], 127).

37. On the legal system's "investment in conjuring the domain of law as a space where emotion is kept at bay," see Austin Sarat, Lawrence Douglas, and Martha Umphrey, *Law's Madness* (Ann Arbor: University of Michigan Press, 2006), 4.

38. Cited in Rosenberg, *The Trial of the Assassin Guiteau*, 51.

39. For a discussion of a strain of Gilded Age fiction that offered an ambivalent negotiation of the tension between lynch law and modern jurisprudence, thereby complicating an easy regional mapping of the modern city vs. the "backward" frontier, see Mark Storey, *Rural Fictions, Urban Realities* (New York: Oxford University Press, 2015), 121. The Guiteau trial troubles this same binary but from the other direction: we see an outright endorsement of lynch law in the heart of the nation's capital.

40. Cited in Sandra Gunning, *Race, Rape, and Lynching: The Red Record of American Literature, 1890–1912* (New York: Oxford University Press, 1996), 52. Jacqueline Goldsby argues that Twain's work (in *Huckleberry Finn* and *A Connecticut Yankee*, for example) often turns lynching into farce or robs it of its specificity by staging it as violence against whites. See Jacqueline Goldsby, *A Spectacular Secret: Lynching in American Life and Literature* (Chicago: University of Chicago Press, 2006), 36. For an overview of the ways "lynching" can be alternately seen as a synonym for anti-black violence, or as a phenomenon that encompasses extralegal violence against other racial groups and among whites, see Storey, *Rural Fictions*, 120.

41. To extol the mob as embodying the ideals that animate modern jurisprudence is of course surprising, given that the exclusion of the mob is often central to descriptions of the function of legal procedure: "The mob may have their faces pressed hard against the courthouse windows…but the achievement of the trial is to keep those forces at bay, or at least to transmute their energy into a stylized formal ritual of proof and judgment" (Sarat et al., *Law's Madness*, 4). See also *Rural Fictions*, 127.

42. Cited in Paul Schmidt, "Mark Twain's Satire on Republicanism," *American Quarterly* 5 (1953): 354.

43. Later Twain works such as 1893's *Those Extraordinary Twins* highlight the absurdity that can arise when an over-rigid method for assessing legal responsibility is applied to "extraordinary" situations. In that text, the law's struggle to assess responsibility leads, again, to a lynching. On this dynamic, see Gillman, *Dark Twins*, 68–9.

44. If this seems an unlikely icon of legal rationality, we might note that the twenty-first century is rife with instances where politicians have performed their pugnacious realism by

executing mentally ill inmates. The 2016 campaign of Hillary Clinton brought Bill Clinton's execution of Ricky Ray Rector back into the spotlight. For an account of how the Rector case was used as an opportunity to perform an antisentimental "tough on crime" stance, see Michelle Alexander, *The New Jim Crow: Mass Incarceration in the Age of Colorblindness* (New York: The New Press, 2013), 54.

45. The prosecutor's insistence on casting Guiteau's extravagant lunacy as a form of rational egotism culminated in the public's bloodthirsty call for the assassin's execution in the name of reason. In this it dramatizes a version of what Paul Campos has called "jurismania," a madness that comes from excessive rationalism. Campos's work also highlights how the putative certainty of legal reason leads to a system of law so complex that "only rich defendants have the resources to exploit the exceedingly complex structure of contemporary American jurisprudence" (Paul F. Campos, *Jurismania: The Madness of American Law* [New York: Oxford University Press, 1998], 10, 18).

46. While I am thus suggesting that Twain's early works functioned as an unwitting accomplice to the rationalist lynch mob, in the years following the trial Twain offered his own commentary on the dangerous recourse to violence in the name of reason. See for example *A Connecticut Yankee in King Arthur's Court* (1889), where the time-traveling Yankee combats deep-rooted prejudice with explosives. See Mark Twain, *A Connecticut Yankee in King Arthur's Court* (New York: Oxford University Press, 1996), 98. On the violence of the novel, see Walter Benn Michaels, "An American Tragedy, or the Promise of American Life," *Representations*, no. 25 (Winter 1989): 71–98.

47. For Shea, "the *Critique of Cynical Reason* is a paean to Bakhtin and the power of carnival to turn the world, with its hierarchies and 'frozen identities,' on its head" (*The Cynic Enlightenment*, 165).

48. John Christian Laursen, "Cynicism Then and Now," *Iris: European Journal of Philosophy & Public Debate* 1, no. 2 (October 2009): 476.

49. In this way I disagree with Timothy Bewes' definition of cynicism; though, to be fair, Bewes makes clear that he sees his version of cynicism as a particularly postmodern phenomenon. For Bewes, "Cynicism denotes a refusal to engage with the world as much as a disposition of antagonism towards it" (*Cynicism and Postmodernity* [London: Verso, 1997], 1). At least in its mid-nineteenth-century forms, however, cynicism appears to be fundamentally a critical orientation *toward* politics, even as the cynic's subsequent recoil is always a foregone conclusion.

50. Bruno Latour, "Why Has Critique Run out of Steam? From Matters of Fact to Matters of Concern," *Critical Inquiry* 30 (Winter 2004): 225–48; Rita Felski, "Digging Down and Standing Back," *English Language Notes* 51, no. 2 (Fall/Winter 2013): 7–23.

51. Lauren Berlant's work helps us see that the cynical posture of universal disillusionment—"everyone knows," "we all know"—mirrors the presumption of the universality of feeling that undergirds the sentimental belief in feeling as a common measure of wrong. See "The Subject of True Feeling: Pain, Privacy and Politics" in *Cultural Pluralism, Identity Politics, and the Law*, eds. Austin Sarat and Thomas R. Kearns (Ann Arbor: University of Michigan Press, 1999): 49–84.

52. Mark Twain, *The American Claimant* (New York: Oxford University Press, 1996). All references to this text are hereafter cited parenthetically by page number and abbreviated *A*.

53. See Schmidt, "Mark Twain's Satire on Republicanism."

54. The name's connotation of insanity is noted in Clyde L. Grimm, "The American Claimant: Reclamation of a Farce," *American Quarterly* 19 (1967): 91.

55. Sellers's fantasy of "spontaneous" selection parodies a Whitmanian conception of democracy that differentiates institutional strictures from genuine popular sovereignty: "I have found that not one in a hundred has been chosen by any spontaneous selection of the outsiders, the people, but all have been nominated and put through by little or large caucuses of the politicians, and have got in by corrupt rings and electioneering, not capacity or desert" (Walt Whitman, *Democratic Vistas*, ed. Ed Folsom [Iowa City: University of Iowa Press, 2010], 30).

56. Lawrence Howe, *Mark Twain and the Novel: The Double-Cross of Authority* (Cambridge: Cambridge University Press, 1998), 179.

57. José Martí, reporting on the trial for a Venezuelan audience, underscored this point: Guiteau "acted on God's orders, not out of rage at seeing himself passed over or in hopes of gaining something by his crime; the division within the Republican Party was not a pretext, concealing the real reason for his act, it was the real reason for it" (José Martí, *Selected Writings* [New York: Penguin Classics, 2002], 98).

58. The trial testimony of Guiteau's brother records a representative sample of this rhetoric: "He had said that he acted under inspiration, and that he was willing to suffer or die for the principle of inspiration. He talked a good deal in that way.... I asked him, 'Are you willing to be sacrificed for this principle, as Christ was?' He said, 'I am' " (*R*, 487–8).

59. The humorist Sarah Vowell makes a related point in *Assassination Vacation* (New York: Simon & Schuster, 2005), 174.

60. "The pathological public sphere is crossed by the vague and shifting lines between the singularity or privacy of the subject, on the one side, and collective forms of representation, exhibition, and witnessing, on the other" (Mark Seltzer, *Serial Killers: Death and Life in America's Wound Culture* [New York: Routledge, 1998], 254).

61. Twain's account of the quotidian banality of modern life looks like a maddening version of the flat, secular time–space of the modern nation that Benedict Anderson describes as "homogeneous empty time" in *Imagined Communities: Reflections on the Origin and Spread of Nationalism* (New York: Verso, 1991), 35.

62. For a resonant consideration of the media's careful tracking of Garfield's slow death as promising "social unity" through mass media but ultimately producing "mass amnesia," see Richard Menke, "Media in America, 1881: Garfield, Guiteau, Bell, Whitman," *Critical Inquiry* 31 (2005): 638–64.

63. George Beard saw a cognate solar intensity in Guiteau: "The mind of Guiteau is never free from eclipse, though it is never totally eclipsed; but the splendor of the corona, the unexpected streams of light, keep us in constant surprise" ("The Case of Guiteau—A Psychological Study," *The Journal of Nervous and Mental Disease* 9, no. 1 [1882]: 111).

64. As early as 1868 Twain expressed a fascination with the figure of the political aspirant: "These office-seekers are wonderfully seedy, wonderfully hungry-eyed, wonderfully importunate, and supernaturally gifted with 'cheek'.... Their desires are seldom as modest as their qualifications" ("Special Correspondence of the Alta California," *San Francisco Alta California*, January 15, 1868). Even with Guiteau's crime as evidence of the dangers of this form of ambition, it's clear that Twain never abandons his fascination with outsized political desire.

65. Cited in Zournazi, *Hope: New Philosophies for Change* (New York: Routledge, 2003), 23.

66. Christopher Castiglia, *Interior States: Institutional Consciousness and the Inner Life of Democracy in the Antebellum United States* (Durham: Duke University Press, 2008), 13.

67. Van Wyck Brooks, *The Ordeal of Mark Twain* (London: W. Heinemann, 1922), 1.

68. Bernard Augustine de Voto, *Forays and Rebuttals* (Boston: Little, Brown and Company, 1936), 370–1.

69. Cited in Zournazi, *Hope*, 44.

70. John Carlos Rowe, *At Emerson's Tomb: The Politics of Classic American Literature* (New York: Columbia University Press, 1997), 1.

71. Ibid., 178.

72. Sloterdijk, "Cynicism: The Twilight of False Consciousness," 194.

73. Twain's productively irrational attachment to democracy emerges as a species of what Lauren Berlant calls cruel optimism: "the condition of maintaining an attachment to an object in advance of its loss." In one of Berlant's literary case studies from "Cruel Optimism," she describes a character who "to protect her last iota of optimism…goes crazy" ("Cruel Optimism," *Differences: A Journal of Feminist Cultural Studies* 17 [2006]: 21, 34). I am suggesting that a similar logic shapes Twain's conflicted engagement with politics through a discourse of insanity.

74. Beard, *American Nervousness: Its Causes and Consequences*, 124.

75. Ibid.

76. William James, "Is Life Worth Living?" in *Writings, 1878–1899* (New York: Library of America, 1992), 481.

77. Again, Christopher Castiglia's work offers an important recent correlate to this effort, as he returns to Ernst Bloch's writing on utopia to help articulate a form of optimism that is also critical. Castiglia warns that "when we deny the simultaneity of critique and hope, phrases like 'dream world' and 'enchantment' too easily rhyme with 'trivial,' 'frivolous,' 'naïve,' and 'escapist' " ("Twists and Turns" in Hester Blum, ed., *Turns of Event: Nineteenth-Century American Literary Studies in Motion* [Philadelphia: University of Pennsylvania Press, 2016], 70).

Coda

1. Jeffrey Gottfried, "Most Americans Already Feel Election Coverage Fatigue," July 14, 2016, http://www.pewresearch.org/fact-tank/2016/07/14/most-americans-already-feel-election-coverage-fatigue/.

2. Jenny Gold, " 'Post-election Stress Disorder' Sweeps the Nation," *PBS Newshour: The Rundown*, February 23, 2017, http://www.pbs.org/newshour/rundown/post-election-stress-disorder-sweeps-nation/.

3. Horace Traubel, *With Walt Whitman in Camden April 8–September 14, 1889* (Carbondale: Southern Illinois University Press, 1964), 194.

4. Walt Whitman, *Leaves of Grass and Other Writings*, ed. Michael Moon (New York: W.W. Norton, 2002), 200. The poem first appeared in *Drum-Taps* (1865).

5. Peter Coviello, *Intimacy in America: Dreams of Affiliation in Antebellum Literature* (Minneapolis: University of Minnesota Press, 2005), 129.

6. Walt Whitman, *Walt Whitman's Drum-Taps* (New York: [Peter Eckler, printer], 1865, 52). This line was cut in the poem's later incorporation into *Leaves of Grass*.

7. Part of this elitism derives from the fact that *Not Quite Hope* has explored something like the eccentric political fantasies of the "professional-managerial class" that soon would characterize the rationalist tenor of twentieth-century progressivism. Barbara and John Ehrenreich first coined the phrase "professional-managerial class" in order to define an emerging demographic with unstable political affinities. See Barbara Ehrenreich and John Ehrenreich, "The Professional-Managerial Class," in *Between Labor and Capital*, ed. Pat Walker (Boston: South End Press, 1979). I take up this class's political sensibilities in Chapters 2 and 3 in particular.

8. On the marginalization of "sexual and gender deviants...by means of the allegation of backwardness," see Heather Love, *Feeling Backward: Loss and the Politics of Queer History* (Cambridge: Harvard University Press, 2010), 6. Love recasts historical anachronism as a source of creativity and critique.

9. "Homogeneous empty time" is Walter Benjamin's phrase for the calendric simultaneity that organizes national time, but it is most closely associated with Benedict Anderson's development of the concept in *Imagined Communities* (New York: Verso, 1991). Elizabeth Freeman argues that homogeneous empty time undergirds not only nationalist coherence but also a wider range of normative discourses that queer temporalities may work to interrupt. See *Time Binds: Queer Temporalities, Queer Histories* (Durham: Duke University Press, 2010), xxii. On "straight time" and "chronobiopolitics" see, respectively, Valerie Rohy, *Anachronism and Its Others: Sexuality, Race, and Temporality* (Albany: SUNY Press, 2009), and Dana Luciano, *Arranging Grief: Sacred Time and the Body in Nineteenth-Century America* (New York: New York University Press, 2007).

10. Freeman, 22.

11. In Allen's account, "heterogenous temporalities" are not necessarily "resistant to the nation"; rather, "they are themselves the threads out of which the fabric of national belonging has long been woven" (Thomas Allen, *A Republic in Time: Temporality and Social Imagination in Nineteenth-Century America* [Chapel Hill: North Carolina Press, 2008], 11).

12. Allen's caution relates to Postcolonial and "New Americanist" explorations of subaltern alternatives to imperial time and nationalist sequence. But his warning bears consideration in the context of queer theory, as well—especially in a moment when queer love sometimes looks like the cornerstone of liberalism's self-congratulatory "presentness." In the wake of *Obergefell v. Hodges*, much of corporate America has seemed eager to tout gay marriage's economic benefits while depicting its opponents as behind the times, on the wrong side of history, or rural relics of a stalled modernity. Making a related point, Carla Freccero notes that "not all nonlinear chronological imaginings can be recuperated as queer" and Valerie Rohy warns that "anachronism and chronology have no essential political valence." See Elizabeth Freeman, ed., "Theorizing Queer Temporalities: A Roundtable Discussion," *GLQ: A Journal of Lesbian and Gay Studies* 13, nos. 2–3 (2007): 187; and Rohy, xv.

13. The novel takes its title from Bertha's joke that a rival socialite might recycle her well-worn demeanor: "For sale. A neatly fitting suit of good manners. Used through one Administration." Frances Hodgson Burnett, *Through One Administration* (Boston: James R. Osgood and Company, 1883), 51. Future citations will be given parenthetically in the text and abbreviated *T*.

14. Much of *Through One Administration* focuses on the slow process by which Richard begins to strategically prostitute his wife, relying on her charms to further his political and financial prospects, and asking her to take her place among "those historical charmers

before whom prime ministers trembled, and who could make and unmake a cabinet with a smile" (*T*, 155). In short, she becomes a "female lobbyist."

15. Arbuthnot might be seen as queer kin to those "little brothers of the rich"—something like a pre-Freudian sexuality that was equally a class position—Stephanie Foote has studied in "Little Brothers of the Rich: Queer Families in the Gilded Age," *American Literature 79*, no. 4 (December 2007): 701–24. Foote's case study is Harry Lehr whose tenuous class position and effeminacy marked him as outside the upper echelons of wealth and normative heterosexuality, even as his wit, creativity, and facilities as a marriage-market confidant made him the center of Gilded Age social circles in Newport and elsewhere.

16. As Bertha's father instructs Tredennis: "You are fond of her children, talk to her of them. When you see her inclined to be silent and unlike herself, bring them to her mind" (*T*, 90).

17. Richard makes explicit the association between Bertha and Arbuthnot's modernity, queerness, and shallowness: " 'There is no denying that you two are the outgrowth of an effete civilization…'That is true,' said Bertha, in her soft, mocking voice. 'We are battered and worldly wise and we have no object' " (*T*, 57).

18. See especially the contributions by Britton, Dollimore, Ross, and Butler in Fabio Cleto, ed., *Camp: Queer Aesthetics and the Performing Subject: A Reader* (Ann Arbor: University of Michigan Press, 1999).

19. Again, the phrase "ugly feelings" comes from Sianne Ngai's book of the same name, in which she studies those "minor affects that are far less intentional or object-directed, and thus more likely to produce political and aesthetic ambiguities, than the passions in the philosophical canon" (Sianne Ngai, *Ugly Feelings* [Cambridge: Harvard University Press, 2005], 20).

20. See Christopher Castiglia, *Interior States: Institutional Consciousness and the Inner Life of Democracy in the Antebellum United States* (Durham: Duke University Press, 2008).

21. Cited in Michael Bronski, *A Queer History of the United States* (Boston: Beacon Press, 2011), 82.

22. An outspoken critic of marriage, Burnett would have learned of Woodhull's "free love" platform from Isabella Hooker during their time together at Nook Farm. See my first chapter for more on Hooker's admiration for Woodhull. Later in life, Burnett's much publicized divorce led critics to scour her works for signs of sex radicalism. Her first best-selling children's book, *Little Lord Fauntleroy* (1886), sparked a craze for dressing little boys in effeminate costumes; some accused the novel of the mass emasculation of an entire generation. *The Secret Garden* (1911), now her most famous work, appeared to some as an allegory of sexual awakening. Burnett always contrasted the constrictions of her abusive and unsatisfying marriages with the freedom of complex forms of kinship and affiliation. Her most recent biographer considers her only fully satisfying romantic relationship to have been with the writer and editor Elizabeth Jordan. For more details of Burnett's life, see Gretchen Gerzina, *Frances Hodgson Burnett: The Unexpected Life of the Author of The Secret Garden* (New Brunswick, NJ: Rutgers University Press, 2004).

23. Seltzer, *Serial Killers: Death and Life in America's Wound Culture* (New York: Routledge, 1998), 35. For another version of the dynamic in which a seemingly salacious interest in the scandals of democracy may constitute a meaningful, or at least inescapable, relation to the workings of American politics, see the essays in Lauren Berlant and Lisa Duggan, eds., *Our Monica, Ourselves: The Clinton Affair and the National Interest*

(New York: New York University Press, 2001), and Eric Lott's discussion of this volume in "The First Boomer: Bill Clinton, George W., and Fictions of State," *Representations* 84 (2004): 103.

24. The primary message of Warner's chapter "Something Queer About the Nation State" was that there is nothing queer about the nation state. Warner argues it is "only when [queerness] is opposed to normal society and the representative state [that] it acquire[s] the sense of transformative significance that it now displays" (*Publics and Counterpublics* [Cambridge: Zone Books, 2005], 221).

25. Warner, 223.

26. Lauren Berlant, *Cruel Optimism* (Durham: Duke University Press, 2011), 227.

27. This artificiality disarticulates history and chronology, depicting an administration as a structure of feeling rather than as a link in the forward march of national time. Jordan Stein has argued that "to assume a stance that challenges the perceived naturalness or neutrality of the sequential movement of time is already to make a queer argument—and that argument will be queer regardless of whether the person making it self-ascribes as queer or purports to speak for or about queer people" ("American Literary History and Queer Temporalities," *American Literary History* 25, no. 4 [Winter 2013]: 867).

28. Heather Love writes, "Public time is collective time, measured by the clock, whereas in psychic life the trains hardly ever run on time" (Love, 11). Yet the regularity of American elections (which one does not necessarily have, for example, in the British and Canadian parliamentary systems) and its predictable set of political feelings mean that some aspects of US citizens' affective, interior lives are remarkably punctual. For another lament about predictable political exhaustion, see a letter to the editor in the *Los Angeles Times*, in which a reader diagnosed the early onset—in April 2015!—of 2016 election fatigue: "Readers React: 2016 election fatigue in 2015," *Los Angeles Times*, April 15, 2015 (http://www.latimes.com/opinion/readersreact/la-le-0415-wednesday-hillary-clinton-2016-20150415-story.html).

29. Charles Olson, "Call Me Ishmael," in *Collected Prose* (Berkeley: University of California Press, 1997), 20.

{ WORKS CITED }

Abbott, Carl. *Political Terrain: Washington, D.C., from Tidewater Town to Global Metropolis.* Chapel Hill: University of North Carolina Press, 2005.

Adams, Henry. *The Letters of Henry Adams, Volume 1.* Edited by J.C. Levenson. Cambridge, MA: Belknap Press of Harvard University Press, 1982.

Adams, Henry. "Civil Service Reform." *The North American Review* 109, no. 225 (October 1869): 443–76.

Adams, Henry. *Democracy: An American Novel.* New York: Penguin Books, 2008.

"A Doomed Wretch's Laugh. Like That of the Hyena, a Hollow, Melancholy Mockery of a Laugh." *The Daily Inter Ocean*, December 14, 1881.

Agamben, Giorgio. *Homo Sacer: Sovereign Power and Bare Life.* Stanford, CA: Stanford University Press, 1998.

"agitation, n." *OED Online.* Oxford University Press. http://www.oed.com/view/Entry/4011.

Ahmed, Sara. *The Promise of Happiness.* Durham, NC: Duke University Press, 2010.

Alexander, Michelle. *The New Jim Crow: Mass Incarceration in the Age of Colorblindness.* New York: The New Press, 2013.

Allen, Thomas. *A Republic in Time: Temporality and Social Imagination in Nineteenth-Century America.* Chapel Hill: North Carolina Press, 2008.

Allewaert, Monique. *Ariel's Ecology: Plantations, Personhood, and Colonialism in the American Tropics.* Minneapolis: University of Minnesota Press, 2013.

Allgor, Catherine. *Parlor Politics: In Which the Ladies of Washington Help Build a City and a Government.* Charlottesville: University Press of Virginia, 2000.

Altschuler, Glenn C. and Stuart M. Blumin. *Rude Republic: Americans and Their Politics in the Nineteenth Century.* Princeton: Princeton University Press, 2001.

Anderson, Amanda. "Postwar Aesthetics: The Case of Trilling and Adorno." *Critical Inquiry* 40, no. 4 (2014): 418–38.

Anderson, Benedict. *Imagined Communities: Reflections on the Origin and Spread of Nationalism.* New York: Verso, 1991.

Arendt, Hannah. *On Revolution.* New York: Penguin, 1990.

Badiou, Alain and Nicolas Truong. *In Praise of Love.* Translated by Peter Bush. London: Serpent's Tail, 2012.

Banta, Martha. "Being a 'Begonia' in a Man's World." In *New Essays on the Education of Henry Adams*, edited by John Carlos Rowe, 49–86. Cambridge: Cambridge University Press, 1996.

Barnes, Elizabeth. *States of Sympathy: Seduction and Democracy in the American Novel.* New York: Columbia University Press, 1997.

Beard, George Miller. *American Nervousness: Its Causes and Consequences.* New York: G.P. Putnam's Sons, 1881.

Beard, George Miller. "The Case of Guiteau: A Psychological Study." *The Journal of Nervous and Mental Disease* 9, no. 1 (1882): 90–125.

Bell, Michael Davitt. *The Development of American Romance*. Chicago: The University of Chicago Press, 1981.

Benhabib, Seyla. *Democracy and Difference: Contesting the Boundaries of the Political*. Princeton: Princeton University Press, 1996.

Bentley, Nancy. "Warped Conjunctions: Jacques Rancière and African American Twoness." In *American Literature's Aesthetic Dimensions*, edited by Cindy Weinstein and Christopher Looby, 291–312. NY: Columbia University Press, 2012.

Beringer, Alex J. " 'Some Unsuspected Author': Ignatius Donnelly and the Conspiracy Novel." *Arizona Quarterly: A Journal of American Literature, Culture, and Theory* 68, no. 4 (2012): 35–60.

Berlant, Lauren. "Cruel Optimism." *Differences: A Journal of Feminist Cultural Studies* 17 (2006): 20–36.

Berlant, Lauren. *Cruel Optimism*. Durham, NC: Duke University Press, 2011.

Berlant, Lauren. *Desire/Love*. Brooklyn, NY: Punctum Books, 2012.

Berlant, Lauren. *The Female Complaint*. Durham, NC: Duke University Press, 2008.

Berlant, Lauren. "Love, a Queer Feeling." In *Homosexuality and Psychoanalysis*, edited by Tim Dean and Christopher Lane, 432–51. Chicago: University of Chicago Press, 2001.

Berlant, Lauren. "A Properly Political Concept of Love: Three Approaches in Ten Pages." *Cultural Anthropology* 26, no. 4 (2011): 683–91.

Berlant, Lauren. *The Queen of America Goes to Washington City: Essays on Sex and Citizenship*. Durham, NC: Duke University Press, 1997.

Berlant, Lauren. "Slow Death (Sovereignty, Obesity, Lateral Agency)." *Critical Inquiry* 33 (2007): 754–80.

Berlant, Lauren. "The Subject of True Feeling: Pain, Privacy and Politics." In *Cultural Pluralism, Identity Politics, and the Law*, edited by Austin Sarat and Thomas R. Kearns, 49–84. Ann Arbor: University of Michigan Press, 1999.

Berlant, Lauren and Lisa Duggan, eds. *Our Monica, Ourselves: The Clinton Affair and the National Interest*. New York: New York University Press, 2001.

Berthoff, Warner. *American Trajectories: Authors and Readings 1790–1970*. University Park, PA: Pennsylvania State University Press, 1994.

Best, Stephen and Sharon Marcus. "Surface Reading: An Introduction." *Representations* 108, no. 1 (2008): 1–21.

Bewes, Timothy. *Cynicism and Postmodernity*. London: Verso, 1997.

Bird, Robert Montgomery. *Sheppard Lee*. New York: New York Review Books, 2008.

Blanchard, Mary Warner. *Oscar Wilde's America: Counterculture in the Gilded Age*. New Haven: Yale University Press, 1998.

Blanchot, Maurice. *Friendship*. Stanford: Stanford University Press, 1997.

Boggs, Colleen Glenney. *Animalia Americana*. New York: Columbia University Press, 2013.

Bovee, John R. "Doctor Huguet: Donnelly on Being Black." *Minnesota History* 41, no. 6 (Summer 1969): 286–94.

Brennan, Teresa. *The Transmission of Affect*. Ithaca: Cornell University Press, 2004.

Bronski, Michael. *A Queer History of the United States*. Boston: Beacon Press, 2011.

Brooks, David. "The Republicans' Incompetence Caucus." *The New York Times*, October 13, 2015. http://www.nytimes.com/2015/10/13/opinion/the-republicans-incompetence-caucus.html.

Brooks, Van Wyck. *The Ordeal of Mark Twain*. London: W. Heinemann, 1922.

Brown, Bill. *A Sense of Things: The Object Matter of American Literature.* Chicago: University of Chicago Press, 2003.

Brown, Gillian. *Domestic Individualism: Imagining Self in Nineteenth-Century America.* Berkeley: University of California Press, 1990.

Brown, Wendy. "Resisting Left Melancholy." *Boundary 2* 26, no. 3 (1999): 19–27.

Bruyneel, Kevin. *The Third Space of Sovereignty: The Postcolonial Politics of U.S.–Indigenous Relations.* Minneapolis: University of Minnesota Press, 2007.

Buhle, Mari Jo and Paul Buhle, eds. *The Concise History of Woman Suffrage.* Urbana: University of Illinois Press, 2005.

Burke, Edmund. *The Portable Edmund Burke.* Edited by Isaac Kramnick. New York: Penguin Books, 1999.

Burnett, Frances Hodgson. *Through One Administration.* Boston: J.R. Osgood and Co., 1883.

Caldwell, Wilber W. *Cynicism and the Evolution of the American Dream.* Washington, DC: Potomac Books, Inc., 2011.

Campos, Paul F. *Jurismania: The Madness of American Law.* New York: Oxford University Press, 1998.

Carlo, Paula Wheeler. *Huguenot Refugees in Colonial New York: Becoming American in the Hudson Valley.* Brighton: Sussex Academic Press, 2014.

"Cartoons and Comments." *Puck*, July 13, 1881.

Castiglia, Christopher. "Critiquiness." *English Language Notes* 51, no. 2 (Fall/Winter 2013): 79–85.

Castiglia, Christopher. *Interior States: Institutional Consciousness and the Inner Life of Democracy in the Antebellum United States.* Durham, NC: Duke University Press, 2008.

Castiglia, Christopher. *The Practices of Hope: Literary Criticism in Disenchanted Times.* New York: New York University Press, 2017.

Castiglia, Christopher. "Twists and Turns." In *Turns of Event: Nineteenth-Century American Literary Studies in Motion*, edited by Hester Blum, 61–78. Philadelphia: University of Pennsylvania Press, 2016.

Castronovo, Russ. *Necro Citizenship.* Durham, NC: Duke University Press, 2001.

Cavell, Stanley. *The Senses of Walden.* Chicago: The University of Chicago Press, 1992.

Chakkalakal, Tess. " 'Whimsical Contrasts': Love and Marriage in 'The Minister's Wooing' and 'Our Nig.' " *The New England Quarterly* 84, no. 1 (March 2011): 159–71.

Chapin, E.H. *The Philosophy of Reform: A Lecture Delivered Before the Berean Institute.* New York: C.L. Stickney, 1843.

Child, Lydia Maria. *A Lydia Maria Child Reader.* Edited by Carolyn L. Karcher. Durham, NC: Duke University Press, 1997.

Ciuraru, Carmela. *Nom de Plume: A (Secret) History of Pseudonyms.* New York: Harper Perennial, 2012.

Cleto, Fabio, ed. *Camp: Queer Aesthetics and the Performing Subject: A Reader.* Ann Arbor: University of Michigan Press, 1999.

"Correspondence: A Washington Winter." *The Literary World: A Monthly Review of Current Literature*, September 8, 1883.

"Correspondence: Novels of Washington Life." *The Literary World: a Monthly Review of Current Literature,* August 25, 1883.

Cott, Nancy F. *Public Vows: A History of Marriage and the Nation*. Cambridge, MA: Harvard University Press, 2000.

Coulthard, Glen Sean. *Red Skin, White Masks: Rejecting the Colonial Politics of Recognition*. Minneapolis: University of Minnesota Press, 2014.

Coviello, Peter. "Intimacy and Affliction: DuBois, Race, and Psychoanalysis." *MLQ: Modern Language Quarterly* 64, no. 1 (March 2003): 1–32.

Coviello, Peter. *Intimacy in America: Dreams of Affiliation in Antebellum Literature*. Minneapolis: University of Minnesota Press, 2005.

Coviello, Peter. *Tomorrow's Parties: Sex and the Untimely in Nineteenth-Century America*. New York: New York University Press, 2013.

Craig, Robert H. *Religion and Radical Politics: An Alternative Christian Tradition in the United States*. Philadelphia: Temple University Press, 1995.

Cvetkovich, Ann. *Depression: A Public Feeling*. Durham, NC: Duke University Press, 2012.

Cvetkovich, Ann. "Everyday Feeling and its Genres." In *Political Emotions*, edited by Janet Staiger, Ann Cvetkovich, and Ann Reynolds, 4–12. New York: Routledge, 2010.

"cynic, adj. and n." *OED Online*. Oxford University Press. http://www.oed.com/view/Entry/46638.

Dando-Collins, Stephen. *Standing Bear Is a Person: The True Story of a Native American's Quest for Justice*. Cambridge, MA: Da Capo Press, 2004.

Daston, Lorraine. "Baconian Facts, Academic Civility, and the Prehistory of Objectivity." In *Rethinking Objectivity*, edited by Allan Megill, 337–63. Durham, NC: Duke University Press, 1994.

Davis, Noah K. "The Moral Aspects of Vivisection." *The North American Review* 140, no. 340 (March, 1885): 203–20.

De Voto, Bernard Augustine. *Forays and Rebuttals*. Boston: Little, Brown and Company, 1936.

Dean, Jodi. *Publicity's Secret: How Technoculture Capitalizes on Democracy*. Ithaca: Cornell University Press, 2002.

Deloria Jr., Vine and Clifford M. Lytle. *The Nations Within: The Past and Future of American Indian Sovereignty*. Austin: University of Texas Press, 1984.

DeLyser, Dydia. *Ramona Memories: Tourism and the Shaping of Southern California*. Minneapolis: University of Minnesota Press, 2005.

Derrida, Jacques. "The Law of Genre." *Critical Inquiry* 7, no. 1 (Autumn 1980): 55–81.

Derrida, Jacques. "Politics of Friendship." *American Imago* 50 (1993): 353–91.

Donnelly, Ignatius. *Doctor Huguet: A Novel*. Chicago: F.J. Schulte & Co., 1891.

Donnelly, Ignatius. *The Great Cryptogram: Francis Bacon's Cipher in the So-Called Shakespeare Plays*. London: S. Low, Marston, Searle & Rivington, 1888.

Dougherty, Michael Brendan. "Henry Adams and the Gift of Pessimism." *The Week*, April 13, 2014. http://theweek.com/articles/444563/henry-adams-gift-pessimism.

Douglas, Ann. *The Feminization of American Culture*. New York: Avon, 1977.

Du Bois, W.E.B. *Black Reconstruction in America: An Essay Toward a History of the Part Which Black Folk Played in the Attempt to Reconstruct Democracy in America, 1860–1880*. New York: Oxford University Press, 2014.

Du Bois, W.E.B. *The Quest of the Silver Fleece*. Boston: Northeastern University Press, 1989.

Du Bois, W.E.B. *The Souls of Black Folk*. New York: Penguin Books, 1989.

Edelman, Lee. *No Future: Queer Theory and the Death Drive*. Durham, NC: Duke University Press, 2004.

Edwards, Rebecca. *Angels in the Machinery: Gender in American Party Politics from the Civil War to the Progressive Era*. New York: Oxford University Press, 1997.

Ehrenberg, Alain. *Weariness of the Self: Diagnosing the History of Depression in the Contemporary Age*. Montreal, QC: McGill-Queen's University Press, 2010.

Ehrenreich, Barbara and John Ehrenreich. "The Professional-Managerial Class." In *Between Labor and Capital*, edited by Pat Walker, 243–78. Boston: South End Press, 1979.

Eng, David L. and Shinhee Han. "A Dialogue on Racial Melancholia." In *Loss: The Politics of Mourning*, edited by David L. Eng and David Kazanjian, 343–71. Berkeley: University of California Press, 2003.

Fanon, Frantz. *Black Skin White Masks*. New York: Grove Press, 1967.

"fascinate, v." *OED Online*. Oxford University Press. http://www.oed.com/view/Entry/68362.

Felski, Rita. "Digging Down and Standing Back." *English Language Notes* 51, no. 2 (Fall/Winter 2013): 7–23.

Field, David Dudley. *Emotional Insanity*. New York: Russell Brothers, 1873.

Fisher, Philip. *The Vehement Passions*. Princeton: Princeton University Press, 2003.

Flatley, Jonathan. *Affective Mapping: Melancholia and the Politics of Modernism*. Cambridge, MA: Harvard University Press, 2008.

Foote, Stephanie. "Little Brothers of the Rich: Queer Families in the Gilded Age." *American Literature* 79, no. 4 (December 2007): 701–24.

Foucault, Michel. *Ethics: Subjectivity and Truth*. New York: New Press, 1997.

Foucault, Michel. *Madness and Civilization: A History of Insanity in the Age of Reason*. New York: Vintage Books, 1988.

Frank, Jason. "Democracy and Disgust." *J19* 5, no. 2 (Fall 2017): 396–403.

Frank, Thomas. *What's the Matter with Kansas? How Conservatives Won the Heart of America*. New York: Metropolitan Books, 2004.

Fraser, Nancy. "Rethinking the Public Sphere: A Contribution to the Critique of Actually Existing Democracy." *Social Text* 25/26 (1990): 56–80.

Freeman, Elizabeth. "Theorizing Queer Temporalities: A Roundtable Discussion." *GLQ: A Journal of Lesbian and Gay Studies* 13, nos. 2–3 (2007): 177–95.

Freeman, Elizabeth, ed. *Time Binds: Queer Temporalities, Queer Histories*. Durham, NC: Duke University Press, 2010.

French, Bryant Morey. *Mark Twain and The Gilded Age*. Dallas: Southern Methodist University Press, 1965.

French, Bryant Morey. "Mark Twain, Laura D. Fair, and the New York Criminal Courts." *American Quarterly* 16, no. 4 (Winter 1964): 545–61.

Freud, Sigmund. *Three Essays on the Theory of Sexuality*. New York: Basic Books, 1975.

Gandhi, Leela. *Affective Communities: Anticolonial Thought, Fin-De-Siècle Radicalism, and the Politics of Friendship*. Durham, NC: Duke University Press, 2006.

Gerzina, Gretchen. *Frances Hodgson Burnett: The Unexpected Life of the Author of The Secret Garden*. New Brunswick, NJ: Rutgers University Press, 2004.

Geuss, Raymond. *Philosophy and Real Politics*. Princeton: Princeton University Press, 2008.

Gillman, Susan. *Dark Twins: Imposture and Identity in Mark Twain's America*. Chicago: University of Chicago Press, 1989.

Gillman, Susan. "Whose Protest Novel? Ramona, the Uncle Tom's Cabin of the Indian." In *The Oxford Handbook of Nineteenth-Century American Literature*, edited by Russ Castronovo, 376–91. New York: Oxford University Press, 2012.

Ginzberg, Lori D. *Women and the Work of Benevolence: Morality, Politics, and Class in the Nineteenth-century United States*. New Haven: Yale University Press, 1990.

Gold, Jenny. "'Post-election Stress Disorder' Sweeps the Nation." *PBS Newshour: The Rundown*, February 23, 2017. http://www.pbs.org/newshour/rundown/post-election-stress-disorder-sweeps-nation/.

Goldsby, Jacqueline. *A Spectacular Secret: Lynching in American Life and Literature*. Chicago: University of Chicago Press, 2006.

Goldsmith, Barbara. *Other Powers: The Age of Suffrage, Spiritualism, and the Scandalous Victoria Woodhull*. New York: A.A. Knopf, 1998.

Gonzalez, John M. "The Warp of Whiteness: Domesticity and Empire in Helen Hunt Jackson's Ramona." *American Literary History* 16, no. 3 (2004): 437–65.

Goodman, Nan. *Shifting the Blame: Literature, Law, and the Theory of Accidents in Nineteenth Century America*. Princeton: Princeton University Press, 1999.

Goodrich, Peter. "The New Casuistry." *Critical Inquiry* 33, no. 4 (Summer 2007): 673–709.

Goodwyn, Lawrence. *The Populist Moment: A Short History of the Agrarian Revolt in America*. New York: Oxford University Press, 1978.

Gottfried, Jeffrey. "Most Americans Already Feel Election Coverage Fatigue." *Pew Research Center*, July 14, 2016. http://www.pewresearch.org/fact-tank/2016/07/14/most-americans-already-feel-election-coverage-fatigue/.

Gray, John. "The Guiteau Trial." *The American Journal of Insanity* 38 (1882): 303–448.

Gregg, Melissa and Gregory J. Seigworth, eds. *The Affect Theory Reader*. Durham, NC: Duke University Press, 2010.

Griffin, Robert J. "Anonymity and Authorship." *New Literary History* 30, no. 4 (1999): 877–95.

Grimm, Clyde L. "The American Claimant: Reclamation of a Farce." *American Quarterly* 19, no. 1 (Spring 1967): 86–103.

Gunning, Sandra. *Race, Rape, and Lynching: The Red Record of American Literature, 1890–1912*. New York: Oxford University Press, 1996.

Gustafson, Sandra. "Democratic Fictions." In *A Companion to American Fiction 1780–1865*, edited by Shirley Samuels, 31–9. Malden, MA: Blackwell Publishing, 2004.

Gustafson, Sandra. *Imagining Deliberative Democracy in the Early American Republic*. Chicago: University of Chicago Press, 2011.

Gutiérrez-Jones, Carl. *Rethinking the Borderlands: Between Chicano Culture and Legal Discourse*. Berkeley: University of California Press, 1995.

Haber, Carole. *The Trials of Laura Fair: Sex, Murder, and Insanity in the Victorian West*. Chapel Hill: The University of North Carolina Press, 2015.

Hamilton, Allan McLane. "The Case of Guiteau." *The Boston Medical and Surgical Journal* 106 (March 9, 1882): 235–8.

Hanson, Ellis. "The Future's Eve: Reparative Reading after Sedgwick." *South Atlantic Quarterly* 110, no. 1 (2011): 101–19.

Hardt, Michael. "For Love or Money." *Cultural Anthropology* 26, no. 4 (2011): 676–82.

Hardt, Michael and Antonio Negri. *Commonwealth*. Cambridge, MA: Harvard University Press, 2009.

Hardt, Michael and Antonio Negri. "Foreword: What Are Affects Good For." In *The Affective Turn: Theorizing The Social*, edited by Patricia Ticineto Clough, ix–xiii. Durham, NC: Duke University Press, 2007.

Harris, Susan. "Four Ways to Inscribe a Mackerel: Mark Twain and Laura Hawkins." *Studies in the Novel* 21 (1989): 138–53.

Hartman, Saidiya. *Scenes of Subjection: Terror, Slavery, and Self-Making in Nineteenth-Century America*. New York: Oxford University Press, 1997.

Havard, John C. "Sentimentalism, Interracial Romance, and Helen Hunt Jackson and Clorinda Matto De Turner's Attacks on Abuses of Native Americans in *Ramona* and *Aves Sin Nido*." *Intertexts* 11 (2007): 101–21.

Hawthorne, Nathaniel. *The House of the Seven Gables*. New York: Penguin, 1986.

Hibbard, Andrea L. and John T. Parry. "Law, Seduction, and the Sentimental Heroine: The Case of Amelia Norman." *American Literature* 78, no. 2 (June 2006): 325–55.

Hirschman, Albert. *The Passions and the Interests: Political Arguments for Capitalism Before Its Triumph*. Princeton: Princeton University Press, 1977.

Hitchens, Christopher. "In Search of the Washington Novel: A Colorful Genre Awaits Its Masterpiece." *City Journal* 20, no. 4 (Autumn 2010). www.city-journal.org/2010/20_4_urb-the-washington-novel.html.

Hofstadter, Richard. *The Age of Reform: From Bryan to F. D. R*. New York: Vintage Books, 1955.

"home-wrecker, n." *OED Online*. Oxford University Press. http://www.oed.com/view/Entry/248675.

Hoogenboom, Ari Arthur. *Outlawing the Spoils: A History of the Civil Service Reform Movement, 1865–1883*. Westport, CT: Greenwood Press, 1982.

Hopkins, Sarah Winnemucca. *Life Among the Piutes*. Reno, Nevada: University of Nevada Press, 1994.

Howard, June. "What Is Sentimentality?" *American Literary History* 11, no. 1 (March 1999): 63–81.

Howe, Lawrence. *Mark Twain and the Novel: The Double-Cross of Authority*. Cambridge: Cambridge University Press, 1998.

Howells, W.D. "Mark Twain." *Century Illustrated Magazine* 24 (September 1882): 780–4.

"hypocrisy, n." *OED Online*. Oxford University Press. http://www.oed.com/view/Entry/90491.

Jackson, Helen Hunt. *A Century of Dishonor: A Sketch of the United States Government's Dealings with Some of the Indian Tribes*. New York: Harper and Bros., 1881.

Jackson, Helen Hunt. *The Indian Reform Letters of Helen Hunt Jackson, 1879–1885*. Edited by Valerie Sherer Mathes. Norman: University of Oklahoma Press, 1998.

Jackson, Helen Hunt. *Ramona*. New York: Avon Books, 1970.

Jackson, Holly. "The Marriage Trap in the Free-Love Novel and Queer Critique." *American Literature* 87, no. 4 (December 2015): 681–708.

Jacob, Kathryn A. *King of the Lobby: The Life and Times of Sam Ward, Man-About-Washington in the Gilded Age*. Baltimore: Johns Hopkins University Press, 2010.

James, Henry. *Literary Criticism: Essays on Literature, American Writers, English Writers*. Edited by Leon Edel and Mark Wilson. New York: Library of America, 1984.

James, William. *Writings, 1878–1899*. New York: Library of America, 1992.

Jameson, Fredric. *The Antinomies of Realism*. London: Verso, 2013.

Jones, William P. "Something to Offer." *Jacobin*, August 11, 2015. https://www.jacobinmag.com/2015/08/debs-socialism-race-du-bois-socialist-party-black-liberation/.

Kant, Immanuel. *The Metaphysics of Morals*. Translated by Mary Gregor. London: Cambridge University Press, 1991.

Kaplan, Amy. *The Anarchy of Empire in the Making of U.S. Culture*. Cambridge, MA: Harvard University Press, 2002.

Karcher, Carolyn L. *The First Woman in the Republic: A Cultural Biography of Lydia Maria Child*. Durham, NC: Duke University Press, 1994.

Kennedy, John F. "Commencement Address at American University, Washington D.C., June 10, 1963." http://www.jfklibrary.org/Research/Research-Aids/JFK-Speeches/American-University_19630610.aspx.

Kete, Mary Louise. *Sentimental Collaborations: Mourning and Middle-Class Identity in Nineteenth-Century America*. Durham, NC: Duke University Press, 2000.

Kilgore, John Mac. *Mania for Freedom: American Literatures of Enthusiasm from the Revolution to the Civil War*. Chapel Hill: University of North Carolina Press, 2016.

King, James T. "A Better Way: General George Crook and the Ponca Indians." *Nebraska History* 50 (1969): 239–56.

Kirk, Russell. *The Conservative Mind From Burke to Eliot*. Washington, DC: Regnery Publishing Inc., 2001.

Kramer, Peter D. *Listening to Prozac: The Landmark Book About Antidepressants and the Remaking of the Self*. New York: Penguin Books, 1997.

Kramer, Peter D. *Against Depression*. New York: Penguin Books, 2006.

Latour, Bruno. "What If We Talked Politics a Little?" *Contemporary Political Theory* 2 (2003): 143–64.

Latour, Bruno. "Why Has Critique Run out of Steam? From Matters of Fact to Matters of Concern." *Critical Inquiry* 30 (Winter 2004): 225–48.

"lobbyist, n." *OED Online*. Oxford University Press. http://www.oed.com/view/Entry/109499.

Laursen, John Christian. "Cynicism Then and Now." *Iris: European Journal of Philosophy & Public Debate* 1, no. 2 (October 2009): 469–82.

Le Bon, Gustave. *The Crowd: A Study of the Popular Mind*. New York: The Macmillan Co., 1897.

Lears, T.J. Jackson. *No Place of Grace: Antimodernism and the Transformation of American Culture, 1880–1920*. New York: Pantheon Books, 1981.

Lehmann, Christopher. "Why Americans Can't Write Political Fiction." *The Washington Monthly*, October 1, 2010.

Leys, Ruth. "The Turn to Affect: A Critique." *Critical Inquiry* 37, no. 3 (Spring 2011): 434–72.

Lippard, George. *The Quaker City; or, The Monks of Monk Hall: a Romance of Philadelphia Life, Mystery, and Crime*. Amherst: University of Massachusetts Press, 1995.

Lott, Eric. "The First Boomer: Bill Clinton, George W., and Fictions of State." *Representations* 84, no. 1 (2004): 100–22.

Love, Heather. *Feeling Backward: Loss and the Politics of Queer History*. Cambridge, MA: Harvard University Press, 2010.

Luciano, Dana. *Arranging Grief: Sacred Time and the Body in Nineteenth-Century America*. New York: New York University Press, 2007.

Maeder, Thomas. *Crime and Madness: The Origins and Evolution of the Insanity Defense*. New York: Harper & Row, 1985.

Margolis, Stacey. *The Public Life of Privacy in Nineteenth-Century American Literature*. Durham, NC: Duke University Press, 2005.

Martí, José. *Selected Writings*. New York: Penguin Classics, 2002.

Marx, Karl. *Grundrisse*. New York: Penguin Books, 1973.

Massumi, Brian. *Parables for the Virtual: Movement, Affect, Sensation*. Durham, NC: Duke University Press, 2002.

Mathes, Valerie Sherer and Richard Lowitt. "Helen Hunt Jackson and the Campaign for Ponca Restitution, 1880–1881." *South Dakota History* 17 (Spring 1987): 23–41.

Mathes, Valerie Sherer and Richard Lowitt. *The Standing Bear Controversy: Prelude to Indian Reform*. Urbana: University of Illinois Press, 2003.

Mazella, David. *The Making of Modern Cynicism*. Charlottesville: University of Virginia Press, 2007.

Mazzarella, William. "The Myth of the Multitude, or, Who's Afraid of the Crowd?" *Critical Inquiry* 36, no. 4 (Summer 2010): 697–727.

McDougall, William. *The Group Mind*. London: Cambridge University Press, 1920.

McGrath, Conor and Phil Harris. "The Creation of the U.S. Lobbying Industry." In *The Routledge Handbook of Political Management*, edited by Dennis W. Johnson, 407–19. New York: Routledge, 2009.

Mee, Jon. *Romanticism, Enthusiasm, and Regulation: Poetics and the Policing of Culture in the Romantic Period*. New York: Oxford University Press, 2005.

Melville, Herman. *The Confidence Man*. New York: Penguin Books, 1990.

Menke, Richard. "Media in America, 1881: Garfield, Guiteau, Bell, Whitman." *Critical Inquiry* 31 (2005): 638–64.

Menninghaus, Winfried. *Disgust: Theory and History of a Strong Sensation*. Translated by Howard Eiland and Joel Golb. Albany, NY: State University of New York Press, 2003.

Merish, Lori. *Sentimental Materialism*. Durham, NC: Duke University Press, 2000.

Michaels, Walter Benn. "An American Tragedy, or the Promise of American Life." *Representations* 25 (Winter 1989): 71–98.

Michaels, Walter Benn. "Romance and Real Estate." In *The American Renaissance Reconsidered*, edited by Walter Benn Michaels and Donald E. Pease, 156–82. Baltimore: Johns Hopkins University Press, 1985.

Michaels, Walter Benn. *The Trouble with Diversity: How We Learned to Love Identity and Ignore Inequality*. New York: Macmillan, 2007.

Miller, William Ian. *The Anatomy of Disgust*. Cambridge, MA: Harvard University Press, 1997.

"Miscellaneous Books." *The American Bookseller*, July 15, 1878.

Mizruchi, Susan L. *The Science of Sacrifice: American Literature and Modern Social Theory*. Princeton: Princeton University Press, 1998.

"More Medical Opinions; New York Doctors Disagree in Guiteau's Case." *The New York Times*, December 14, 1881.

Muller, Jerry Z. "What is Conservative Social and Political Thought?" In *Conservatism: An Anthology of Social and Political Thought from David Hume to the Present*, edited by J.Z. Muller, 3–31. Princeton: Princeton University Press, 1997.

Muñoz, José Esteban. *Cruising Utopia: The Then and There of Queer Futurity*. New York: New York University Press, 2009.

Muñoz, José Esteban. "Feeling Down, Feeling Brown: Latina Affect, the Performativity of Race, and the Depressive Position." *Signs* 31, no. 3 (Spring 2006): 675–88.

Nevins, Allan. "Helen Hunt Jackson, Sentimentalist vs. Realist." *The American Scholar* 10, no. 3 (Summer 1941): 269–85.

Ngai, Sianne. *Ugly Feelings*. Cambridge, MA: Harvard University Press, 2005.

Nussbaum, Martha. *Hiding from Humanity: Disgust, Shame, and the Law*. Princeton: Princeton University Press, 2004.

Oliver, Charles M. *Critical Companion to Walt Whitman: A Literary Reference to His Life and Work*. New York: Facts on File, Inc., 2006.

Oliver, Kelly. *Colonization of Psychic Space: A Psychoanalytic Social Theory of Oppression*. Minneapolis: University of Minnesota Press, 2004.

Olson, Charles. *Collected Prose*. Berkeley: University of California Press, 1997.

Paine, Albert Bigelow. *Mark Twain: A Biography*. New York: Harper and Brothers, 1912.

Papacharissi, Zizi. "Affective Publics and Structures of Storytelling: Sentiment, Events and Mediality." *Information, Communication & Society* 19, no. 3 (2016): 307–24.

Passet, Joanne E. *Sex Radicals and the Quest for Women's Equality*. Chicago: University of Illinois Press, 2003.

Patterson, John S. "Alliance and Antipathy: Ignatius Donnelly's Ambivalent Vision in Doctor Huguet." *American Quarterly* 22 (1970): 824–45.

Pfeifer, Michael James. *Rough Justice: Lynching and American Society, 1874–1947*. Urbana and Chicago: University of Illinois Press, 2004.

Piatote, Beth H. *Domestic Subjects: Gender, Citizenship, and Law in Native American Literature*. New Haven: Yale University Press, 2013.

Pierce, Charles P. *Idiot America: How Stupidity Became a Virtue in the Land of the Free*. New York: Anchor Books, 2009.

Pinch, Adela. *Strange Fits of Passion: Epistemologies of Emotion, Hume to Austen*. Stanford: Stanford University Press, 1996.

Poe, Edgar Allan. *Essays and Reviews*. New York: The Library of America, 1984.

Pollack, Norman. *The Just Polity: Populism, Law, and Human Welfare*. Urbana: University of Illinois Press, 1987.

Posnock, Ross. "The Distinction of Du Bois: Aesthetics, Pragmatism, Politics." *American Literary History* 7, no. 3 (Autumn 1995): 500–24.

Priest, Loring Benson. *Uncle Sam's Stepchildren: The Reformation of United States Indian Policy, 1865–1887*. New York: Octagon Books, 1969.

Protevi, John. *Political Affect: Connecting the Social and the Somatic*. Minneapolis: University of Minnesota Press, 2009.

Prucha, Francis Paul. *The Great Father: The United States Government and the American Indians*. Lincoln: University of Nebraska Press, 1986.

Rampersad, Arnold. *The Art and Imagination of W.E.B. Du Bois*. Cambridge, MA: Harvard University Press, 1976.

Rancière, Jacques. *Disagreement: Politics and Philosophy*. Minneapolis: University of Minnesota Press, 1999.

Ray, Isaac. *A Treatise on the Medical Jurisprudence of Insanity*. Cambridge, MA: Belknap Press of Harvard University Press, 1962.

"Readers React: 2016 election fatigue in 2015." *Los Angeles Times*, April 15, 2015. http://www.latimes.com/opinion/readersreact/la-le-0415-wednesday-hillary-clinton-2016-20150415-story.html.

"Recent Fiction." *The Critic: A Weekly Review of Literature and the Arts*, no. 405 (October 03, 1891): 164–5.

Recker, Astrid. "To Market! Consuming Women in Harriet Beecher Stowe's *My Wife and I* and *We and Our Neighbors*." In *Beyond Uncle Tom's Cabin*, edited by Sylvia Mayer and Monika Mueller, 209–35. Madison: Fairleigh Dickinson University Press, 2011.

Reik, Louis E. "The Doe–Ray Correspondence: A Pioneer Collaboration in the Jurisprudence of Mental Disease." *Yale Law Journal* 63 (1953): 183–96.

Report of the Proceedings in the Case of the United States vs. Charles J. Guiteau. Tried in the Supreme Court of the District of Columbia, Holding a Criminal Term, and Beginning November 14, 1881. Washington, DC: Government Printing Office, 1882.

Reynolds, David S. *Walt Whitman's America: A Cultural Biography.* New York: Vintage Books, 1996.

Ridge, Martin. *Ignatius Donnelly: The Portrait of a Politician.* St. Paul: Minnesota Historical Society Press, 1991.

Rifkin, Mark. "Indigenizing Agamben: Rethinking Sovereignty in Light of the 'Peculiar' Status of Native Peoples." *Cultural Critique* 73 (2009): 88–124.

Robertson, Andrew W. *The Language of Democracy: Political Rhetoric in the United States and Britain, 1790–1900.* Charlottesville: University of Virginia Press, 2005.

Rohy, Valerie. *Anachronism and Its Others: Sexuality, Race, and Temporality.* Albany, NY: SUNY Press, 2009.

Romero, Lora. *Home Fronts: Domesticity and Its Critics in the Antebellum United States.* Durham, NC: Duke University Press, 1997.

Rosenberg, Charles E. *The Trial of the Assassin Guiteau: Psychiatry and Law in the Gilded Age.* Chicago: University of Chicago Press, 1968.

Rosenberg, Emily S. *Spreading the American Dream: American Economic and Cultural Expansion, 1890–1945.* New York: Hill and Wang, 1982.

Rosse, Irving. "Washington Malaria and Politics as Genetic Factors in Nervous Disease." *Virginia Medical Monthly* 18, no. 7 (October 1891): 525–32.

Rossiter, Clinton, ed. *The Federalist Papers.* New York: Penguin Putnam, 1999.

Rowe, John Carlos, ed. *New Essays on the Education of Henry Adams.* Cambridge: Cambridge University Press, 1996.

Rowe, John Carlos, ed. *At Emerson's Tomb: The Politics of Classic American Literature.* New York: Columbia University Press, 1997.

Runciman, David. *Political Hypocrisy: The Mask of Power, from Hobbes to Orwell and Beyond.* Princeton: Princeton University Press, 2010.

Ryan, Susan M. *The Moral Economies of American Authorship: Reputation, Scandal, and the Nineteenth-Century Literary Marketplace.* New York: Oxford University Press, 2016.

Salazar, James B. *Bodies of Reform: The Rhetoric of Character in Gilded Age America.* New York: New York University Press, 2010.

Samuels, Ernest. *Henry Adams, the Middle Years.* Cambridge, MA: Belknap Press, 1958.

Samuels, Shirley, ed. *The Culture of Sentiment: Race, Gender, and Sentimentality in the Nineteenth-Century.* New York: Oxford University Press, 1992.

"Sam Ward's Career." *The National Police Gazette* 44, no. 350 (June 7, 1884): 6.

Sanchez-Eppler, Karen. *Touching Liberty: Abolition, Feminism, and the Politics of the Body.* Berkeley: University of California Press, 1993.

Sandage, Scott. "The Gilded Age." In *A Companion to American Cultural History*, edited by Karen Halttunen, 139–53. Malden, MA: Blackwell Publishing, 2008.

Sarat, Austin, Lawrence Douglas, and Martha Umphrey. *Law's Madness.* Ann Arbor: University of Michigan Press, 2006.

Schiesl, Martin J. *The Politics of Efficiency: Municipal Administration and Reform in America, 1800–1920.* Berkeley: University of California Press, 1980.

Schlesinger, Arthur. "On Henry Adams and Democracy." *New York Review of Books* 50, no. 5 (March 27, 2003). https://www.nybooks.com/articles/2003/03/27/on-henry-adamss-democracy/.

Schmidt, Paul. "Mark Twain's Satire on Republicanism." *American Quarterly* 5 (1953): 344–56.

Sedgwick, Eve Kosofsky. *Touching Feeling: Affect, Pedagogy, Performativity*. Durham, NC: Duke University Press, 2003.

Seltzer, Mark. *Serial Killers: Death and Life in America's Wound Culture*. New York: Routledge, 1998.

Senier, Siobhan. *Voices of American Indian Resistance: Helen Hunt Jackson, Sarah Winnemucca, and Victoria Howard*. Norman, OK: University of Oklahoma Press, 2001.

"Several Recent Novels." *Christian Union* 21, no. 17 (April 28, 1880): 398.

Shea, Louisa. *The Cynic Enlightenment*. Baltimore: The Johns Hopkins University Press, 2010.

Shklar, Judith N. *Ordinary Vices*. Cambridge, MA: Harvard University Press, 1984.

Silberman, Bernard S. *Cages of Reason: The Rise of the Rational State in France, Japan, the United States, and Great Britain*. Chicago: University of Chicago Press, 1993.

Silbey, Joel H. *The American Political Nation, 1838–1893*. Stanford: Stanford University Press, 1991.

Simpson, Audra. *Mohawk Interruptus: Political Life Across the Borders of Settler States*. Durham, NC: Duke University Press, 2014.

Simpson, Brooks D. *The Political Education of Henry Adams*. Columbia: University of South Carolina Press, 1995.

"SLC to OLC, 3 Oct 1872, London, England (UCCL 00817)." In *Mark Twain Project Online*. Berkeley: University of California Press, 2007. http://www.marktwainproject.org/xtf/view?docId=letters/UCCL00817.xml;style=letter;brand=mtp.

Sloterdijk, Peter. *Critique of Cynical Reason*. Minneapolis: University of Minnesota Press, 1987.

Snediker, Michael. *Queer Optimism: Lyric Personhood and Other Felicitous Persuasions*. Minneapolis: University of Minnesota Press, 2009.

Solomon, Andrew. *The Noonday Demon: An Atlas Of Depression*. New York: Scribner Classics, 2001.

Spurlock, John C. *Free Love: Marriage and Middle-Class Radicalism in America, 1825–1860*. New York: New York University Press, 1990.

Starita, Joe. *"I Am a Man": Chief Standing Bear's Journey for Justice*. New York: St. Martin's Press, 2008.

Stein, Jordan. "American Literary History and Queer Temporalities." *American Literary History* 25, no. 4 (Winter 2013): 855–69.

Storey, Mark. *Rural Fictions, Urban Realities*. New York: Oxford University Press, 2015.

Stowe, Harriet Beecher. *My Wife and I: Or, Harry Henderson's History*. New York: Fords, Howard & Hulbert, 1871.

Summers, Mark Wahlgren. *The Era of Good Stealings*. New York: Oxford University Press, 1993.

Susman, Warren. *Culture as History*. New York: Pantheon Books, 1984.

Taylor, Matthew. *Universes Without Us: Posthuman Cosmologies in American Literature*. Minneapolis: University of Minnesota Press, 2013.

Terada, Rei. *Feeling in Theory: Emotion After the Death of the Subject*. Cambridge, MA: Harvard University Press, 2003.

"The Old and New Cynics." *The Eclectic Magazine of Foreign Literature* (March 1884): 408–10.

Thrailkill, Jane. *Affecting Fictions: Mind, Body, and Emotion in American Literary Realism.* Cambridge, MA: Harvard University Press, 2007.

Tibbles, Thomas Henry. *Hidden Power. A Secret History of the Indian Ring, Its Operations, Intrigues, and Machinations. States Government. A Defense of the U.S. Army, and a Solution of the Indian Problem.* New York: G.W. Carleton and Co., 1881.

Tibbles, Thomas Henry. *The Ponca Chiefs: An Account of the Trial of Standing Bear.* Lincoln: University of Nebraska Press, 1972.

Tighe, Janet A. "Francis Wharton and the Nineteenth-Century Insanity Defense: The Origins of a Reform Tradition." *The American Journal of Legal History* 27, no. 3 (July 1983): 223–53.

Tocqueville, Alexis de. *Democracy in America.* Translated by Harvey C. Mansfield and Delba Winthrop. Chicago: University of Chicago Press, 2000.

Tompkins, Jane. *Sensational Designs: The Cultural Work of American Fiction, 1790–1860.* New York: Oxford University Press, 1985.

Trachtenberg, Alan. *The Incorporation of America: Culture and Society in the Gilded Age.* New York: Hill and Wang, 1982.

Traubel, Horace. *With Walt Whitman in Camden April 8–September 14, 1889.* Carbondale: Southern Illinois University Press, 1964.

Twain, Mark. *The American Claimant.* New York: Oxford University Press, 1996.

Twain, Mark. *Collected Tales, Sketches, Speeches & Essays.* New York: The Library of America, 1992.

Twain, Mark. *A Connecticut Yankee in King Arthur's Court.* New York: Oxford University Press, 1996.

Twain, Mark. "Special Correspondence of the Alta California." *San Francisco Alta California,* January 15, 1868.

Twain, Mark and Charles Dudley Warner. *The Gilded Age: A Tale of Today.* New York: Penguin Books, 2001.

Tyree, J.M. "Ignatius Donnelly, Prince of Cranks." *The Believer* 3 (2005).

Vandersee, Charles. "The Pursuit of Culture in Adams' *Democracy.*" *American Quarterly* 19 (1967): 239–48.

Vendler, Helen. *Invisible Listeners: Lyric Intimacy in Herbert, Whitman, and Ashbery.* Princeton: Princeton University Press, 2009.

Venegas, Yolanda. "The Erotics of Racialization: Gender and Sexuality in the Making of California." *Frontiers: A Journal of Women Studies* 25 (2004): 63–89.

Vowell, Sarah. *Assassination Vacation.* New York: Simon & Schuster, 2005.

Warner, Charles Dudley. "How I Killed a Bear." *Outlook,* June 4, 1898.

Warner, Charles Dudley. *In the Wilderness.* Boston: Houghton, Mifflin, 1878.

Warner, Charles Dudley. *Publics and Counterpublics.* Cambridge: Zone Books, 2005.

Warner, Michael. *The Letters of the Republic: Publication and the Public Sphere in Eighteenth-Century America.* Cambridge, MA: Harvard University Press, 1990.

Warren, Joyce W. *Fanny Fern: An Independent Woman.* New Brunswick, NJ: Rutgers University Press, 1992.

Warren, Kenneth. " 'As White as Anybody': Race and the Politics of Counting as Black." *New Literary History* 31, no. 4 (2000): 709–26.

Warren, Kenneth. *What Was African American Literature?* Cambridge, MA: Harvard University Press, 2011.

Weheliye, Alexander. *Habeas Viscus: Racializing Assemblages, Biopolitics, and Black Feminist Theories of the Human*. Durham, NC: Duke University Press, 2014.

Weiner, Mark S. *Americans Without Law: The Racial Boundaries of Citizenship*. New York and London: New York University Press, 2006.

Weinstein, Cindy. "From True Woman to New Woman to Virgin." In *Henry Adams and the Need to Know*, edited by William Merrill Decker and Earl N. Harbert, 300–14. Charlottesville: University of Virginia Press, 2005.

Wells, Susan. *Sweet Reason: Rhetoric and the Discourses of Modernity*. Chicago: University of Chicago Press, 1996.

Wexler, Laura. *Tender Violence: Domestic Visions in an Age of U.S. Imperialism*. Chapel Hill: University of North Carolina Press, 2000.

Whitman, Walt. *Democratic Vistas*. Edited by Ed Folsom. Iowa City: University of Iowa Press, 2010.

Whitman, Walt. *Leaves of Grass and Other Writings*. Edited by Michael Moon. New York: Norton, 2002.

Whitman, Walt. *Leaves of Grass: The Original 1855 Edition*. New York: Dover Publications, Inc., 2007.

Whitman, Walt. *Walt Whitman's Drum-Taps*. New York: [Peter Eckler, printer], 1865.

Wiegman, Robyn. "The Times We're in: Queer Feminist Criticism and the Reparative 'turn.' " *Feminist Theory* 15, no. 1 (April 1, 2014): 4–25.

Wilkins, David E. *American Indian Sovereignty and the U.S. Supreme Court: The Making of Justice*. Austin: University of Texas Press, 1997.

Wilkins, David E. and K. Tsianina Lomawaima. *Uneven Ground: American Indian Sovereignty and Federal Law*. Tulsa: University of Oklahoma Press, 2002.

Williams, Raymond. *Marxism and Literature*. New York: Oxford University Press, 1977.

Wilson, Christopher P. "Secrets of the Master's Deed Box: Narrative and Class." In *A Companion to American Fiction 1865–1914*, edited by Robert Paul Lamb and G.R. Thompson, 340–55. Malden, MA: John Wiley & Sons, 2008.

"Women at the Capital." *Every Saturday: A Journal of Choice Reading*, August 12, 1871.

Wyman, Margaret. "Harriet Beecher Stowe's Topical Novel on Woman Suffrage." *The New England Quarterly* 25, no. 3 (1952): 383–91.

Zheng, Da. "Twain's and Warner's The Gilded Age: The Economy of Insanity." *College Language Association Journal* 39 (1995): 71–93.

Ziarek, Eva. "Bare Life on Strike." *South Atlantic Quarterly* 107, no. 1 (2008): 89–105.

Žižek, Slavoj. "Against the Populist Temptation." *Critical Inquiry* 32, no. 3 (Spring 2006): 551–74.

Žižek, Slavoj. *The Sublime Object of Ideology*. London and New York: Verso, 1989.

Zournazi, Mary. *Hope: New Philosophies for Change*. New York: Routledge, 2003.

{ INDEX }